THE
DEATHLY HALLOWS
LECTURES

The Hogwarts Professor
Explains the Final
Harry Potter
Adventure

JOHN GRANGER

Zossima Press titles may be purchased for business or promotional use or special sales.

second edition August 2008
10-9-8-7-6-5-4-3-2

Zossima Press

ISBN 0-9723221-7-5

Table of Contents

Introduction

Learning the Passwords for the Magical Paintings on Display

Thank you for choosing to read this book on *Harry Potter and the Deathly Hallows*, the capstone and most intriguingly complex book of author J.K. Rowling's seven-book series. As this book itself is unusual, in light of most books on Harry Potter, I'll preface it with an explanation of its more peculiar features and vocabulary, and list several operating assumptions which might strike the reader as foreign, even bizarre.

In exploring Ms. Rowling's artistry and meaning, the first "given" is that her writing deserves to be taken seriously. This is a credible assumption, because the author has said many times that she planned the whole series and each book for the "obsessive" or serious reader.[1] The books themselves – which include paintings opened by a secret word or knowing touch to a greater, concealed world within, offer repeated examples of an "inside being greater than its outside," [2] and eyes with more and less penetrating insight or vision[3]--indicate that they work on levels beneath the surface narrative.

The tradition in which Ms. Rowling writes, too, requires attentive reading. It is the Romantic, subversive tradition of symbolist literature beginning with Chaucer, Dante, and Shakespeare, which is to say, the Medieval imagination as understood by Blake, Coleridge, and Ruskin and furthered by 19th and 20th Century satirists and fantasy writers, to include MacDonald, Orwell, Chesterton, Sayers, Goudge, Lewis, and Tolkien. In reading Ms. Rowling as a writer of this tradition, I have tried to follow the examples of D.W. Robertson's work on Chaucer, Northrop Frye reading Spencer, John Ruskin on landscape painting, Coleridge's "transforming vision" and natural theology, and Dante in his instruction about unveiling his own work.

This path is a departure from the dismissive analysis of critics as notable as Harold Bloom and A.S. Byatt who think Ms. Rowling's books "puerile" and "slop" and even from admirers who write patronizing reviews of the Potter books as edifying books for children. Harry Potter, as James Thomas of Pepperdine has noted, seems "too juvenile, too popular, and too current" to deserve the kind of serious reading we feel obliged to give acknowledged classics or literary canon.[4] I therefore feel obliged to explain in this book why I believe (beyond the author's suggestion and telling signs in her books) Harry Potter merits canonical status and respect.

First, Rowling novels hold up to close reading. My first two books— *How Harry Cast His Spell* and *Unlocking Harry Potter*—examine in depth the series' alchemical artistry, narrative misdirection, postmodern themes, Christian content, hero's journey structure, and the meaning of various recurrent symbols and images in the series. This study was anything but wasted time. These books are now used in classrooms from Princeton to Pepperdine, because exploring the books as vessels of meaning (rather than cultural artifacts or sociological curiosities) is as rewarding as reading Shakespeare, Dickens, and Swift.

More important, the specific school of criticism from which I interpret the books, what Frye calls the "iconological tradition" of Dante, Spencer, and Ruskin,[5] is especially illuminating when its tools are applied to Rowling's work. The two parts of the word "iconological" – *icon* and *logos* –the utility of this neglected method in understanding both Ms. Rowling's artistry and the profound resonance of her meaning in the hearts of her international reading audience.

An "icon" is a painting, usually religious, that, as an image portraying something or someone else (its "referent"), is less about exactitude in representative detail than it is about likeness in meaning and substance. "Symbol" is closer to the meaning of icon than "picture," because an icon is less like a photograph or exact likenesses than a defining image or transparency to the referent. As C.S. Lewis said about Spencer[6] and his own work,[7] their starting point and strength is not in their faithful representation but in the power and translucency, to use a Coleridgian phrase, of their key images.

Iconological criticism, then, is the work of penetrating the surface of these images and symbols to discover the "greater substance inside," which is to say, their several levels of meaning. Dante urged his readers to look under the veils of his poetry, and, specifically, to understand them as working on four levels – the surface, moral, allegorical, and anagogical meanings that exist simultaneously in his work.[8]

As D.W. Robertson explains, this was not a superhuman expectation on Dante's part, but just the Medieval baseline understanding of how to understand reality, man, Scripture, and any work of art, especially literature. [9] Most of a poem's or painting's meaning was assumed to require penetrating vision or puzzle solving and readers of Shakespeare and Chaucer, as well as Dante devotees, are obliged to look beneath the surface, moral, and allegorical levels – political and theological – to get at their most important meaning, the anagogical.

"Anagogical" is not a word we use very often but it is important to know and understand it to grasp the purpose of traditional iconological criticism. "Anagogical" literally means "leading upwards" and "leading back." When applied to story or symbol, it refers to the transcendent meaning or metaphysical referent of the icon or parable. Living as we do in an ontologically flat world, in which the "Great Chain of Being," instead of reaching from lifeless matter to the Supreme Reality, is stretched instead horizontally across the gateway to meaning, even the best books of the Western Canon are rarely "mined slowly" and meditatively as Ruskin said they must be [10] to be understood at the anagogical level.

"Slow mining" in a rich text, contrary to the mental picture I have of working in a mine, is delightful work with remarkable rewards. It does require, however, a transformed and transforming vision, another Coleridgian notion. Which brings us to the "logical" part of "iconological" criticism. To get to the anagogical or spiritual realities at the heart of profound writing means understanding, as C. S. Lewis put it, that "the world is mental."[11] Ron Weasley asks Harry rhetorically if he is "mental" at two critical points in *Deathly Hallows*,[12] meaning, "You're crazy!" But Harry is indeed "mental," even a symbol of the Intellect.

As explained in Chapter 5, what Lewis meant in saying the world is mental is that the principle and unity of existence is the divine *Logos*, which our Intellect or noetic faculty (not to be confused with discursive reasoning or academic intelligence) is "continuous with," if not identical to. This inner *logos*—what Lewis calls conscience and others the Eye of the Heart—recognizes the divine *Logos* in created things (their "inner principles," the *logoi* of St. Maximos), as well as in truth, beauty and goodness. The *logos* within sees the *Logos* without in the way a knowing subject recognizes itself in a mirror's reflection.

Iconological criticism is the exercise of this "seeing eye" and "sacred I" within us in the penetration of surface meanings to recognition of itself in the anagogical or transcendent level of nature, art, and literature. Time spent in reflection on a landscape painting by Turner, a lyrical ballad of Coleridge or Wordsworth, an Inkling novel, a Harry Potter adventure, or the ocean at sunset fosters our sense of the sublime and of the metaphysical beneath the physical, so that, as Sir Philip Sydney put it, the focus of our reflection is "instructing while delighting" us.

I have argued since 2002 that the symbols or images central to Harry Potter are the trio of Harry, Hermione and Ron as, first, a soul triptych of Spirit, Mind, and Body, and, second, as an alchemical work in progress, with Ron and Hermione acting as alchemical mercury and sulfur and Harry as leaden Philosophical Orphan becoming the Philosopher's Stone. The publication of *Deathly Hallows* only confirmed the validity of that argument. I will explain *Deathly Hallows* as the series' alchemical finale in Chapter 3, but Harry as an icon of Intellect or the Spirit within us is probably the more important image of the two.

Harry beneath the Invisibility Cloak, alone or with his two friends, is a story-symbol of the invisible, "seeing eye" or *logos*-Intellect within. His seven staged story, then, is the adventure of his noetic purification or "corrected vision," an alchemical allegory of human apotheosis. Ms. Rowling's books, as has frequently been noted, are about life and death. The reason they resonate with a worldwide audience, though, is because Harry's journey to and from King's Cross is the story of our hoped for spiritual perfection and immortality in the Eye of the Heart – the "sacred I" and "seeing eye."

The *Deathly Hallows Lectures* in this book are organized into two parts and seven chapters to mine that meaning. The first three-chapter part is an examination of *Deathly Hallows* in light of my previous books' ideas: the 5 keys that unlock the series, literary alchemy, and Christian content. Ms. Rowlings' books are not evangelical or an invitation to devotional Christianity, per se; Harry's transformation however, is an engaging and edifying story-symbol or parable of Everyman's life in Christ – the Word or *Logos* living in us and behind the veil of all surfaces.

The second part, the four last chapters, are the "slow mining" for the anagogical aspect of the eye symbolism that is the larger part of *Deathly Hallows'* meaning. I explore the eyes as the avenue of ego-transcendence in detailing the connections between Lily's green eyes and the eyes of Dante's Beatrice in the *Divine Comedy;* in unveiling the eye in the mirror shard contrasted with the two eyes of the Locket Horcrux; and, finally, in explaining the "triangular eye" Hallows symbol and its three dimensional story echo in the burial of Moody's Mad Eye. I end the book with a collection of thirty-one frequently-asked questions.

This book has been a lot of fun for me to write and is my personal thank you to Ms. Rowling for years of reading pleasure. I need and want to thank, as well, the many friends at HogwartsProfessor.com who have joined me in conversation about books in general and Harry Potter specifically for the last four years. Robert Trexler of Zossima Press midwifed this book through its long delivery, Deborah Chan (aka "Arabella Figg" at HogPro) edited it with invaluable and patient attention so it is as intelligible as it is, and Joyce Odell gave it the "eye-catching" cover it enjoys. I owe at least a tip of the hat here, too, to Travis Prinzi of TheHogsHead.org, whose book *Harry Potter & Imagination: The Way Between Two Worlds* is the most cogent exploration of the allegorical and political level of meaning in the Potter series I have read, for his many kindnesses to me. Conversations with and the efforts of Deborah, Travis, Robert, Joyce and the HogPro All Pros about all things Potter have made this a better book; the failings and mistakes that remain are all mine.

Summing up, the *Harry Potter* series, full of edifying symbols, is an evocative parable of human perfection and ego transcendence. As you'll discover in the coming pages, *Deathly Hallows* is all that *and* a book about how to read books like *Deathly Hallows.* I understand these ideas are difficult for most readers to grasp or accept, being contrary to prevailing opinions about *Harry Potter* and conventional thinking about what it is that books do, even about what reality is. As Coleridge, Lewis and others insist, however, matter and energy's measurable and sense-perceptible surfaces are *not* the greater reality of our lives and world; they are visible obstacles or veils which must be penetrated to know the Absolute beneath their surface. Because *Harry Potter and the Deathly Hallows* is a book illustrating this fact and because its symbols are largely about interpreting the world as symbol, and demonstrating the value of stories, it deserves a symbolic and subversive reading ("subversive" understood literally as "turning the underside or inside up").

The Deathly Hallows Lectures is your password to enter the much larger world of fun and meaning behind the gargoyle guardians and Pink Lady artistry of Ms.Rowling's novels and especially *Deathly Hallows*, the series finale. Thank you for joining me on this adventure of meaning-mining and, in advance, for writing me with your comments and corrections when you're done.

Gratefully,

John Granger

John Granger

www.HogwartsProfessor.com
Feast of the Dormition, 2008

Post:
All book page and chapter references are to Scholastic hard cover editions

Endnotes

1   For Ms. Rowling's interview comments that suggest a serious reading of her work is in order, see Chapter 6, pp. 192-195

2   For a listing of several "Inside greater than outside" references, see Chapter 5, pp. 184-185 (note 8).

3   For discussion of Ms. Rowling's eye symbolism in *Deathly Hallows*, see Chapters 4-7.

4   For Bloom and Byatt criticism of the Potter books, see http://hogwartsprofessor.com/?p=34, http://hogwartsprofessor.com/?p=391; for patronizing reviews see http://hogwartsprofessor.com/?p=166 or http://www.scriptoriumdaily.com/2007/07/24/potter-narnia-and-spiderman-matter-in-a-serious-world/; James Thomas was quoted in *Time* magazine's 2007 Person of the Year Runner-Up profile of Ms. Rowling that can be read at http://www.time.com/time/specials/2007/personoftheyear/article/0,28804,1690753_1695388_1695436,00.html

5   Northrop Frye, *Anatomy of Criticism*, Princeton: Princeton University Press, 1957, page 10; see discussion here in Chapter 6, pp. 204-208.

6   C. S. Lewis, *Oxford History of the English Language, 16ᵗʰ Century (Excluding Drama)*, Oxford: Oxford University Press, 1952, pp. 387-388; see discussion here in Chapter 6, pages 211-212.

7   "All my seven Narnian books, and my three science-fiction books, began with seeing pictures in my head. At first they were not a story, just pictures. The *Lion* began with a picture of a Faun carrying an umbrella and parcels in a snowy wood. This picture had been in my mind since I was about sixteen. Then one day, when I was about forty, I said to myself: 'Let's try to make a story about it'." C. S. Lewis, *It All Began With a Picture*, cited in *C. S. Lewis: Companion and Guide*, Walter Hooper (ed.), New York: HarperCollins, 1996, page 401.

8   Dante Alighieri, *Convivio*, 2.1; see discussion in Chapter 4, page 138, and Chapter 6, page 205.

9   "[T]he underlying logic of the four senses of Scripture became a habit of mind." D. W. Robertson, Jr., *A Preface to Chaucer: Studies in Medieval Perspectives*, Princeton: Princeton University Press, 1962, page 355 (cf. *Preface*, Chapter 4, "Allegory, Humanism, and Literary Theory"). See pages 15 and 32 for his discussion of how "a work of art was frequently a puzzle to be solved" in the Medieval "habit of mind."

10   John Ruskin's "slow mining" quotation can be found in full with citation in Chapter 6, pp. 212-214.

11 For discussion of "the world is mental," see Chapter 5, pp. 188-189

12 "Are – you – *mental?*" (*Hallows*, Chapter 19, page 371: Ron has just rescued Harry from pool in Forest of Dean); "What?' said Ron loudly. "Are you mental?" (*Hallows*, Chapter 36, page 748; Harry has just said he doesn't want the Elder Wand)

Chapter 1

Unlocking Deathly Hallows:

Five Keys to Open the Last and Best Harry Potter Novel

Of all the lectures in this book, 'Unlocking Deathly Hallows' is the only one I'm presenting here as the talk as it was given. This chapter is largely the lecture I gave to college students at Washington & Lee University and the Torrey Honors College at Biola University in the Fall of 2007.

Good Evening! Are we ready to open up the meaning and artistry of *Harry Potter and the Deathly Hallows*? All right!

First, though, some precaution. Is there anyone here who hasn't read *Deathly Hallows* yet? (Two people raise their hands.) And who let these people in here? Before we start, someone get spoiler release forms from these people so I don't have 'Ruined the Ending Karma' the rest of my life.

Okay, we're good? Then let's begin.

You have grown up with Harry so you understand that life wasn't always as much fun for *Harry Potter* readers as it is now that we have all seven books. Most people your age remember when reading Harry's adventures was, well, a little *edgy*. How many of you had friends with mothers who were convinced that Harry Potter was the gateway to the occult if he wasn't the Anti-Christ himself? (Almost every hand goes up.) How many had a mom or dad who felt this way? (Many hands.) How many felt this way themselves at one time? (Quite a few hands.)

Great. I can tell you, as one of the first eggheads to try to explain the literary merit, not to mention the Christian content, of the *Harry Potter* novels, that the years when the opinion that Harry was an occult gateway was mentioned in every news story about Harry or Ms. Rowling were very long years indeed. The thought persists, of course, but it is no longer everyone's first thought.

The thesis of tonight's talk is that *Harry Potter* is not only *not* the gateway to the occult but that he *is*, in fact, really a gateway to the best in

English Literature and much of world literature as well. You need keys to get through the gateways, of course, tools that will help us understand the books, why we love them so much, and how they have become such a big part of our lives. I'm going to give you five of these keys tonight.

To use them it helps if you have read a lot of good books. But even having read more of the Western Canon than anyone your age can do without having that slightly bug-eyed look, my bet is that you scratched your head when reading *Deathly Hallows* this summer and wondered "Why does the dragon in the Gringotts vault have 'pale scales' with 'milkily pink' eyes?" (If you saw the cover of the deluxe U.S. edition, the dragon was green with red wings and white eyes – nothing pale about the poor creature's scales).

You're "close readers," right? So this bothered you. Some of you probably even thought it had something to do with literary alchemy – and, of course, if you did, you were right. Those milkily pink eyes and pale scales are important details because they appear near the end of the *albedo* or white stage of the alchemy.

This is no accident. It's brilliant artistry. To spot and understand details like these you need special eyeglasses or keys to open. The five literature keys we'll pass out tonight – with the authors most often identified with their use – will open the locks on Moody's magical trunk that keep you from the deeper magic of the books: The keys are:

1. Narrative Misdirection from Miss Jane Austen

2. Literary Alchemy via Shakespeare and Charles Dickens

3. The Hero's Journey, let's say from Homer, Virgil, and Dante

4. Traditional Symbolism a la Messrs. Tolkien and Lewis – and

5. Postmodern Themes (Ms. Rowling is the most notable author on the short PoMo list, so we'll leave this without a "great" dead writer for now.)

If you understand these five keys tonight, the next time you reread *Deathly Hallows,* you'll slap your head at the appropriate time and say, "I get it; the traditional symbolism is why I cried when Dobby died." Anyone here cry when Dobby died in *Deathly Hallows*? How many? Hand's up. (Most of audience raises their hands.)

If you didn't cry when Dobby died, let's be frank, there's something wrong with you. I've heard of guys that sell crack and pornography to school children in Philadelphia who cried when Dobby died. Okay, hands down. Here's my pledge. Listen closely and you'll get these five keys. Smart as you all are, that means you'll be well on your way to understanding *Harry Potter*, the shared text of your generation and our times. Extra bonus: you'll know five reasons Harry was able to defeat the Dark Lord that aren't in the storyline. And, if you're really listening closely, you'll understand better how you think and how stories work.

Narrative Misdirection

One joke about Harry Potter in the literature wing of the Ivory Tower is that it's really just *"Pride and Prejudice* with wands." Ms. Rowling is always asked in interviews who her favorite author is and what her favorite book is. For over ten years she has always given the same answers: "Jane Austen is my favorite writer and her *Emma* is my favorite book." She added one time that she read *Emma* 20 times in a row.[1]

That may strike you as borderline obsessive. I've learned, though, that reading this way is anything but unusual for real Austen or devoted Harry Potter fans. C. S. Lewis was a Jane Austen reader, by the way. He said there were only two faults with Austen's work, both of which faults were damnable: her novels were too few and too short. One Lewis expert told me that the Narnian read the complete works of Austen every year from the age of 17. Prime Minister Disraeli may have been his role model. He read *Pride and Prejudice* 17 times straight.[2]

Rereading a book isn't the sign of a fanatic or someone who just can't get it the first time; it's the hallmark of a *serious* reader. None of us really understand what we've read until we've read and reread it, especially books of any length or substance.

Deathly Hallows is already being read and reread; I have no doubt it stands up to this kind of scrutiny because I've looked at it myself once or twice since the first run-through in July. It's the best thing Ms. Rowling has written. And, like her other books, much of the genius of *Deathly Hallows* is in her creative borrowings from Jane Austen.

What Rowling takes from Miss Austen, and from *Emma* specifically, is narrative misdirection. "Misdirection" is what a running back does in the open field to get a tackler to think he is moving in one direction when he is about to reverse field. Misdirection is also what a street magician does with sleight-of-hand to make you think the little red ball is under that cup (it isn't). *Narrative* misdirection is telling a story in such a way that readers believe they know for sure what is going on and then feel like fools, just like the football safety and con-man's shell game flunky, when it turns out they are very wrong.

There are several ways to pull off this misdirection trick in a novel. Ms. Rowling's method is pulled straight out of Austen's *Emma,* namely, in choosing the right voice with which to tell her story.

The "voice" we're talking about is called "third-person limited-omniscient." The shortcut to understanding this is to imagine a house-elf perched on Harry's right shoulder. The elf's got a magical minicam that allows him to show you not only everything Harry sees from a point of view just over the boy wizard's head, but allows the elf to also film what Harry is thinking and feeling (by pointing the camera lens in Harry's ear, I'm guessing). The "film" from this magical camera is, with few exceptions, the Harry Potter epic.

We don't get views of Dumbledore in the Hufflepuff common room or the Headmaster *anywhere* except on those occasions when he interacts with Harry. All the action, with three chapter exceptions in the 4100 pages of the books, is captured by the house-elf cameraman. This means that everything we learn as the story is told comes from just above or inside Harry's point of view.

The effect of this perspective is subtle but almost impossible to escape. It gives us the mistaken impression that we understand what's going on because we can see everything that Harry sees and thinks. And, indeed, we do have a pretty good picture of what Harry sees and thinks. Better than he has, in fact. We think, because Harry is not telling us the story (and distorting it with his prejudices), that we have a larger perspective than he does. Something like "distance" or "objectivity."

But we don't. *All* we get is Harry's view and, even if it's a bit bigger than Harry's, it isn't significantly bigger. Third Person Limited Omniscient storytelling is no better than the hero telling you the story himself. If anything, it's worse. If the hero tells you the story, you realize the hero has blind spots; the house-elf version is the same information but we think we have an objective, bird's-eye view.

Nope, not close.

The hard thing to remember when reviewing the magical minicam video is that we're on the shoulder of a teenage boy. However brave and earnest Harry is, there are few things as stupid in the entire world as a teenage boy. Sorry, guys. It's a universal truth almost globally acknowledged ... and you'll think so, too, in few years.

Anyway, at the end of every *Harry Potter* book we find out (surprise!) this perspective was wrong or, at least, laughably incomplete and filled with mistaken ideas of what was really happening at Hogwarts and elsewhere. This boy, alas, is like all teenage boys; again, my apologies, but he's a moron. Because the minicam is held just above Harry's point of view we forget after awhile that he doesn't know everything.

At the end of the story, having identified with this heroic young man and his fun friends, we've bought the whole package of his beliefs and imaginings. You'd think by the time Barty Crouch, Jr., is revealed as the faux Alastar Moody – the fourth Defense Against the Dark Arts teacher in as many years who turns out in the end to not be what he seemed – that we might have been a little less credulous or willing to believe *anything* Harry believes to be true, especially about a DADA professor.

The only story where we're not surprised at the end, because we accepted Harry's opinion, is *Half Blood Prince*. But, of course, we should have suspected something was crazy about the sixth book's finish. All the major characters except Dumbledore and Snape line up to tell Harry, "Doggone it, you were right. Snape was evil and Dumbledore was wrong to trust him!" And sure enough, in the seventh book we learn that all these people, in accepting Harry's view of the events on the Astronomy Tower, were wrong, just as we readers had been wrong in all six books. The assassination on the Tower had been staged.

We were all, I submit, Confundus-charmed by the narrative misdirection magic of Ms. Rowling's choice of positions for her storytelling minicam.

Ms. Rowling pulls off the signature surprise ending in every single book. Go ahead and ask yourself: "If I could see this story from any perspective, over whose shoulder would I place the house-elf cameraman?" How about Dumbledore? Good choice. You know he knows more of what's going on, even about Harry, than Harry does, not to mention the doings of Lord Voldemort, the Ministry, or the Potions teacher, about which Harry (and we readers) have no idea.

How about Severus Snape? I dread the idea of these stories told from Snape's perspective and I *really* feel for the house-elf, but, yes,

Snape also has to have a better idea of what's going on than Harry. Lord Voldemort, Professor McGonagall, even Moaning Myrtle: we want *anybody's* perspective but Harry's.

But we don't get this kind of surprise at the end of *Deathly Hallows*. What happened? Harry finally filled in the big circles.

Imagine three intersecting circles shaped something like a pretzel or the five Olympic rings (minus two rings). The area of each of these rings contains the sum total of a major character's knowledge. One is Voldemort's, one is Snape's, and the last is Dumbledore's. The area where these circles intersect are the things that two or all three know.

Where does Harry fit in here? He has a circle, too. Harry's is just a very small circle, proportionate to what he is able to figure out, and his circlet is placed right at the intersection of the three bigger circles. Harry may know something the three big players don't know, but it's pretty small compared to what each of the others knows, not to mention all three combined.

What changes by the end of *Deathly Hallows* is that Harry has finally learned much of what is going on in those big three rings. He learns Voldemort's secrets from Dumbledore in *Half-Blood Prince* and through better control of his and Voldemort's mind-link in *Deathly Hallows*. Near the end of the seventh book, Hermione says to Harry, "Wow, you really know how this guy [Lord Voldemort] thinks." Harry responds, "Yeah, I wish I understood how Dumbledore thought." Don't we all wish we knew what Dumbledore was thinking.

Most of *Deathly Hallows* is spent throwing a light into the late Headmaster's dark, locked head-space. We learn the dirt on Dumbledore from Doge, Aunt Muriel, the *Daily Prophet* interview with Rita, Rita's book, from Aberforth, and finally from Dumbledore himself at Harry's King's Cross Station. And what we learned from Severus' memories in the Pensieve is the narrative misdirection shocker of all the books, the "big twist" at which Ms. Rowling promised she was aiming. Too simplify horribly, Snape was a very good guy and Albus was more than a little Machiavellian.

Harry, armed with this larger perspective (having expanded his knowledge from his narrow view minicam to include the Dark Lord, Severus Snape, *and* the late great Dumbledore), of course, kicks butt in the Battle of Hogwarts. He's hit the epistemological trifecta. He's not going to be doing the usual dance with Ron and Hermione at the end of this book, chanting "Oh my goodness, I was totally flummoxed. How could we have known?" Harry finally knows and believes more than what he's seen.

So what? What do we get for understanding narrative misdirection and how Ms. Rowling pulls it off?

Beyond some appreciation of the artistry and genius of her story telling, not to mention her debt to Austen, what we get is a repeated experience of the wisdom in the saying "Don't believe everything you think." Harry's perspective, after all, is the conscious individual's perspective: what we can sense and some awareness of what we are thinking and feeling filtered through our prejudices and mental ruts. Ms. Rowling is telling us that, like the teenage boy we've been following, our perspectives are also dangerously limited and untrustworthy.

We also know *why* Harry was able to defeat Lord Voldemort. We know from traditional epistemology that we are or we become, in some fashion, what we know and that we are our knowing faculty [see chapter 5]. Harry, by the end of *Deathly Hallows* and his final battle with the Dark Lord, has become the greater part of the three rings of knowledge previously unknown to him. He has become Albus-Severus-Potter, if you will, with all their knowledge of Tom Riddle, Jr.

Voldemort, in contrast, is put in the position Harry has been in every previous story's ending, namely, surprised at all he doesn't know because of his narrow perspective. Unlike Harry, though, he denies all that Harry reveals to him in their Great Hall confrontation. Feeling remorse would have been a better choice!

We'll come back to this idea of the power of a larger perspective when we get to the fifth key, Postmodern Themes. Jane Austen, the queen of narrative misdirection and the "big twist" according to Ms. Rowling, delivered the same message to the Empiricists of her pre-modern era as Ms. Rowling does as a post-modern. Which explains why Jane Austen is as popular as she is right now. If you wondered why you can't turn on a teevee or go to a movie without seeing an Austen flick or spinoff, it's because she's stunningly current.

But I'm jumping the gun on that subject. Time for the alchemy.

Literary Alchemy

Tonight, as you can see, I am dressed as an alchemist, or, really, like an alchemical novel: the suit is black, the shirt is brilliantly white, and the signature bow tie is red. I dressed up this way to illustrate the second key for unlocking *Deathly Hallows*: literary alchemy. Let's leave the sartorial illustration, or object lesson, to talk about what alchemy was and what literary alchemy is. When I talk about the colors, though, check out the clothes again as visual reminders – black, then white, then red.

Alchemy, in a nutshell, was the science for the perfection or sanctification of the alchemist's soul. This heroic venture is all but impossible today because the way we look at reality, at "things," *per se,* makes the Great Work itself almost an absurdity. Unlike the medieval alchemists, we moderns and postmoderns see things with a clear subject/object distinction; that is, we believe you and I and that table are entirely different things and between them is there is no connection or relation. The knowing subject is one thing and the observed object is completely "other."[3]

To the alchemist that is not the case. His efforts in changing lead to gold are based on the premise that he, as the subject, will go through the same types of changes and purifications as the materials he is working with. In sympathy with these metallurgical transitions and resolutions of contraries, his soul will be purified in correspondence as long as he is working in a prayerful state within the Mysteries (sacraments) of his revealed tradition.

Now, historically there was an Arabic alchemy, a Chinese alchemy, a Kabbalistic, as well as a Christian alchemy; each differs superficially with respect to their spiritual traditions but, in every one, the alchemist was working with a sacred natural science or physics to advance his spiritual purification. This was only possible because he looked at the metal he was working with as something with which he was not "other" but with which he was in relationship. The alchemist and the lead becoming gold are artifex and artifact imitating and accelerating the work of the Creator creating a bridge so that, as lead changes to gold or material perfection, the alchemist's soul in sympathy goes through similar transformations and purifications.

How does this edifying magic become the scaffolding for Harry's adventures? Largely through the genius of William Shakespeare. Hermetic wisdom and alchemical efforts were such commonplaces in Elizabethan England that Shakespeare and his contemporaries recognized the magic of staged drama as essentially alchemical. If we groundlings are all watching what's going on up on the stage and everything is working the way it's supposed to, the subject-object distinction dissolves, inasmuch as we identify with the characters and their agonies. As they go through their changes, like the metals in a crucible, we identify with them and pass through the same cathartic moment.[4]

The great dramatists of that period realized, "if what we're doing is alchemical, why don't we use alchemical imagery and language, too?" And, voila, literary alchemy was born. This stream of English literature, in which narrator or characters and the reader or audience pass, in correspondence, through the stages of the alchemical work, runs through the next five centuries of poetry, stage work, stories, and novels. You may not have recognized it, but it's a big part of things you have read or viewed.

Shakespeare's *Romeo and Juliet*, for instance. This play you've all read and probably seen on stage or screen has a black and a white and a red stage that ends in gold. You remember Romeo's melancholic beginnings, and the strife and division in the streets of Verona. The white stage begins when the young lovers meet. The division between Capulet and Montague is joined when this couple is bound by the sacrament of marriage. The story is essentially over when they're married in the church service and the marriage is consummated. But the accomplishments of the white stage that are hidden have to be revealed on a larger stage in the crucible of the red stage. Through the deaths of Romeo and Juliet in the Capulet tomb, greater life comes to Verona. Juliet's parents and Romeo's father promise to erect golden statues of the star-crossed lovers and the city is at peace at last.

Dickens does much the same thing in *Tale of Two Cities*. As you probably remember, *Tale* is divided into three books. The first is about the recovery of a man "buried alive" in the Bastille and about the darkness in both England and France. The second is about the doppelganger of Darney and Carton and how each loves Lucie Manette, who is almost always in white. And the third book is the crucible of Revolutionary Paris with Carton's simultaneously spectacular and sublime sacrifice to save the wedded Charles and Lucie.

If Dickens the Alchemist makes you raise your eyebrows, remember there was a Coleridge inspired Shakespearean revival in the early 19th century in London, a time when Dickens was in love with the stage. His most dramatic novel is his shortest, that is *Tale of Two Cities,* and, sure enough, it's a play in 3 Acts about the resolution of contraries featuring a wedding in the second act and a sacrificial death that "saves" a city in some fashion in the third. Think about all the "resurrection men," the several mirrored figures there are in *Tale,* and the power of the finish. Is there a better line in any language than ""It is a far, far better thing that I do, than I have ever done; it is a far, far better rest that I go to than I have ever known"? Joanne Rowling has said it's the best one-liner in English and I think she's right.[5]

Shakespeare, the Metaphysical Poets, Blake, Dickens, Yeats, Eliot, even C. S. Lewis after Charles Williams – a large part of their magical artistry and transforming imagery is alchemical. Ms. Rowling is a Shakespeare lover, a fan of Dickens, and a Lewis admirer; we shouldn't be too surprised, then, to find that she swims in the same stream of English literature as her favorites do. *Harry Potter* is an alchemical drama, pure and simple.

We first see that the books are largely about the resolution of contraries, especially the battle between the hot and dry Gryffindors up in their tower and the cold and moist Slytherins in the dungeons beneath the lake. Harry's adventures are about his transcending this polarity, marrying the contraries, which purification happens in, you guessed it, a black and a white and a red stage. Every book and the series as a whole come with a complete set.

In the individual books, the black stage, or *nigredo,* is almost always launched on Privet Drive, where Harry is treated horribly and, at least in *Philosopher's Stone,* lives in a cupboard under the stairs. The work of breaking Harry down continues each year when he gets to Hogwarts and Severus Snape takes over, a black figure if there ever was one. But Hogwarts is the home of Albus Dumbledore, whose first name means "white," and Hogwarts, the "white house" if you will, is where Harry is purified of the failing identified at the Dursleys as he and the Quarreling Couple solve that year's mystery. The understanding he gains through these trials is revealed in the book's crisis, the confrontation with the bad guys, in which he always dies a figurative death and is reborn. From Privet Drive to his chat with Dumbledore at book's end, Harry is always purified and transformed.

The clearest illustration of this is in *Prisoner of Azkaban*. At the start, this is one angry teenage boy. He blows Aunt Marge up, quite literally, because she has a little too much to drink and, in a flood of Thatcherisms (Aunt Marge and her bulldogs being Margaret Thatcher and the Conservatives after all), says unkind things about Harry's parents. At the end of same book he is so much changed that he throws himself in front of Pettigrew, the man who actually betrayed his parents and was almost solely responsible for their deaths, because he felt his father wouldn't want his best friends to kill Peter Pettigrew. James Dean to sacrificial savior is a lead-to-gold transformation, right?

The series taken altogether has a black, white and red stage, too: *Order of the Phoenix* is the series "black book," *Half-Blood Prince* is the White, and *Deathly Hallows* is the *rubedo* or Red stage. Let's review them quickly.

The *nigredo* is the stage in which the subject is broken down, stripped of all but the essential qualities for purification in the *albedo* or white work. *Order of the Phoenix*, darkest and most disturbing of all the *Harry Potter* novels, is this stage in the series; Ms. Rowling cues us to this not only in the plot points, all of which are about Harry's loss of his identity, but in the "black"-ness of the book. No small part of it takes place in the House of Black and it ends, of course, with the death of Sirius Black. More important, though, is that *Phoenix details* Harry's near complete dissolution. Every idea he has of himself is taken from him. Dolores Umbridge teaches him that Hogwarts can be hell. He learns his father was a jerk. No Quidditch! Ron and Hermione outrank him on the Hogwarts totem pole. The entire "girl thing" eludes him except for agonizing confusion and heartbreak. Everything, in brief, is a nightmare for him in his fifth year. His self-understanding and identity are shattered – except, at the very end, after Sirius' death and with it any hope of a family life with his godfather, Harry learns about the Prophecy. That understanding replaces everything else. And that's the end of the black work.

When *Half-Blood Prince* begins, we feel we are in a different universe. Albus Dumbledore is not only back in Harry's life, he comes to pick him up at Privet Drive! The Headmaster, largely absent in *Phoenix*, is everywhere in *Prince*. This is his book, which, given the meaning of his name and the work that is accomplished, might be called the "white book." Not to mention, like Sirius at the end of the "black book," Albus dies at the end of the "white." Through the tutorials with Dumbledore and the tasks he is given, Harry comes to a whole new understanding of himself in terms of the Prophecy *and* his relationship to Lord Voldemort. Harry doesn't get the whole truth from the Headmaster, but at the end of *Prince,* he has been transformed from a boy who doesn't believe Dumbledore will show up to one that defiantly tells the Minister of Magic, "I'm a Dumbledore man through and through."

Deathly Hallows, you probably guessed, being last, is the 'Red book,' the *rubedo.* If you've read the alchemy chapters in *Unlocking Harry Potter,* you know what has to happen in the *rubedo.* Just like *Romeo and Juliet* and *Tale of Two Cities,* a wedding has to be revealed, contraries have to be resolved, and a death to self must lead to greater life. We should expect to see a philosopher's stone and a philosophical orphan, as well. The *rubedo* of *Deathly Hallows* is the crisis of the whole series we waited two years to read – and it is everything alchemical we could have hoped for.

We start off with Bill and Fleur's alchemical wedding, in which France and England are married in the *sitzkrieg* before the shooting war with Voldemort's Nazis begins. The first eight chapters of *Deathly Hallows* are lead up to this union of opposites, of choler and phlegm. As you'd expect, the wedding itself is a meeting of contraries, of solar and lunar. That's why, in addition to the Gallic/Briton jokes, we have the lunar Lovegoods show up in sunlight-bright yellow. Luna, the moon in solar outfit, explains that it's good luck to wear gold at a wedding. This isn't just loony Luna; everything at the wedding is golden: the floor, the poles, the band jackets, the bridesmaids' dresses, even Tonks' hair!

We have a long way to go, though, before the conjunction of the Slytherin and Gryffindor opposites. The wedding breaks up with the arrival of Kingsley's lynx Patronus with the message that Rufus Scrmgeor is dead and the Death Eater *blitzkrieg* has begun. With wedding and the death of the first character whose name means 'red,' the real action of *Deathly Hallows'* alchemical work begins.

The rest of the book is best understood as black, white, and red stages. For those of you taking notes (who let them in here?), the *nigredo* stretches painfully from Ch. 9, "Place to Hide," to Ch. 18, "The Life and Lies of Albus Dumbledore." Harry's purification and illumination begin in Ch. 19, "The Silver Doe," and end with the trio's return to Hogsmead in Ch. 28, "The Missing Mirror." The crisis of the book and the series, of course, is in Harry's return to Hogwarts, destruction of the remaining

Horcruxes, and victory over Lord Voldemort, as told in the last eight chapters of *Deathly Hallows*.

The ten *nigredo* chapters are as dark and gothic as any reader could want. We get a trip to the House of Black, we visit the Orwellian "Magic is Might" black statue in the new Ministry (accessible only by flush toilet . . .), and we go camping, where, for some reason, it's always night, or overcast, or the three friends can't get along. Ron finally just up and leaves. Can you say "dissolution"? Ask anyone what the longest part of *Deathly Hallows* is. The answer is always "the camping trip." It *is* nine chapters (that's 14 through 21) but only three are agony, the three after Ron departs.

These Christmas chapters about Harry's holiday trip with Hermione to Godric's Hollow are the climax of the *nigredo* and end with Harry's crisis of faith. We left Harry at the end of *Prince* proclaiming that he was "a Dumbledore man." In *Hallows*, he reads one article by Rita Skeeter and his faith is shaken. He talks to Aunt Muriel and Dogbreath at the wedding, his faith takes another blow, and now he is struggling to believe. At the end of the *nigredo*, when Harry reads *The Life and Lies of Albus Dumbledore*, he denies Dumbledore, denies that he loves Albus, denies that Dumbledore loved him, etc. Harry's holly and phoenix wand has been broken in battle with Nagini and he is left with a broken wand, a broken piece of mirror, and shattered faith. He keeps these fragments, though, in a bag around his neck. He denies Dumbledore, denies his mission, and, in something like despair, he keeps these remnants or relics of the person he once was close to his heart.

And just when I almost closed the book, feeling a little despair myself just before dawn, the *nigredo* ends with the brilliance reflecting off the Silver Doe in the snow-covered Forest of Dean. This chapter, a meeting of Christian, alchemical and Arthurian images in one spot, is probably the height of Ms. Rowling's achievement as a writer. A detailed look at the alchemy of *Deathly Hallows* is a talk longer than this one [see Ch. 2] and most of it is in the white stage: Ron the Baptist saving Harry, Ron's exorcism in destroying the Horcrux, Harry's death to self and discovery of remorse, repentance, faith, *and* love in Dobby's grave, and the pale dragon in Gringott's are all images of purification, with water on hand or nearby.

The white stone on the red earth of Dobby's grave and the "milkily" pink eyes are chromatic signs of the story's movement from white to red. The *rubedo* of *Deathly Hallows* begins, I think, when Harry refuses to listen to Aberforth's complaints and criticism of his brother Albus. When Harry shows his faith and his *choice* to believe, Neville appears to take him into the castle and the battle for Hogwarts begins. You could say the red stage really begins when Rubeus, the half-giant whose name means "red," flies through the window of Hogwarts Castle. In this battle, which includes Harry's sacrifice in the Forbidden Forest and his ultimate victory over Voldemort, the contraries are resolved and all the Houses sit down at one table. The battle also causes the creation of the "philosophical orphan" when Nymphadora and Remus Lupin are killed. And we get a Philosopher's Stone, too; Hermione and Ron's daughter, we learn in the epilogue, is named 'Rose,' which is another name for the Stone.

Three quick alchemical points before we hurry on to our next key:

The turning-into-its-opposite transformation in the last novel of the series shows how the world has been changed by Harry's internal victory and destruction of the scar-Horcrux. Lord Voldemort tortures and murders the Hogwarts Muggle Studies Teacher in the first chapter of the book. Her name is *Charity* Burbage and her corpse is dinner for Nagini. *Charity or Love is destroyed by Death.* Via Harry's death to self in the white stage's Dobby burial, revealed in his willing self-sacrifice before Voldemort, death's power is broken. *Lily and Harry's sacrificial and selfless love sustains life and has its victory over death.*

We see a complete transformation in Harry, too. He is a Dumbledore man by confession as the story begins but his disbelief and lack of trust come to the fore after his fight with Nagini in Godric's Hallow. After choosing to believe, however, when he is in Dobby's grave and choosing to pursue the Horcruxes as instructed rather than Hallows, he becomes almost Christlike in dying and rising from the dead to vanquish death. Even the near-omnipotent Dumbledore begs Harry's forgiveness and tells him he has known for a long time that Harry was "the better man."

What has made Harry the better man was becoming the Gryffindor/ Slytherin union himself; again, call him 'Albus Severus Potter,' as Harry and Ginevra name their younger son. He becomes the conjunction of contraries, we learned in the first key, by acquiring the seemingly contradictory views of both Albus Dumbledore, champion Gryffindor, and Severus Snape, Slytherin House Master and icon by the end of *Deathly Hallows.*

When he fights Lord Voldemort in the Great Hall, Harry has achieved an understanding and perspective that is essentially all-knowing. Voldemort, in contrast, has the limited ego view that we had at the end of every previous book (because that was all the perspective Harry's house-elf with magical minicam gave us!). Remember, to a classicist *and* postmodern like Rowling, "knowing" is in large part a measure of "being." In becoming relatively 'omniscient' as Albus Severus Potter, Sr., Harry, the Hogwarts Hermaphrodite and *de facto* Philosopher's Stone, is "love on legs" and, as such, virtually omnipotent.

Voldemort didn't stand a chance.

The Hero's Journey

Literary alchemy is a pretty complicated subject. Not only do you need to understand the specific symbolism of the tradition used by writers from Shakespeare to C.S. Lewis and now Ms. Rowling (things like what a grave, a dragon, and references to Mercury refer to in the work and as symbols), but you have to get your head around the alchemy of literature, how identifying with the action and characters transform us the way observing metallurgical transformations purified the soul of the traditional alchemist. It's something serious readers experience every day in their favorite books and it is the heart of all stage productions. But, because it means seeing beyond or around one of our core beliefs as modern people – that subjects and objects are distinct or separate and that observation doesn't change one or the other– the magic of stories, the real alchemy, escapes us.

The Hero's journey isn't nearly so hard to understand. In large part, it's a story formula each writer adapts to his or her purposes. Once you recognize it and pin down the author's tweaking and meaning, you've almost mastered the third key. Seeing how Harry's annual journey and especially the one he takes in Deathly Hallows ensures – and I mean 'guarantees' – his victory over Voldemort, though, will require another stretch of our thinking very similar to the one we just made with alchemy. Let's identify the stages of Harry's hero journey first and then get to Ms. Rowling's meaning and how we are changed by it.

You all came to this school for a hardcore classical education and I know you read the *Iliad*, the *Odyssey*, the *Aeneid*, and Dante's *Comedia* "before breakfast" as the Japanese would say. No doubt your teachers introduced you to the idea of "monomyth," as the Hero's Journey is often called, in your discussions of these myths and epic poems. Just in case we have visitors without this background, I'll make a few quick comments as a review.

There seems to be a common pattern in the foundational myths of cultures around the world. Here is the fire-hose version: the hero of the story is called to an adventure and eventually separates from his mundane existence for a journey to a magical place. On this journey he encounters a series of trials and deceives or defeats the enemy with the help of a goddess. The hero becomes something like a god. He returns to the mundane plane of existence to share the graces consequent to his journey and victory. This journey formula is such a commonplace in literature, and has been since the Homeric poems were sung, that one serious reader has even suggested that the Book of Acts was composed *on the model of* Virgil's Aeneid with St. Paul standing in for Aeneas.[6]

We've already seen that Ms. Rowling writes with a three-stage alchemical formula in her books, in which Harry is downtrodden, purified, and revealed as transformed, black, to white, to red. I think a moment's reflection will be enough for you to see that every year Harry *separates* from his Muggle home on Privet Drive, is *initiated* and transformed in a series of magical trials and adventures, and *returns* to Muggledom or to the Dursleys, at least, at the end of each school year.

Ms. Rowling's annual journey formula for Harry, though, is more detailed than Privet Drive to Hogwarts and back to Privet Drive. Harry's journey has ten steps we see every year:

1. **Privet Drive:** Home Sweet Home!

2. **Magical Escape:** the intrusion of the magical world into profane existence – and the adventure begins!

3. **Mystery:** Harry, Ron, and Hermione's extracurricular assignment each year.

4. **Crisis:** the mystery comes to a head – and Harry chooses to do the right, difficult thing!

5. **Underground:** Harry and one or both of his two friends go underground to confront the evil to be overcome!

6. **Battle:** and we have a fight!

7. **Loss and Death:** a fight Harry loses every single year . . . and seems to die.

8. **Resurrection:** but he rises from the dead, in the presence of a

symbol of Christ.

9. **Dumbledore Denouement:** the Headmaster explains what happened that Harry missed.

10. **King's Cross:** Harry rides the Hogwarts Express back to the conjunction of his magical and Muggle lives.

If you want to see how each *Harry Potter* novel satisfies every point on this checklist, with only one or two exceptions in seven years of adventures, pick up *How Harry Cast His Spell* (Tyndale, 2008, 3rd edition) or *Unlocking Harry Potter* (Zossima, 2008, 2nd edition) where there are charts and long explanations. Here I just want to point out three curious things about how *Deathly Hallows* satisfies this formula.

First, the ten steps above can be divided pretty neatly into the divisions of separation: (steps one and two), initiation (three to eight), and return (nine and ten). The fifth step, though, "going underground," is a bit of a head-scratcher. Sure, Odysseus journeys to the land of the dead, Aeneas follows suit, and Dante, boy, does he go underground! There is even the pointer to Christ's Harrowing of Hades.

But in the Rowling formula, it just seems bizarre and mechanical. We go through the Trap Door Fluffy protects in *Stone*. In *Chamber*, it's down the long slide under the sink in Myrtle's bathroom to the Chamber of Secrets, again, "miles beneath Hogwarts." *Prisoner* has the most token underground travel: through the roots beneath the Whomping Willow to the tunnel leading to the Shrieking Shack. Harry doesn't go underground in *Goblet* but to a graveyard, which, because most of the people "present" *are* underground, has the same symbolic weight. In *Phoenix*, Harry and friends battle the Death Eaters in the Department of Mysteries in the lowest level of the Ministry of Magic. Dumbledore takes Harry into a subterranean cave and lake in *Prince* before making his notable, if solo, descent from the Astronomy Tower.

What is Ms. Rowling after here? I think it's safe to assume if we see an event or action recur without fail in each book, it has been put there intentionally and for a reason beyond a hat-tip to Homer and Joseph Campbell.

In *Deathly Hallows* Harry and friends go underground, too, right? Again and again. And again. I counted seven times – and yes, that number is meaningful. They flush themselves into the Ministry and descend to the Wizengamot chambers to rescue the Cattermoles. Harry and Ron dive into the pool in the Forest of Dean to get the Sword of Gryffindor. There's a regular reunion in the dungeon beneath Malfoy Manor. Harry digs himself a hole to get underground and bury Dobby. The Terrific Trio and Griphook descend to the depths below Gringotts to liberate and hitch a ride on a pale dragon. We get back into the Shrieking Shack via the tunnel beneath the Whomping Willow. And Harry enters the London "Underground" in King's Cross, his very real and 'in his head' meeting place with the late Headmaster (King's Cross is the busiest platform on the London Underground subway system).

In every one of these trips, a spelunker ascends in a lifesaving rescue (the Cattermoles, Harry from the pool, Dobby's group rescue from the Malfoy's, and the Gringotts dragon), with an invaluable magical object (the Sword of Gryffindor, twice, the cup Horcrux, and Snape's memories), or forever changed (Ron post-baptism, Harry after burying Dobby, Harry rising from King's Cross). Could the previous six novels' underground passages have just been foreshadowing all these descents in *Deathly Hallows*? Hold on to this question. We'll have to come back to it.

Second, another signature of Ms. Rowling's Hero's Journey is Harry's annual figurative death and resurrection from the dead in the presence of a symbol of Christ. There are only two lines we read in every book, I think, three if you include Hermione's pleas for Ron and Harry to read *Hogwarts: A History*. One is "and Harry's scar hurt worse than it had ever hurt before." The third time that occurs in a book, my head begins to ache. The other and more important repeatable line is Harry's dying thought, "so this is what it's like to die." Battling Quirrell, fanged by a Basilisk, kissed by a Dementor, tortured by the reborn Dark Lord, possessed by Voldemort in the Ministry, carried by the Inferi into the lake, and just flat-out killed by Voldemort in the finale, Harry dies a figurative death in every single book.

And in every book except the last, he comes back from this faux death either because of or just in the vicinity of a symbol of Christ. I'll talk more about that symbolism in the next section, but here you just have to note for six books, Harry's resurrection is cued or caused by a potent Christian reference. Fawkes the Phoenix plays this part in *Chamber, Goblet,* and *Order of the Phoenix.* It's a Philosopher Stone in his pocket in the first book, a Stag Patronus in *Prisoner,* and both a Hippogriff and the Half-Blood Prince in *Prince.* [For explanations of these symbols, see *How Harry Cast His Spell, Chapter 9* (Tyndale, 2008).]

And *Deathly Hallows*?

In *Deathly Hallows*, Harry doesn't rise from the dead *in the presence of* a symbol of Christ. He rises *as* a symbol of Christ. I think it's safe to say here that all the previous deaths and resurrections were just pointers and prefigurings of Harry's ultimate victory, his "mastery of death." Ms. Rowling has said that the last third of *Deathly Hallows* was the fixed part of the storyline that drove every other element of the previous books. All the stories do point to Harry's trip into "The Forest Again."

Third, two violations of journey formula happen at the end of *Half-Blood Prince*: we don't get our meeting with Dumbledore (he's attending his own funeral) and we don't go to King's Cross station. That omission is understandable; as Ms. Rowling said before the finale, books six and seven slide together at the end into one story. We make up for it, though, in *Deathly Hallows,* where we get *two* Dumbledore denouement scenes and *two* trips to King's Cross. Harry's encounter with his mentor at his King's Cross vision is the most curious of these scenes and trips.

Ms. Rowling said in the 2007 Bloomsbury chat that this meeting took place in King's Cross because "the name worked rather well." On her Open Book Tour press conference in Los Angeles, she said she thought the Christian content of the books was "obvious."[7] I think we can all agree that Harry's arriving at 'King's Cross' after his sacrificial death in love for his friends is a pointer to Calvary and not an especially obscure reference. But why meet with Dumbledore there? and underground?

To answer those questions, I think we have to discuss why poets and novelists return again and again to the Hero's Journey or Monomyth. If you grasp this, you'll understand why Harry's final return from the dead *guaranteed* his eventual victory over the Dark Lord.

The Hero's Journey isn't a story formula, ultimately, or just a mechanical structure to hang a plot on. It's really about the symbolism of the Circle and the Center, a symbolism Mircea Eliade discusses in *Myth of the Eternal Return*.[8] This gets a little heady, so pay attention here.

Harry's adventure completes a circle every year: from his life with the Dursleys at Privet Drive, through his adventures in the magical world, back to being picked up by the Dursleys at King's Cross Station at year's end. Draw a circle with the beginning point at the bottom being the Dursleys, Hogwarts being diametrically across from it (up in Scotland?), and the circle coming to close again at the Dursleys, who meet Harry at King's Cross.

Now every hero's journey is a figurative, completed circle, if not a geometric one, so let's think about what a circle is. Anyone want to define "circle" for me? Not even the note-takers? I doubt this is Euclid's definition, but it should help us understand what a Hero's Journey is and does. *A circle is the uniform radiation of a spaceless point, the center, into space.*

All points of a circle are equidistant from a center point, right? This center, then, really *defines* the circle, of which it is only an extension. Think of a ripple moving away from a rock dropped in the pond. The rock at the center causes and defines the circle rippling away from it. A circle, which is visible, is only intelligible and understandable because of the defining and spaceless center that is usually invisible and unknowable in itself. (This, incidentally, is why a circle is an adequate, even a profound representation of God as Trinity with God the Father as Center, the Word as Circle, and Holy Spirit as proceeding radiation from the Center. The Father is only knowable through His Word and because of the Holy Spirit; each is distinct and the center is logically, but not temporally, prior).

And this has *what* to do with Harry's annual journey? I'm getting there!

A hero completing a circular journey has ritually arrived at the defining center because the circle he or she has completed is one with the center. Harry ends every year and the story has its most important turn at King's *Cross* because the cross, like the circle, is defined by the center point at which a horizontal and vertical line meet. Draw a cross in your circle to divide your circle into four pie pieces. This point which defines the cross, the circle and the end (*telos* in Greek; the goal or purpose) of the journey brings the hero into the "sacred space" or point creating the world,

Harry makes this trip to the crossing point defining the circle of his journey *seven* times. I explain the symbolism and importance of the number seven in *Unlocking Harry Potter* but, as you've read the stories you know how central that number is: the number of Quidditch players, Horcruxes, Years of Magical Education, Harry-clones escaping Privet Drive in *Deathly Hallows*, etc. If you've studied Arithmancy with Professor Vector or Pythagoras or even Lord Voldemort, you know this is the most "magically powerful" number. Having completed the circle and achieved the center the seventh time, this last time by sacrificing himself without hope of gain, Harry, in effect, has executed his ego or died to himself, thereby returning to the center or transpersonal self before Voldemort kills him.

Harry survives the Killing Curse *again*. How? In the story, it's a function of his connection with the sacrificial death of his first savior, Lily Potter, and the magic of this sacrifice that exists in her blood, blood that flows in both Voldemort and Harry. I think it is as credible – and maybe even easier to understand – to think that Harry survives as the center because no point on the circle can destroy the center defining that circle. By transcending himself, Harry steps out of time and space, if you will, and into eternity and infinite, which Ms. Rowling portrays quite appropriately as a place called King's Cross.

When Harry tells Dumbledore he thinks they are at King's Cross, do you remember the Headmaster's reaction?

> "King's Cross Station!" Dumbledore was chuckling immoderately.
> "Good gracious, really?" (*Deathly Hallows*, Ch. 35, page 712)

Dumbledore, unlike Harry, undoubtedly has studied Arithmancy, sacred geometry, and Christian scripture (hence the tombstone verses in Godric's Hollow). Of course, he finds Harry's intuitive choice of "locations" (after his sacrifice makes him "master of death") quite humorous. Dumbledore laughs because the hero's journey is a circle for much the same reason that the events of Calvary (the King's Cross) have their meaning and why Christ died on a geometric cross [see Chapter 7 and its discussion of Rene Guenon, *The Symbolism of the Cross*, Sophia Perennis, 1998]. In achieving the center, Harry has become if not one, then "not two" with the transcendent Absolute.

By choosing to return to time and space after this apotheosis, Harry broke the power of the Dark Lord. Harry went underground repeatedly in *Deathly Hallows*, most importantly in choosing to dig Dobby's grave, because each descent into the underworld was a dying to himself from which, remember, he either saved lives, recovered lost treasure, or was enlightened. Imagine the world as a circle; every descent was Harry's movement toward the center and source of life and away from the periphery of ego and the fear of death.

It's important to note that the end of *Deathly Hallows* is not just the completion of Harry's journey in his seventh year, but the joining of the circle with the beginning of his journey in *Philosopher's Stone*.

There are too many connecting points and echoes to go into here [see Question 20 in FAQ Chapter 8 for a chart of 26 parallels] but you probably noticed in the first book that Hagrid carries Harry's body from the ruins of his childhood home to safety on Sirius' motorcycle and he escorted Harry from his about-to-be-destroyed house on Privet Drive on the same motorcycle and, in the last, carries Harry's body on the same motorcycle from the Forbidden Forest to Hogwarts as an echo of that event.

Harry returns to Godric's Hollow in *Deathly Hallows* for the first time since Hagrid took him to the Dursleys and learns on Christmas morning what happened to him and his parents on that Halloween long ago. Ted Lupin becomes the philosophical orphan whose parents were murdered by the Dark Lord's Death Eaters, completing and repeating another circle.

There is Neville Longbottom, too. In *Philosopher's Stone*, Dumbledore awards Gryffindor House the five points it needs to overcome Slytherin, because of Neville's courage. In *Deathly Hallows*, of course, it is Neville's courage and faith in the face of almost certain death that brings him the Sword of Gryffindor to destroy Nagini, the last Horcrux.

And remember Harry's "resurrection" in *Philosopher's Stone*? He doesn't quite get to King's Cross in his first year, but it does take him *three days* to return to life. No doubt, Dumbledore "chuckled immoderately" then on the Chosen One's rising on the third day.

Mircea Eliade in *Myth of the Eternal Return* explains the difference between archaic, primitive man and modern people.[9] The former are creatures who understand reality as cosmos, myth, and cycles in which he can participate ritually to transcend himself and enter the center of sacred space and time. In this, he becomes more real and has more being because, to use spatial terms in metaphor, he is closer to the fount of Being, the Supreme Reality. Modern people, in contrast, live in an ontologically flat world of time, space, matter, and linear, sequential history. We cannot, as Moderns at least, "approach the center" anymore than we can become alchemists.

In myth and story, however, as well as religious ritual, we can reenter an ontologically rich "place" in which we can transcend ourselves and "have" more being. Eliade argues in *The Sacred and the Profane* that this is the reason for modern people's preoccupation with entertainments, movies, story, and novels. In a secular culture, he says, entertainment serves a mythic or religious function. These are the activities in which even the atheist and ideologically secular person can have mythic, even religious experience of a world other than that defined by the ego-self of the individual.[10]

The Hero's Journey in *Harry Potter,* especially the journey he starts and finishes in *Deathly Hallows* which also completes the circle and finds the center and crossing point of the whole series, explains in large part why we love the books and why Voldemort couldn't defeat Harry in the end. Having achieved the Absolute and Transcendent, Harry could not be defeated by the fraction of a man fearing death that Voldemort had become.

And we, having experienced Harry's journey alongside him, had some imaginative experience of our own hope of defeating death. No wonder we read and reread these books!

Which brings us to key number four, traditional symbolism.

Traditional symbolism

First, let's say what symbolism isn't.

As I wrote in *How Harry Cast His Spell:*

> Symbolism is not something 'standing in' for something else, a tit-for-tat allegory. An allegory is a story or word picture in which something existing on earth is represented by another earthly character or image. Some critics, for example, have written that *The Lord of the Rings* is an allegory of the Second World War, with Sauron and the forces of darkness standing in for the Axis powers, while the Fellowship of the Ring and other white hats represent the Allies. As readers, we don't interpret allegories as much as we translate them; allegories, unlike symbols, are just a translation of one story into another language or story. Neither are symbols simply signs, or at least they are not like street signs, which are simple representations for earthly instructions or things (such as "Stop" or "Deer Crossing").
>
> Literary characters and stories are not necessarily symbolic. Great novels like *The Pilgrim's Progress* are allegorical both in regard to their characters and story line. Christian's journey in *Progress* is a detailed picture of events and people met on every Christian's earthly journey. The men that he meets—I think immediately of "Mr. Worldly Wiseman" (a great stand-in for television talking heads!)—are cardboard cutouts of people we

meet every day who support or obstruct us in our passage to the heavenly kingdom.

Many stories that are symbolic, however, are often mistakenly explained (and dismissed) as allegories. Please note that little else disturbed C. S. Lewis and J. R. R. Tolkien more than critical explanation of their fiction as "allegorical" (as in the WWII analogy). The reason their books touch us so deeply and have endured in popularity as long as they have is because of their symbolic meaning.

Symbols, rather than analogies for other earthly events, are transparencies through which we see greater realities than we can see on earth (see 1 Corinthians 13:12 and 2 Corinthians 3:18). The ocean as it stretches to the distant horizon is a symbol of the infinite power and breadth of the spiritual reality human beings call God. In seeing the one, we can sense the other. The ocean as a body of water has no power in itself to stir the heart; it's just an oversized bathtub. But as a symbol of God, a way of seeing the unseeable, it can take our breath away or bring tears to our eyes.

Symbols are windows, too, through which otherworldly realities (powers, graces, and qualities) intrude into the world. This is the traditional or theocentric understanding of Creation—that all earthly things and events testify to "the invisible things of him from the creation of the world" (Romans 1:20, KJV). This testimony includes the power of natural beauty and grandeur (think of mountain ranges, a field of flowers, or a lion on the savanna). It also includes sacred art, architecture, and liturgy, which are by definition symbolic in their portrayal of greater value than earthly realities . . ..

The great revealed traditions teach that man, as an image and likeness of God, is a living symbol—both in the sense of transparency through which we look and of an opening through which God enters the world. Mankind is created in the image of God so that the world will reverence the God who cannot be seen (see 1 John 4:20 and the sequence of the Great Commandments in Mark 12:30-31). Humanity also is designed to be a vehicle of God's grace, power, and love intruding into the world of time and space. The tragedy of man's "fall" is that, because most people no longer believe they are symbols of God, shaped in His likeness, it is more difficult to see God in our neighbor, and the world is often denied access to God through His chosen vessel.

We are still moved, however, by the symbols in nature and the symbols that we experience in story form. This is the power of myth: that we can experience invisible spiritual realities and truths greater than visible, material things in story form. Tolkien described Christianity as the "True Myth," the ultimate intrusion of God into the world through his incarnation as Jesus of Nazareth. Tolkien's explanation of this idea was instrumental in C. S. Lewis's conversion to Christianity; it is this understanding of the purpose and power of story that gives his fiction its depth, breadth, and height.

Symbols in stories, just as the symbols in nature, sacred art, and edifying myths, are able to put us in contact with a greater reality than what we can sense directly. They do this through our imagination. The power of Lewis's and Tolkien's writing is found in their profound symbolism; *The Lord of the Rings* is not a strained allegory or retelling of WWII, but a dynamic symbol of the cosmic struggle between good and evil of which WWII was also but a real-world representation."[11]

Literary Alchemy and the Hero's Journey, then, are best understood as story formulas that are essentially symbolic. The alchemy is a transparency of accelerated human transformation from spiritual lead to gold, God's image to His likeness. By looking through this transparency, the subject/object distinction dissolves and we experience some part of this apotheosis. Likewise, by accompanying the Hero on his Journey, each of us completes the circle or cycle and experiences the metaphysical center or Absolute, if only in our imaginations.

Ms. Rowling's use of symbols, though, isn't restricted to the traditional narrative schemes and structures on which she builds her stories, as remarkably rich in significance and important as alchemy and monomyth are in understanding her novels. Some of her most remarkable spiritual-transparencies and reality-windows are stand-alone characters lifted straight from the backlot of traditional literature and art, others are less in-your-face but still not especially unusual, some are remarkably subtle, almost invisible.

I mentioned that Harry rises from the dead in the presence of a symbol of Christ in every book, didn't I? What I probably didn't mention was that these symbols of Christ, specifically, and resurrection in general – the phoenix, the philosopher's stone, the white stag, and the hippogriff – aren't the only Christ symbols in the book. As I explain in *How Harry Cast His Spell*, the Red Lion of Gryffindor, the Centaur, the

Unicorn, the Goblet of Fire, and every book title, believe it or not, are pointers to the God-Man. It's not something a medievalist or pedestrian Christian struggles to see; as the author says, it's "obvious."

C. S. Lewis wrote that "an influence which cannot evade our consciousness will not go very deep" [12] and the planetary symbolism that supports his more obvious Christian images in the *Narniad* is correspondingly subtle and penetrating.[13] Ms. Rowling's artistry, too, is not just blatant stand-ins and pointers, as we've seen in her alchemical backdrops. The meaning evident in her major characters and Ollivander's wand cores when viewed diagonally, that is, as symbols, are examples of her subtlety and profundity.

Harry, Ron, and Hermione, for example are both an alchemical experiment in progress and a tryptich of the soul's faculties. Alchemy is the purification of lead into gold by the action of alchemical mercury ("quicksilver") and sulphur. These two reagents represent the contraries of existence: mercury is the feminine and intellectual pole, sulphur is the masculine, choleric aspect, and their catalytic work is antagonistic, hence their being called the "quarreling couple." I've talked tonight about Harry's transformations from lead to gold. Is it hard to see Ron and Hermione as alchemical sulfur and mercury?

It's in their names and characters. "Hermione" is the feminine for "Hermes," another name for 'Mercury;' her initials (Hg) are the chemical sign for mercury, her parents are dentists (who, of course, make fillings with mercury), and she is the incarnation of intellect in a woman's body. Hotheaded Ron's middle name is "Bilious,' a synonym for "choleric" or hot and dry. And do they quarrel?

As traditional and more conventional are the trio's symbolic meaning as body, mind, and spirit. The human person has to have these three elements in good health and in the right order to function effectively. Whenever Ron the body decides he's going to take charge, everything goes wrong. If the trio misses a piece (remember how Hermione was treated in *Prisoner*?), it's like a wheel comes off the bike. This isn't Ms. Rowling's invention; you can see similar body/mind/spirit trios in the hobbits on Mt. Doom; Kirk, Spock, and 'Bones' on the original *Star Trek*, Luke and Leia Skywalker and Hans Solo in the *Star Wars* films of the 70's; even Dmitri, Ivan, and Alyosha in Dostoevsky's *The Brothers Karamazov*.

She may not have come up with this triptych on her own, but none of her predecessors were able to tell the story of the importance of the soul's purity through their three characters representing the soul's aspects or faculties *and* introduce and illustrate this importance as part of the story-line. Ms. Rowling's popularity is so great and so much a common-place of our times, and her work is still so often pigeonholed by even her admirers as "kid stuff," that we miss the amazing artistry in her use of story-symbols.

And if "evading consciousness" is one measure of a symbol's power or penetration, check out Ollivander's wand cores. Ms. Rowling says almost anything can be used as a wand core (Fleur's, remember, is a Veela hair), but that Mr. Ollivander used the most powerful substances in his wands: phoenix feather, unicorn hair, and dragon's heartstring. Why are these the most magically powerful? For the same reason that wands are "quasi sentient." Ms. Rowling said in a 2008 interview:

> Essentially, I see wands as being quasi-sentient. I think they awaken to a kind of – They're not exactly animate, but they're close to it, as close to it as you can get in an object, because they carry so much magic. So that's really the key point about a wand.[14]

Now, wandlore plays a pretty big part in *Deathly Hallows*, so this isn't just trivia. Harry's wand goes on autopilot during his battle with the Dark Lord and blasts Voldemort out of the skies. Dumbledore explains at King's Cross that Harry's wand "had imbibed some of the power and qualities of Voldemort's wand" in their battle at the end of *Goblet* so that it

> recognized him when he pursued you, recognized a man who was both kin and mortal enemy, and it regurgitated some of his own magic against him . . .. Your wand now contained the power of your enormous courage and Voldemort's own deadly skill . . . (Deathly Hallows, Ch. 35, page 711).

This "quasi-sentience" is what enables Harry's wand to "recognize" Voldemort and save Harry by its own spell-making and magic on reserve. We have known since *Philosopher's Stone* that "wands choose the wizard," but who knew they were almost "minds-in-a-stick"? Not I. But we might have guessed.

The clue is in the wand cores that Ollivander prefers. In brief, each is taken from a magical creature that is a symbol of God the Word, the *Logos*, or Christ. The Phoenix is the "resurrection bird" of tradition, and the unicorn in tapestries and stories has been a stand-in for Christ for so long that neither of these animals' feather or hair requires much explanation. The dragon heartstring is a powerful magic substance because "Dragon's Blood" is a euphemism for the Elixir of Life that comes from the Philosopher's Stone. This elixir, in being a "fountain of immortality, is a reflection of the blood of Christ in Communion. A little less obvious but there it is: another strong connection to a story-transparency for God the Son, the Word made flesh.

This *Logos*-connection is the source of a wand's "powerful magic" and "quasi-sentience" because of what the Word is. The Word is not just the historical Jesus of Nazareth; the Word is what incarnates as Jesus. Remember the symbolism of the circle and the center? The Word is the visible and creative (though begotten, not created itself) God "through which all things are made." The Center or Absolute, "God the Father . . . maker of everything visible and invisible," is unknown except through the Circle, His "Word" that creates. Just as God creates through His *Logos*, so men in His image can co-create (at least in literature!) with speech that harmonizes with his Word (Latin, for the most part) and with wands that have cores taken from symbols resonating with the Word's qualities. As explained at length in *How Harry Cast His Spell*, the incantational or harmonizing magic of Ms. Rowling's world requires a trinitarian cosmology and traditional metaphysics to make sense.

And the sentience? The Word or *Logos* "through whom all things are made" is in all things as the *logoi* or raison d'etre of its existence. The *Logos* is also the substance of our knowing faculty, our reason. The sympathy or likeness of our reason is how we are able to understand anything about any existent thing that would otherwise be completely unknowable. We add the "-ology" suffix to so many of the subjects we study because, traditionally at least, it was understood that it was our reason/logos studying the logoi specific to life in "bio-logy," stars in "astr-ology," and beginnings in "arche-ology." This is spiritual anthropology and theocentric epistemology, by golly-ology.

The wand cores are Logos echoes and symbols. What else could they be but semi-divine in power and quasi-sentient? They are shades of the Creative Principle and the source of knowing Itself.

What I enjoy about Ms. Rowling's symbolism is the care she takes to layer it. If you ever hear my talks on the Alchemy and Christian Content of *Deathly Hallows* [see Chs. 2 and 3]. you'll hear how the three stages – please tell me you can look at my clothes by now and say the three stage colors in order – are told in correspondence with the three Christian holidays of the year. In brief, the *nigredo* or black stage hits its nadir on Christmas Eve in Godric's Hollow. Harry's wand and faith are broken on the night of darkness before light came into the world. The white stage's purifying work begins when Ron the Baptist pulls the story's Christ figure out of the baptismal pool in the Forest of Dean soon after, just as Theophany, the Baptism of Christ is only two weeks after Nativity.

And Harry's trip to King's Cross, sacrificial death for his friends, and victory over the Dark Lord are all but a Passion Gospel narrative of Calvary and Easter in the story's *rubedo* or red stage. Ms. Rowling matches the exoteric celebration of events in the life of Christ and His Church with the esoteric, alchemical meaning of same in the life of an individual seeker. No small trick. We saw this same kind of layering with her choice of King's Cross for Harry's afterlife denouement with the Headmaster.

In our previous three keys, we saw how each explained how Harry was able to defeat the Dark Lord. The traditional symbolism key is similarly helpful. Just as Harry was changed into something semi-transcendent and absolute by his completion of the alchemical work and hero's journey in general, and, specifically, by his dying to self and sacrificing himself for his friends, so understanding what symbolism is helps us grasp why Lord Thingy was doomed in the final battle.

A symbol is a transparency of a referent or reality greater than earthly reality and being: a transparency through which we can look or, by which some quality or grace of that referent, can enter the world and the minds and hearts of readers. By the choices and changes Harry has made and experienced, he rises from the dead in *Deathly Hallows*, as I said earlier, not in the presence of a symbol of Christ like he did in the first six books, but as a symbol of Christ himself. No wonder he is so confident he knows how the wand cores will work in the last standoff. He is, metaphorically at least, of one substance with them.

Why do people around the world love Ms. Rowling's stories? I think at least half the answer is because of her inspired use of symbols that open us to an edifying, imaginative experience of realities greater than our own. It's not the religious or Christian content *per se*, though, for Western readers, this sort of thing "evades the consciousness" and penetrates very deeply into our hearts. The power and joy of myth is in every reader's connection with the symbols' referents, the spiritual realities.

Ms. Rowling's writing is not evangelical in nature or proselytizing in any way for a specific, exoteric faith; her comments about her struggles to believe and with Christian believers make that very clear. It is the magic of story and myth that Ms. Rowling crafts, using imagery and symbols from the Christian tradition, to make accessible, even delightful, metaphysical and human truths readers can experience, embrace, and embody regardless of their tradition.

Which leaves us with only more key, postmodern themes.

Postmodernism

Hey we're on the last key! Where has all the time gone?

I mentioned earlier that symbolism and mythic experience account for maybe half of Potter-mania, which caused at least one of the note-takers up front to lift his head with a look that said, "we have four of five keys but we have only half the answer . . ." The other half, the fifth key, is two parts common sense and one part looking at your own eyeballs.

The common sense parts are (1) there is *no way* symbols of Christ, alchemical imagery and other traditional cargo are driving this freight train and (2) this book, like every other novel, poem, or play, is written by an author of a historical period for an audience of that historical period. Let's give these points the acknowledgment they merit.

If being Christian iconography in story form, with an engaging adventure and edifying ending in each episode, was what got the Harry firestorm started, I'll eat my hat. If that were the kind of story we all wanted and couldn't get more of, we'd all be reading *The Faerie Queen*, *Orlando Furioso*, and *The Pilgrim's Progress*. Or just Homer and Dante.

I realize all of you *do* read Homer and Dante, but I hope all of you are willing to admit, even boast, that this qualifies you as members of the freaky geeks fraternity and sorority. I have argued and will continue to make the point that the *substance* of Ms. Rowling's novels is what *sustains* their hold on readers. But the subliminal artistry of her symbols and story architecture are not what hooks readers to Harry's adventures – readers age six to sixty, from Boston to Bangladesh and back again.

As Andrew Lazo at the University of Houston has established,[15] Lewis and his Inkling freaky geek friends like you may have imagined themselves as literary dinosaurs out of step with their times, but their methods, concerns, and answers are all very much of the modern period. They are Victoria's children and WWI survivors stepping out of the wreckage left them after Versailles, to a world unstrung from its moorings. Their literary output, like their explicit and implicit social criticism, *had to* reflect the age in which they wrote and it does.

Lewis criticized his contemporaries for what he called their "chronological snobbery," by which phrase he meant to point out that historical blind spots, prejudices, and overriding concerns weren't just things that Ancient Romans, Renaissance Italians or Georgian Englishman suffered from unconsciously. Every historical period has its good and bad aspects that color the thinking of every man, woman, and child living in that age – and his and ours are no different.

Half of Potter-mania, the sustaining and largely invisible half below the water line, is its transcendent meaning and the artistry that delivers it. What hooks us, though – what we see, recognize, and agree with in the stories – is their *aboveboard* themes and meaning. Ms. Rowling's hook, the fifth key for unlocking her *Harry Potter* novels, is her use of postmodern themes about which we all agree and celebrate as core truths.

Getting at these requires that we step back and consider how we think as postmodern people. This means looking at our own eyeballs, or, better, at the colored glasses through which we all look at reality. We have to ask ourselves what qualities and perspectives distinguish our historical period from all others and then verify that Ms. Rowling's books are about confirming and advancing these core beliefs.

The best chapters in my book *Unlocking Harry Potter: Five Keys for the Serious Reader* – and you all *are* going to buy that book tonight, right? You think I'm joking but my fourteen year old son needs new running shoes and he wears an 11 1/2 – anyway, the best chapters of the book are the ones on postmodernism, what one friend calls the "Disney Does Derrida" section. I lay out ten different ideas and beliefs that you'll find in every postmodern story, including the holiday teevee special, *Rudolph the Red Nosed Reindeer,* and the movies *Sky High, Ants, Narnia,* well, *any* movie, really – even *Left Behind,* Tom Clancy's books and, of course, *Harry Potter.* I haven't got time to talk about all those so let me focus on the most important core belief of our age.

In technical language, what typifies us as postmoderns is "skepticism about metanarratives." In language you can share with mom, dad, and your little sister, that means the flag we fly that everyone will salute – and I mean everybody: rich, poor, Republican, Democrat, fundamentalists, Libertines, even epistemological existentialists – is that "prejudice is the enemy." That may strike you as a little simplistic, so here's how to see the lens we all see reality through.

Prejudice is by definition an unexamined and deeply held belief that distorts our ability to see things as they are. Because of cultural myths, what are called "metanarratives" – myths are perpetuated by language, institutions like schools, church, family, and media, and the inertia of ideas in those leading an unexamined life – all of us to one degree or another respond to stimuli from the world in obedience to our sexist, racist, homophobic, colonial, elitist, capitalist, individualist prejudices. This colored perception, because it is a consequence of the lens or filter of beliefs we look through, is distorted and somehow exclusive. The lens colors one group or type of behaviors as "good" and another as "other." The "others" are excluded, diminished, or otherwise "discriminated against" because of prejudice – and cannot resist their exclusion except by illuminating those prejudiced against them.

Hence the civil rights movement, the Equal Rights Amendment, political correctness, the Rainbow Coalition, and Barney the Dinosaur. Prejudice is not only the principal evil against which postmoderns battle; our belief that this evil is pervasive, even impossible to avoid or throw off, that prejudice is the "original sin" of the 21st Century from which we must be delivered by something greater than ourselves, say, government regulation and advanced education, makes us doubt that we can know anything certainly and as it is. The metanarratives that cloud, distort, and poison our thinking inevitably blind us to people and reality as it is. Only prejudiced and unloving fundamentalists and ideologues, atheists and Bible-thumpers, abortionists and terrorists, think they have a periscope that sees through prejudice to perceive the truth as such – filter-and-prejudice-free. And these people, who do not embrace relativism and ecumenism as core truths, are the intolerant people postmoderns will not tolerate.

I suspect you see the oddity of having a belief about beliefs as the defining metanarrative of our time. The truth we all hold to be self-evident is that there are no self-evident truths; our postmodern metanarrative is that metanarratives are bad and to be resisted at all costs – all of them, of course, except *this* particular metanarrative. Those who resist the "prejudice is bad" defining myth as another prejudice and intolerance-creating core belief can only do so in the name of their know-better elitist prejudices. Lock 'em up!

Every story, teevee show, blockbuster film, advertisement campaign, and election promise of our time has to confirm and reinforce this core point. Minority opinions are, by definition, more true than majority opinions; the disenfranchised or marginalized are more insightful and kind than the powerful; uniformity is ignorance and pluralism is deliverance.

Harry Potter is in many ways the postmodern epic. Ms. Rowling has told us as much in almost every interview she has given since *Deathly Hallows* was published. In the *Time* magazine 2008 "Person of the Year Runner-Up" article, it was put very succinctly:

> [Y]ou can tell how much this all matters to her, if it weren't already clear from her 4,100-page treatise on tolerance. "I'm opposed to fundamentalism in any form," she says. "And that includes in my own religion."[16]

Like most of us, Ms. Rowling's religion, qua postmodern, *is* being "opposed to fundamentalism in any form." She misuses the word "fundamentalism," which refers to a set of beliefs held by a specific, historic sect of Protestant Christians, the way most everyone else does, that is, as a synonym for "ignorant, prejudiced people who think their beliefs of right and wrong are indisputable – and which blindness causes them to be intolerant, discriminatory, even violent." She, of course, overlooks the irony that she is talking about these evil fundamentalist folk the way Death Eaters talk about Muggles.

Prejudice and discrimination are Voldemort's origin and what the Order was fighting against. As Ms. Rowling said in the 2007 Bloomsbury chat:

> Ravleen: How much does the fact that Voldemort was conceived under a love potion have to do with his nonability to understand love? Is it more symbolic?
>
> J.K. Rowling: It was a symbolic way of showing that he came from a loveless union – but of course, everything would have changed if Merope had survived and raised him herself and loved him. The enchantment under which Tom Riddle fathered Voldemort

is important because it shows coercion, and there can't be many more prejudicial ways to enter the world than as the result of such a union.

....

Leaky Cauldron: What, if anything, did the Wizarding World learn, and how did society change, as a direct result of the war with Voldemort? (i.e., not as a result of Harry, Ron and Hermione's future careers.) J.K. Rowling: The Ministry of Magic was de-corrupted, and with Kingsley at the helm the discrimination that was always latent there was eradicated.[17]

Time magazine still rather overstates the case, as is their wont in highlighting Ms. Rowling's secular agenda, (see Lev Grossman's hilariously misguided "Who Dies in Harry Potter? God," *Time*, July 12, 2007, for a few laughs on this point), in calling *Harry Potter* a "4,100-page treatise on tolerance." But they do get half the story. The hook that catches postmodern readers around the world is about Harry – heroic "excluded other," fighting against the Nazi fundamentalist pureblood Death Eaters and their nightmare leader Voldemort.

Why are these bad guys so bad? It isn't just the murders, the nastiness, or the snobbery; it's the poisoned, prejudicial *thinking* that they are better than others because of their blood-status we are obliged to hate. Being "pure-blood," of course, is just a metaphor for any caste of social class, education, or privilege. They are evil and Dumbledore and Harry are heroic because they are archetypes of postmodern beliefs about good and bad. *Harry Potter* does for us what Augustus hoped the *Aeneid* would do for Rome; *Harry* confirms and buttresses in his readers' minds the core beliefs contra prejudice and ideological thinking of our time.

Battle of the Books? Tradition vs. Modernity

There's a point of conflict, though, between the two half-explanations I've given you for Potter-mania. Like all great books and stories, *Harry Potter* simultaneously delivers transcendent, timeless meaning, and answers to the big, universally human questions, with topical and timely references to concerns of the age. The potential conflict in a postmodern epic, as opposed to the best books of any previous age, is that the anti-metanarrative beliefs and prejudices about prejudices of our time, (again, unlike all others) often *contradict* or deny traditional truths, even the existence of anything "transcendent" or "true." When the only social convention of destroyed traditions left by the revolutionaries is anti-traditionalism, how can *Harry Potter* deliver *both* postmodern skepticism *and* mythic, otherworldly, imaginative experience?

Deathly Hallows, the finale of this "treatise on tolerance," shows us how.

Harry's last adventure is the story, in Ms. Rowling's words, of his "struggle to believe." When *Half-Blood Prince* ended, Harry stood up to the Minister of Magic and all but spat in Rufus' face his loyalty to Albus Dumbledore. This fidelity was inspiring but not especially long-lasting. *Deathly Hallows* is not many chapters old before his faith has been weakened by newspaper reports, the testimony of skeptics and enemies, and by his own discomfort with having been left clueless by his departed guide. By the time Harry reads *The Life and Lies of Albus Dumbledore*, he denies Dumbledore's love for him and his own "trust" in the headmaster. Hermione and Elphias Doge both urge Harry to "choose to believe" in Dumbledore, but this strikes him as nonsensical.

Harry here takes sides with Richard Dawkins, the 21st Century's most strident public atheist (in a crowded field!). Dawkins says[18] it was Pascal, accomplished natural scientist and author of the *Pensees*, who first put forward the "ludicrous idea that believing is something you can *decide* to do" in absence of compelling, material evidence and logic. Harry is unable to decide or choose to believe, because belief is something he does as a conclusion he makes from sensory knowledge and conclusions made after sifting through this experience (not that Harry's track record for successful deduction justifies this empiricism). *Choose to believe*? Harry thinks he could just as soon choose to hear or see whatever he liked; belief has to correspond to perceived reality not personal preferences.

Here Harry is fighting the Dumbledore myth and the Wizarding World metanarrative he grew up with. It is Ms. Rowling's tableau of adolescent atheism or agnosticism that denies the faith of the fathers. I detail Harry's return to trust or faith in Dumbledore in my lecture on the Christian content of *Deathly Hallows* [see chapter three], but the short course is that Dobby's sacrificial death and the remorse Harry feels at his death – "Dumbledore, of course, would have said that it was love" (Ch. 24, page 478) – ignites Harry's faith in the Headmaster and his plan for Harry, a faith that does not waver even in the face of more damning testimony from Aberforth about Albus. [cf., Ch. 28, page 563; "He had made his choice while he dug Dobby's grave, he had decided to continue along the winding, dangerous path indicated for him by Albus Dumbledore, to accept that he had not been told everything that he wanted to know, but simply to trust. He had no desire to doubt again . . .".]

This choice to believe in Dumbledore is not surrender to the anthropomorphic wizard-God Dumbledore and the metanarrative Harry grew up with at Hogwarts. Quite the contrary. Harry has looked the metanarrative of fideism or "belief for its own sake" in the face, rejected it, *and* transcended it. He was liberated from it in Dobby's grave because of his epiphany there. What is it about the graveyard scene that moves Harry's choice?

I would say "Harry's love for Dobby and what Dobby had done for him." Dobby, you recall, was always something of a throwaway comic figure in the series, even in books where he played a big role. What defined Dobby, what made him different from all other house-elves and magical creatures, was his faith in and sacrificial love for Harry Potter as savior. That religious language may strike you as odd, but remember, Dobby served in Malfoy Manor, literally the "house of bad faith," where everyone hated Harry. Dobby risked everything several times in *Chamber of Secrets* to serve and save *Harry* rather than his appointed masters and his own house-elf species. He does this out of a kind of worship, a recognition that Harry is the Chosen One.

Dobby's reward in *Chamber* was Harry's winning him his freedom which, like having Christian faith in a world of cynics, doesn't make Dobby's external circumstances much easier. Happy as he may be, he becomes something of an outcaste among house-elves. When Harry calls for help in *Deathly Hallows* from the bowels of Malfoy Manor, it's the very last place Dobby ever wants to go. But he goes there; he rescues Luna, Dean and Ollivander before returning to confront his former masters as a free house-elf in service to Harry Potter. He catches the knife meant for Harry with his chest and dies in Harry's arms.

Dobby's choice to believe in Harry to the death moves Harry tremendously. As Harry digs the grave by hand, mastering death as it were, "an understanding blossomed in the darkness," ideas came "to him in the grave, ideas that had taken shape in the darkness, ideas both fascinating and terrible" (Ch. 24, pages 479, 481). Harry trusts his intuition, as Lupin recommended, just as he did with the Silver Doe, and makes a decision based on his cardiac rather than cranial intelligence. As Edward Tingley wrote in *Touchstone* magazine, Pascal described this heart discernment:

> It is the heart which perceives God, and not the reason" (424). "The heart has its reasons, which reason does not know" (423). Pascal's reasons of the heart are meant to take over from an intellect that operates on hard evidence but has run out of it. "The heart has its order, the mind has its own, which uses principles and demonstrations. The heart has a different one" (298).
>
> We are not talking here about feelings, which love to cheat us. Pascal says that the heart convinces, makes us rightly sure. "Demonstration is not the only instrument for convincing us" (821).[19]

Deathly Hallows is an anti-metanarrative novel because Harry rejects the Dumbledore-is-God myth when confronted with contrary evidence and then *chooses,* despite this contrary evidence, to believe because of inspired understanding. Harry is enlightened by the heroic example of a house-elf who made a like-minded choice to believe in Harry out of love before ever having met him. The power of Dobby's sacrificial example saves Harry, much as his mother saved him from Voldemort years ago in Godric's Hollow.

Harry transcends one metanarrative, Dumbledore-Deus, with doubt. *And* he overcomes the postmodern skepticism about metanarratives in his choice to believe what he had rejected. This self-actualizing decision for faith transforms Harry, an *albedo* transformation more visible in the last part of the book, the *rubedo.* There, in his walk down the Via Dolorosa to the Forbidden Forest, his 'death,' resurrection after harrowing King's Cross, and victory over the Dark Lord, Harry reveals the victory over death and the prison of his thoughts and prejudices he had won in the grave at Shell Cottage.

Ms. Rowling here orchestrates the postmodern finish of all she has taught us about choice – "choice reveals who we really are," right? – so that it synchronizes and harmonizes with the traditional message of human apotheosis consequent to dying to one self and mastering death in humility and obedience. We readers, just along for the ride, are not only taught the prevailing metanarrative of our times about the evils of prejudice ("boo, Death Eaters!") but also the importance of choosing our beliefs carefully if we want to live relatively free of prejudices.

Following Dumbledore, Dobby, and Harry's examples, we are encouraged to adopt the only cultural myth that has no core-elite and constitutive other, namely, the "metanarrative of love." That Harry's ending looks an awful lot like a Christian transformation is no accident; the Christian God is love (1 John 4:8) and Christians are supposed to be known for the love they have for one another (John 13:35), especially sacrificial love, the love than which there is no greater (John 15:13).

You might say, especially if you're reporting for *Time* magazine, that Harry is "spiritual, not religious." That's almost a postmodern creed because it retains the privilege of choice and distance from any doctrinal authority or prejudice-inducing ideology and myth. Choosing "to be loving," though, really isn't a fair description or summary of what Harry does. He rejects the occult by not pursuing the Hallows instead of Horcruxes, and, with them, the idea of personal power through immortality. He also has only pity touched with disdain for the New Age seeker Xenophilius Lovegood, whose virtue and love of the good, the true, and the beautiful only extended to his loved one in the end.

Again, Harry dies in *obedience*, he dies sacrificially and, most importantly, he dies to himself, effectively executing the Lord Voldemort within him. Though Ms. Rowling doesn't have Harry go to church and receive religious instruction, she presents, in story form, his final journey as Christian everyman and as an echo of Christ's walk to Calvary and resurrection from the dead. [See Ch. 3 for more on these decisions.]

Dobby, Neville, and Harry are all simultaneously postmodern heroes and Christian seekers. The Christian qualities are, as Ms. Rowling said in California, "obvious." Dobby is a cartoon picture of the slave to Christ; Neville is the "good and faithful steward" in Harry's absence from Hogwarts in *Deathly Hallows* (note his joy at Harry's return, despite his suffering: "I knew you'd come! *I knew it, Harry!* . . . I knew you'd come! Kept telling Seamus it was a matter of time!" Chs. 28, 29, pages 570-571); Harry is the willing lamb sacrificed at Golgotha.

Note, though, that none of them are conformists in any way. Each has confronted the myth or controlling idea of their lives and made an inspired decision to choose or reject it, independent of what others think or their personal comfort. Dobby, in embracing his freedom and his love for Harry, becomes something of everything that house-elves are *not*. Neville in his final showdown with Voldemort – a death to self in obedience if there ever was one – denies his pureblood ancestry, denies the possibility of his ever joining Voldemort, and loudly affirms his loyalty to Albus Dumbledore (Ch. 36, page 731). Harry, after his victory in the Great Hall over Voldemort, repairs the holly-and-phoenix-feather wand that chose him and refuses the Elder Wand and the Resurrection Stone.

All three heroes deny what their world had taught them and choose the metanarrative of love that has no prejudices – or restrictions on what it can know and become. Again, poor Voldemort. When Neville bested him and killed Nagini, you'd think he would have had the sense to flee. Facing Harry, freshly liberated from his inner-Voldemort, was nigh on suicidal. Of course, as Dumbledore said to Harry, if Tom Riddle could have understood the power of selfless love, he wouldn't have become Lord Voldemort.

In the conjunction of transcendent meaning and postmodern teaching we see in Dobby's, Neville's, and Harry's choices, that they become "masters of death." Ms. Rowling ties the knot here between the postmodern hook that grabs us in the stories and the greater meaning that resonates in our hearts and brings us back again and again.

Conclusion

We made it! Narrative Misdirection, Literary Alchemy, Hero's Journey, Traditional Symbolism, and Postmodern themes: each unlocks an aspect of Ms. Rowling's artistry and of her meaning. Each also reveals how differently our minds work when reading a story than how they do in "the real world."

The 'Narrative misdirection' key opens the lock that kept us from understanding how Ms. Rowling surprised us in every book. Seeing it in action was also a lesson in postmodern skepticism, i.e., "Don't trust what you think; only a spectrum of perspectives can give us even a hint of the truth." Being burned year after year by believing we had an objective understanding, when all we had was Harry's view, taught us just how narrow our individual perspective is and how dangerous it is to make decisions from a prejudiced view.

The 'Literary Alchemy,' 'Hero's Journey,' and 'Traditional Symbolism' keys all are artistic points that, to understand, require our thinking diagonally or perhaps upside-down from how we usually see things.

• The alchemy of storytelling is about the blurring of the distinction between the subject who is reading and the object hero being read about, if not identification of reader and hero, and how the transformation of the story character affects and transforms the other.

• The Hero's journey, too, involves our completing the escape, initiation, and return circle of the story principal; returning to the symbolic point of origin or center with him or her, and sharing in that transformation.

• Symbols as vessels of grace from, or some experience of, greater realities is another mind-bender and departure from conventional, naturalist thinking.

With the 'Postmodern Themes' key we return to thinking about how we think that we began with 'Narrative Misdirection' somewhat transformed ourselves by the other keys. Ms. Rowling hooks us with the postmodern metanarrative about the evil of prejudices and metanarratives in general. She shifts from Barney and the Berenstein Bears, though, in her story-lesson that the myths about self, power, and what we're about, must all be confronted and transcended by obedience and devotion to Love.

How does Harry defeat the Dark Lord? Simple. The five keys reveal the five ways he has become nigh unto a god.

Narrative misdirection: Unlike the first six books and their narrative misdirection created surprises, Harry has the 'big picture' when he finally goes toe-to-toe with Lord Thingy in the Great Hall. He taunts Voldemort with his mastery of knowledge from Snape and Dumbledore, and about Riddle, Jr. Knowing more, Harry becomes more real than Voldemort and, in that, his master.

Literary Alchemy: Harry has completed the seven cycles of the alchemical Great Work and transformed from lead to gold. By taking in the contraries of Gryffindor and Slytherin, a la Albus and Severus, and resolving them into a unity, he has become the Hogwarts Hermaphrodite or *rebus*. He has the power of the whole, consequently, and the fragmented and broken Dark Lord doesn't have a chance.

Hero's Journey: The end of the seventh book is a return to the end of the first book and, after a fashion, to the very beginning of

Harry's hero's journey the night his parents were murdered. Having completed the circles of these annual separations, initiations and returns to confront the Dark Lord where Gryffindor miraculously defeated Slytherin his first year, Harry has the power of the "circle that has no beginning," "the phoenix and the flame," (Ch. 29, page 587), which is the power of the transcendent center, the creative point. Voldemort, only ego and periphery, is nothing in comparison.

Traditional Symbolism: Ms. Rowling, in her use of resurrection imagery from the Passion Gospels of the New Testament, isn't being obscure in the symbolic presentation of Harry's apotheosis or divinization. Having conquered death or mastered it, defeating Voldemort is a warm-down exercise.

Postmodern Themes: Harry's greatest victory, though, is over the metanarrative of division and prejudice that rules the Wizarding world. He names his second son 'Albus Severus' and, in this and in his comments to this son, he shows how the Gryffindor-Slytherin chasm has been bridged. At the Epilogue's farewell at Platform 9 3/4, the Weasley purebloods, blood-traitors that they are, have married a mudblood and not-quite pureblood – and the subject is a matter of jokes that have little edge.

We can see in this, once again, how the timeless and topical meet in Ms. Rowling's weaving of the transcendent with the obviously postmodern. This meeting jumps at us in Harry's farewell question to Dumbledore at the mystical King's Cross:

> "Tell me one last thing," said Harry. "Is this real? Or has this been happening inside my head?"
>
> Dumbledore beamed at him, and his voice sounded loud and strong in Harry's ears even though the bright mist was descending again, obscuring his figure.
>
> "Of course it is happening inside your head, Harry, but why on earth should that mean that it is not real?" (Ch. 35, page 723)[20]

I think the reader with a grasp of the five keys that unlock Ms. Rowling's Harry Potter novels can read this exchange, the penultimate Dumbledore Denouement, as a conversation between Harry Potter author and reader. The reader asks, "Why does this book mean so much to me? It's just a story I'm reading about in my head; outside my head, these stories have no reality."

The great myth of our times is "naturalism," the belief taught in our schools and media that the only things that are "real" are quantities of matter and energy. Harry's question is one step removed from this; his distinction seems to be between "real life," that is, "conscious experience of time and space," and "imaginary life, a dream experience." He is concerned that the conversation he just had with the Headmaster, if it didn't happen in "real time," was delusional or something he should discount as questionable.

After 4,100 pages and more than a few years of reading, thinking about, and waiting on these stories, I expect many of us – and all of your parents – have wondered what was the point. Maybe you've asked yourself after another all-night read, "Wait a minute, this is *fantasy*; why am I wasting my time with this kid stuff?"

Dumbledore's answer to Harry is best and an apt finish to this talk.

As a good postmodern professor (remember that talk he gave at Harry's Sorting Feast? "Nitwit. Blubber. Oddment. Tweak." Sheesh), he thinks that what happens in your head, how you see things, to what degree your prejudices guide you, *is* your reality. Head-happenings are as close to what is real as we can get. This again is Ms. Rowling's hook; our shared belief that "you are what and how you think" and "prejudice is the enemy."

But Dumbledore also believes and has taught Harry that there are greater truths than "tolerance" and politically correct notions of our age. Love is the power that unites contraries and is our means to victory over death. If we choose to believe in the difficult path of sacrificial love, we will be able to clear our minds and hearts of the Voldemort within us and defeat the almost as real Voldemorts outside us. But it all begins with what you choose to believe and how you choose to see [see chapter 5].

Reading *Harry Potter* fosters our making the heroic right choices to love and to examine and accept or reject ideas others have given us about what life is really about. If we listen to our hearts as much as our heads, we'll make our own trips to King's Cross and defeat death and the evil one in turn.

The magic of story *is* "just in your head." But this magic, the alchemy of literature, is very real; as our thinking becomes like Harry's, to one degree or another, we are transformed by our shared decisions and experiences. God willing, we will trust in his path and share his victory.

Thank you for your attention tonight and for the wonderful dinner. Does anyone have a question?

Endnotes

1   "I re-read Austen's novels in rotation - I've just started *Mansfield Park* again. I could have chosen any number of passages from each of her novels, but I finally settled on *Emma*, which is the most skilfully managed mystery I've ever read and has the merit of having a heroine who annoys me because she is in some ways so like me. I must have read it at least 20 times, always wondering how I could have missed the glaringly obvious fact that Frank Churchill and Jane Fairfax were engaged all along. But I did miss it, and I've yet to meet a person who didn't, and I have never set up a surprise ending in a Harry Potter book without knowing I can never, and will never, do it anywhere near as well as Austen did in *Emma*." http://www.accio-quote.org/articles/2000/0500-heraldsun-rowling. html
2   *Collected Letters of C. S. Lewis, Volume 2*, Hooper,p. 977; Disraeli reading Austen: http://www.1911encyclopedia.org/Jane_Austen
3   The reader is urged to read Titus Burckhardt's *Alchemy* (Penguin, 1971) or *Mirror of the Intellect* (Quinta Essentia, 1987) for a traditional understanding of alchemy rather than a strictly historical treatment or psychological pastiche.
4   For alchemy in Shakespeare and other authors, see Martin Lings' *Secret of Shakespeare* (Inner Traditions, 1984) and Stanton Linden's *Darke Hierogliphicks: Alchemy in English Literature* (University Press of Kentucky, 1996).
5   'Tale of Two Cities: Why We Should Expect a Beheading in Deathly Hallows,' http://hogwartsprofessor.com/?p=89
6   See "An Apostolic Epic," Fr. Patrick Henry Reardon, Touchstone, March, 2003. http://www.touchstonemag.com/archives/article. php?id=16-02-030-f

7   2007 Bloomsbury chat: http://www.bloomsbury.com/jkrevent/; Oct 17 2007,'Harry Potter' Author J.K. Rowling Opens Up About Books' Christian Imagery:'They almost epitomize the whole series,' she says of the scripture Harry reads in Godric's Hollow, Shawn Adler: http://www.mtv.com/news/articles/1572107/20071017/index.jhtml, http://hogwartsprofessor.com/?p=196

8   Mircea Eliade, *Myth of the Eternal Return*, Princeton University Press, 1971, 'The Symbolism of the Center,' pages 12-16

9   Op. cit., pages ix, 3-6

10   Mircea Eliade, *The Sacred and the Profane* , Harcourt, 2007, pages 204-5

11   *How Harry Cast His Spell* ,Tyndale, 2008, Chapter 9, pages 92-93

12   C.S. Lewis, *The Literary Impact of The Authorised Version*. The Ethel M. Wood Lecture delivered before
the University of London on 20 March 1950. London: The Athlone Press, 1950. pg. 22; http://www.biblicalstudies.org.uk/pdf/kjv_lewis.pdf

13   See Michael Ward's *Planet Narnia*, Oxford University Press, 2007

14   http://www.accio-quote.org/articles/2007/1217-pottercast-anelli.html

15   Andrew Lazo, 'Mythic Movements: Inklings, Modernists, and the Problem of Placement,' Past Watchful Dragons C. S. Lewis Conference, Belmont University, 3-5 November 2005

16   *Time* magazine 2008 "Person of the Year Runner-Up;" http://www.time.com/time/specials/2007/personoftheyear/article/0,28804,1690753_1695388_1695436,00.html

17   2007 Bloomsbury chat; http://www.bloomsbury.com/jkrevent/;

18   Cited in 'The Skeptical Enquirer,' Edward Tingley, *Touchstone* magazine, June 2008; http://touchstonemag.com/archives/article.php?id=21-05-020-f

19   Op. cit.,'The Skeptical Inquirer,' June 2008

20   See the much longer discussion of this passage in Chapter 5.

Chapter 2

The Alchemical End Game:

Harry Potter and the Deathly Hallows as Rubedo

What follows is an expanded version of my Keynote Lecture at Prophecy 2007 in Toronto, a presentation I gave two weeks after *Deathly Hallows* was published. That talk, *The Alchemical End-Game: Harry Potter and the Deathly Hallows as Rubedo, the Last Stage of the Alchemical Work* explores the literary alchemy of the last book and it is this artistry that makes *Deathly Hallows* the remarkable literary achievement that it is.

You've just read an introduction to the subject in the first chapter's discussion of alchemy as one of the five keys that unlock the series and each book. I will do my best not to repeat what you have already read, of course, and will try, too, to avoid saying much of what is written about alchemy in the Christian content chapter following this one. Because Ms. Rowling's artistry is very much a weave of different elements, though, however focused any discussion is on any one aspect of her loom work, it inevitably will touch on others as well.

My three tasks here are to explain briefly *why* Ms. Rowling would have gone to the trouble of building her novels on an alchemical scaffolding; then *how* she structures *Deathly Hallows* specifically as an alchemical progression, black to white to red, and how the book serves as the *rubedo* or last stage of the Great Work for the series as a whole. Of these tasks, the *why* question is the natural beginning of our conversation.

Why Literary Alchemy: Subliminal Advertising

Why, after all, does an author use symbols from the hermetic stream of literature that are obscure or unrecognizable to most readers, even very serious ones? That these images and references permeate Ms. Rowling's work makes it even more mysterious, and more important for us to understand. If readers almost certainly won't notice alchemical touches, how does the writer think they can affect their readers' understanding and experience of the story?

Great question. I think the answer is best approached through something we experience much more often than literary alchemy. To understand the traditions of hermetic writing in English literature, forget Shakespeare, Donne, and Joyce. Study advertising.

Though we don't often associate advertising with books we love, Madison Avenue "story board" writers do have the same tools and objectives in many respects as "storybook" writers like Ms. Rowling. By suggestion and setting, as much as by direct speech, these writers deliver messages that are almost entirely subliminal and more effective for being *below* the threshold of consciousness. At least that seems to be what Philip Pullman believes.

In 2002, the "Un-Lewis" (Pullman) told Peter Hitchens:

> All stories teach, whether the storyteller intends them to or not. They teach the world we create. They teach the morality we live by. They teach it much more effectively than moral perceptions and instructions. . . . We don't need lists of rights and wrongs, tables of do's and don'ts: we need books, time, and silence.[1]

Ms. Rowling claims she does not have didactic intentions, "if undeniably morals are drawn,"[2] in her stories, which comes to Pullman's point exactly: "all stories teach, whether the storyteller intends them to or not." Ms. Rowling, the consummate planner and most deliberate of writers, may not have didactic or proselytizing motives in her writing but her artistry is undeniably intentional and this work creates a message for the reader.

Not a little bit like the creative folk making 30 second spots on the teevee that encourage us to buy soap. They know that few people watch these spots with any kind of *conscious* attention; their job is just to catch our eye long enough for a chuckle or cerebral footnote that makes the product or service being touted a part of our mental landscape. Because, like our dreams, much of our "conscious" thinking, and creativity and decision making comes out of the storehouse of images and ideas stored in the unconscious mind.

The most powerful demonstration I have seen of just how much this is true comes from British illusionist Derren Brown.[3] In a short film that can be seen on YouTube.com he uses staged "stray images" that would never penetrate our conscious attention to plant specific ideas he wanted in the minds of two advertising agency story-board writers. Incredibly, he plants these images on the streets down which these writers were driven to get to the filming studio.

The advertising professionals in Brown's stunt produce story boards for a taxidermist shop with words and pictures Brown wants them to use. He doesn't tell them what words and pictures to use, though. He just plants those ideas by exposing the writer and artist to them without speech and without their knowledge and in the most fleeting of moments. We know these are the images he wanted them to use because, after they show him their story boards, he shows the advertising wizards his own storyboards that he had created before their brain-storming as well as the images on the street he had planted. As a master illusionist, he leaves us, his audience, to draw our own conclusions about the power of suggestion in the advertisements we see every day and take no conscious note of.

If you think the way I do, this demonstration of the power of stray images placed in the subconscious staggers you. These advertising professionals – an artist and writer – spilled out a set of pictures and copy that were almost exact reproductions of the images Derren Brown wanted them to produce, all the while believing they were listening to their inner muse. What hope do we have of escaping the unending and heavy barrage of messages to buy, and buy now, that we experience night and day? I think the answer is "Not much hope."[4]

I want to note here that I'm not talking about "subliminal advertising" by "embedded images" or "flashed messages" the unconscious mind cannot see, a technique made famous by Wilson Bryan Key in his book, *Subliminal Seduction*. Key's work and the urban legend of "buy popcorn" messages flashed on movie screens has been dismissed by people who study such things and by advertisers themselves (who wish it worked).[5]

But by dismissing Key's embedded-image "subliminal seduction," we're likely to miss the hidden-in-plain-sight power of suggestion in real advertising that is still subliminal ("under-the-threshold" of our conscious mind) and all the more effective for being discounted. Carrie MacLaren explored this mistake – missing the effectiveness of ads we don't think persuade us in an article titled '*Subliminal Seduction*.'[6]

> Criticism of subliminal advertising [of the sort described in Key's book] benefited sellers in yet a third way. By suggesting that the only kind of advertising manipulation was subliminal manipulation, the controversy deterred more meaningful discussions of advertising influence. The advertising industry couldn't have asked for a better straw man. Once the idea of subliminal advertising could be revealed as bogus, advertising manipulation could be considered fictitious, too. A 1989 New York magazine article mocking subliminal-phobia was typical of the "enlightened" response to the subliminal critics: "People don't walk around in a semi-trance; buying is a rational, cognitive process."

> Yet, as any marketer knows, buying is not simply a rational, cognitive process. Despite his shortcomings, Key was quite correct on this count. The power of advertising, he argued, lay in controlling cultural symbols, in linking virility to hard liquor and soap to safety. Such subtle twists of meaning, he argued, shape the cultural environment and, in doing so, influence people's subconscious. Many scholars of advertising would agree. Indeed, there is a great deal of truth to Key's statement that *"It's What You Don't See That Sells You"*—so long as that claim is read figuratively.....

> Even when one grants that Key had a point, he advocated a dubious form of awareness. Contrary to the "seduction," "sexploitation" and "orgies" implied by his titles, *real advertising manipulation isn't particularly sexy, nor is it easy to grasp.* You can't find it in a mirror or hidden in the shadows or f—ing polar bears in ice cubes. So when everyone started hunting for dog heads in Scotch bottles, *the reality—that advertiser influence is everyday, ordinary, and infinitely more subtle*—became more remote. The hunt for embeds, by presenting itself as advertising education, prevented more substantive discussions of advertising from taking place.....

> In a way, visual drumbeats have less in common with subliminals than other, far more common sales strategies. Packaging design capitalizes on intuitive responses to color, typography, and word choice. Background music in stores and restaurants influences the amount of time people linger. Product placements are among the many ways of marketing "under the radar" by fusing ads and entertainment. Though by no means guaranteed, these time-worn strategies continue to influence people's subconconscious.

And they are not alone. In fact, it could be argued that *most every advertisement is subliminal.* The ubiquity of advertisements means that *people tune out the vast majority of them, only to experience them unconsciously.* Yet, like visual drumbeats, everyday embed-free ads are not considered subliminal. (emphases mine)

Got that? Remember Derren Brown's demonstrated point: even the subtlest subconscious experience can shape your approach to problem solving or just your way of thinking. That's how advertising works and it's the reason Proctor & Gamble, Pepsodent, and Presidential politicians all pay the big bucks to crawl inside our heads through print, display, and projected media ads.

What does this have to do with *Harry Potter* and literary alchemy?

In 2003, I gave a lecture at St. Thomas' Episcopal School in Houston, Texas, about what constitutes a "Great Book." I said there were four qualities almost all books in the western canon had in common: longevity, asking the big questions, answering these questions with an artistry that dovetailed with the author's answers, and giving Christian answers. The third point about artistry, I guess, I picked up from C. S. Lewis because, as Michael Ward argues in *Planet Narnia*, this is what Lewis said the best stories do. As Ward wrote in *Touchstone* magazine ('Narnia's Secret,' December 2007):[7]

> In 1940, at a literary society in Oxford, Lewis read a paper entitled "The Kappa Element in Romance." ("Kappa" is the initial letter of the Greek word meaning "cryptic" or "hidden.")
>
> The thrust of the paper was this: *Stories are most valuable for their quality or atmosphere, not simply their plot.* The example he uses is *The Last of the Mohicans.*
>
> When the hero of the story is half-sleeping by his bivouac fire in the woods while a Redskin with a tomahawk is silently creeping up on him from behind, what makes for the essence of the scene is not simply peril, but the whole world to which this kind of peril belongs: the snow and snow-shoes, the canoes, the wigwams, the feathered headdresses, the war-paint, the Hiawatha names. A crook with a revolver would have conveyed a significantly different experience to the reader, even though the danger he represented might have been greater.
>
> Stories earn our allegiance, Lewis argues, by conveying a distinct and coherent qualitative atmosphere. "To be stories at all," he

says in "On Stories," stories:

> "must be series of events: but it must be understood that this series—the plot, as we call it—is only really a net whereby to catch something else. The real theme may be, and perhaps usually is, something that has no sequence in it, something other than a process and much more like a state or a quality."

> James Fenimore Cooper gives us the state or quality of "redskinnery." Alexandre Dumas in *The Three Musketeers* gives us no such intrinsic atmosphere or spirit. His story is just plot, without any kappa element, and to that extent is, in Lewis's view, a failure. (emphasis mine)

The artistry of the story is much like the stage setting, costume design, and choreography of the actors and actresses in a play. These things are not what we share with friends who ask "what the play was about." We tell them the major plot points and about the actresses and actors with whom we identified (or those for whom we could not suspend disbelief). But the stage setting — from the furniture to the lighting — has to jibe with and buttress the language, plot points, and, ultimately, the meaning of the drama *or it fails.* Lewis' genius in his Narnia novels, as Ward demonstrates, is the nigh-on invisible setting of individual planets and their astrological influences and qualities he gives each of the seven books.

My point? Ms. Rowling's accomplishment and great popularity is similarly due to the alchemical scaffolding and hero's journey structure she uses for each Harry Potter adventure and the series as a whole.

Do we notice the medieval planetary images embedded in Lewis' books? Not before Michael Ward pointed them out, we didn't. And the alchemical artistry of Ms. Rowling? It is also very much under the radar of most readers. The point is, the obscurity or subliminal quality of these structures doesn't make them wasted flourishes; they are the vehicles of Lewis' and Ms. Rowling's larger and more profound meaning and it is largely because they are unnoticed that they gain a foothold in our minds and hearts.

Two conclusions:

First, this is exactly the substance of the objection to the *Harry Potter* novels made by Christians concerned about the occult. The books' magical setting is what makes them dangerous, they argue, rather than specific plot points, because readers who enjoy the books inevitably come away from reading them with the subconscious but very real belief that "magic is okay." It is this belief that opens the door to real-world occult groups. We haven't seen the growth in these groups that the "Vigilants," as Lewis described them, have predicted, but their point is not nonsense for not having played out immediately.

Second, the reason to embrace and celebrate these novels as the countercultural event that they are is due largely to the subliminal messages delivered by Harry and friends in their stolen wheelbarrows. Readers walk away, maybe a little softer on the occult than they were, but with story-embedded messages : the importance of a pure soul; love's power even over death; about sacrifice and loyalty; a host of images and shadows about Christ and how essential 'right belief' is for personal transformation and victory over internal and external evils.

"Smuggling the Gospel" – Lewis' term for this sort of artistry – has an evangelical flavor that I think Ms. Rowling would find repugnant just because it is overly and overtly didactic (assuming the Grossman 2005 interview in *Time* magazine wasn't a fraud).[8] I'd disagree about this estimation of Lewis, but it points to a difference between Lewis' artistry and Ms. Rowling's. Relative to one another, Lewis was an accomplished advertiser who "instructed while delighting" and Ms. Rowling is an illusionist making her points by misdirection and under-the-radar images. Either way, the heart of their messages and the vehicles in which they are delivered are, in both writers, "subliminal" and "seductive," to glorious, edifying effect.

Lewis wrote in *The Literary Impact of the Authorized Version*, "An influence which cannot evade our consciousness will not go very deep."[9] Authors use hermetic images in literature because they are looking for this deep effect. The attachment readers have to both Lewis' *Narniad* and Rowling's *Harry Potter* epic demonstrates that these writers have reached and secured readers' deepest parts, the bottom of our hearts.

Literary Alchemy in *Harry Potter and the Deathly Hallows*

I explain in Chapter 7, "The Triangular Eye," that Ms. Rowling is writing on at least three levels to drive home her theme of "Love's Victory Over Death." There is the surface meaning – how bad the prejudiced Death Eaters are and the importance of making the hard, difficult choices to resist them. There is another layer of meaning just below the surface, filled with the heroic examples of the principal players and familiar (and not so familiar) symbols from the Christian tradition buttressing the "good versus evil" message of the storyline (Sydney's "instructing while delighting").

And underneath this, there is a remarkable third layer of alchemical images and personal change that are about Harry's transformation from spiritual lead into gold – his apotheosis. Here is the subliminal, symbolic, and spiritual artistry that is Ms. Rowling's real magic and the great achievement of *Deathly Hallows*. Let's get into the details of this edifying manipulation of our unconscious minds and hearts.

In a nutshell, *Deathly Hallows*1 has *four distinct parts* that should be understood as parts of the *rubedo* and of Harry's final alchemical transformation.

The first part is the alchemical Wedding, the traditional marker that signals this is the *rubedo* novel in the *Harry Potter* series. It lasts for eight chapters, ends with the announcement of Rufus Scrimgeour's death and the fall of the Ministry, and its signature color is gold.

The black, white, and red stages of the red novel of the series are launched by the death of the red scrimmager (Rufus Scimgeour) and we begin *nigredo* or black stage at that point. It stretches from 'A Place to Hide' (Ch. 9) to "The Life and Lies of Albus Dumbledore" (Ch. 18), the nadir of Harry's doubts and dissolution from the "Dumbledore Man through and through" he imagined himself to be at the end of *Prince*. Its signatures are: the color black, darkness, division, and depression in general.

The *albedo,* or white stage, begins with "The Silver Doe" (Ch. 19), which, with Harry's experience in Dobby's grave, is the central and pivotal point in the book; it continues through Harry's return to Hogwarts and "The Sacking of Severus Snape" (Ch. 30). Its tokens are the colors white and silver and the presence of water or moisture for purification.

The *rubedo* or red stage of *Deathly Hallows*, itself the *rubedo* of the seven book series, begins with "The Battle of Hogwarts" (Ch. 31) and ends after we learn "The Flaw in the Plan" (Ch. 36), which ends the book's essential narrative. The *rubedo* shows itself in the violent or sudden resolution of contraries, conflict, and mysteries, by the color of red, by death, and by the appearance of a *rebis* or double-natured man, of a Philosophical Orphan, and of the Philosopher's Stone.

The Epilogue is the return to the gold of the alchemical Wedding and the peaceful, post-*rubedo* version of the opening chapters' challenge, much as *Deathly Hallows* is a return to and retelling of *Philosopher's Stone*'s story and events. In its seven pages, we meet the *rebis*, the Orphan, and the Stone in the children of the next generation.

To care for this sort of thing and to follow how it all works requires (1) understanding the central place of alchemical imagery and sequencing in Ms. Rowling's work and (2) understanding more than a little bit about alchemy. We can get at the importance of alchemy in comprehending *Harry Potter* because Lisa Bunker at AccioQuotes.com found the 1998 interview in which Ms. Rowling told us so herself:[10]

> "I've never wanted to be a witch, but an alchemist, now that's a different matter. To invent this wizarding world, *I've learned a ridiculous amount about alchemy*. Perhaps much of it I'll never use in the books, but I have to know what magic can and cannot do *in order to set the parameters and establish the stories' internal logic*." (emphases mine)

To understand the literary alchemy of the series, though, beyond its similarities to advertising, is not as easy. Ms. Rowling says she read "a ridiculous amount about alchemy," but she doesn't specify what and by whom she read. And if she had, do you have time to figure out how she turned her alchemical reading and the tradition of using these images and sequences in English literature, especially in Elizabethan drama and by the Metaphysical poets, into Harry's magic? I cannot explain it here at any depth, but I have in *Unlocking Harry Potter: Five Keys for the Serious Reader*, whose three chapters on the alchemy key are the best shortcut to understanding Ms. Rowling's alchemical efforts in all seven books. [End shameless plug.]

Let's walk through the Wedding and the Harry's final turn on the alchemical wheel in *Deathly Hallows*.

The Alchemical Wedding

Here are the events of the first eight chapters in Deathly Hallows:

* Voldemort murders Charity Burbage after Bellatrix is shamed about the marriage of Remus and Tonks, her niece
* "Big D" admires Harry after a fashion and even shakes

his hand in parting
* Seven Potters escape from Privet Drive, Mad-Eye dies in flight, and Hedwig, too, is lost forever
* Harry and Hagrid take another trip on Sirius' bike with Voldemort trying to hitch a ride
* Harry's Wand goes autopilot and Golden to defeat the Dark Lord — and
* The Wedding (Alliance?) of France and England is followed by the Fall of the Ministry

What, if anything, do these events have in common, or to do with the alchemical Wedding?

"The marriage of sulphur and quicksilver, Sun and Moon, King and Queen, is the central symbol of alchemy" (Titus Burckhardt, *Alchemy*).[11] I'm pretty confident that Burckhardt is the best source of alchemic lore in *Harry Potter*, if Jung and MacLean must be considered likely pieces of the puzzle, too; Ms. Rowling has said New Age-ism leaves her cold,[12] so most of the junk on the Internet or on "New Age/Occult" shelves at your local bookstore are not good bets. If Burckhardt says the alchemical Wedding is the "central symbol of alchemy," the wedding deserves our attention.

Alchemy restores Edenic perfection to the soul of the alchemist while he restores the equilibrium of gold (the metallurgical equivalent of Eden) to metals that have lost this balance. The means to this perfection is the action of the "quarreling couple," alchemical mercury (quicksilver) and sulphur, an action of dissipation and the contraction — *solve et coagula* — that breaks down, purifies, and recrystallizes the base metal into the Philosopher's Stone. The "Elixir of Life" or "Dragon's Blood" that drops from this Stone is the end of the alchemical Great Work; it is supposed to turn other metals to gold and give eternal life or immortality to the alchemical adept.

The "wedding of sulphur and quicksilver... is the central symbol of alchemy" because this marriage reveals both the action and the end of the Great Work. Just as in a wedding, two people "die" to themselves, a "married" or "blended" couple is born, and life is conceived in this "deadly" union of contraries. The alchemical wedding, by the "marriage" or "quarrel" of sulphur and quicksilver, creates both an alchemist, that is a *"rebis"* or double-natured person, and the Philosopher's Stone (sometimes called the Philosophical Orphan). The wedding occurs in the *albedo* or before the *rubedo*, the last stage of the seven-cycle work, and is, naturally, both red and gold.

Go ahead and check out the cover of the Scholastic hard cover for *Deathly Hallows*. Note the red and gold.

After opening the book covers, the first eight chapters are the run-up to the wedding of Bill Weasley and Fleur Delacour, the Red King and White Queen, whose marriage has already happened after a fashion at the end of *Prince*. This is the introduction to the end of the series – Harry's last trip through black dissolution, white purification, and red reintegration. And we are shown the resolution of non-essential contraries, the opposition and remaining contraries to resolve and, most importantly, the imperfections in Harry that must be revealed and transcended.

Lyndy Abraham, whose *Dictionary of Alchemical Imagery* is such a boon to understanding both alchemy itself and the use of its images in English Literature, writes that:

> "Metaphysically, the chemical wedding is the perfect union of creative will or power (male) with wisdom (female) to produce pure love (the child, the Stone). The creation of this Stone always involves some kind of sacrifice or death. Thus emblems of the chemical wedding almost always include emblems of death which overshadow the *conjunctio*....
>
> "The death at the wedding symbolizes the extinction of the earlier differentiated state before union, and also powerfully conveys the alacrity with which the festive moment of the *coagula* or wedding is transformed into the lamentation of the solve or death." (*Dictionary of Alchemical Imagery*, pp. 36-37)

Burckhardt adds:

> "On 'chemical marriage' quicksilver takes unto itself sulphur, and sulphur, quicksilver. Both forces 'die,' as foes and lovers. Then the changing and reflective moon of the soul unites with the immutable sun of the spirit so that it is extinguished, and yet illumined, at one and the same time." (*Alchemy*, pp. 155-156)

At the opening of *Deathly Hallows*, then, we meet the character who has divided his soul into seven parts in a horrific attempt to ape alchemy and create an egocentric rather than spiritual immortality. Voldemort is the anti-alchemist of the series and, true-to-form, he inverts the right understanding of "death" and "love." Love's victory over personal or individual death is in the choice to die to one's ego in an act of self-transcendence or love. Voldemort turns this love-death-life right understanding upside-down by mocking the marriage of Remus and Tonks (and calling for their execution) and by murdering Charity (whose name means "Love") himself. This corpse becomes the food of the serpent Nagini who, like Voldemort, is a poetic vision of everything Satanic. This murder and token of death, with the announcement of Rufus Scrimgeour's death, brackets the alchemical Wedding chapters and the introduction to the *Deathly Hallows* alchemical three stages.

But if the Wedding is marked, even "overshadowed" by "tokens of death" (remember Mad-Eye and Hedwig), we should also see signs that the work is coming successfully to an end. Contraries are being resolved. The Dursleys, most obviously, have willingly accepted magical protection and Dudley and Aunt Petunia have come to new understandings of Harry's value as a person. The magical and Muggle worlds coincide as Harry's childhood and maternal protection are willingly, consciously thrown aside; the meeting is spectacular and violent.

Harry escapes from Privet Drive as he first arrived – as Hagrid's passenger on Sirius' motorcycle. In pointed contradiction with Voldemort's Horcrux method of escaping death, Harry becomes seven selves, not by murder and investing his soul into material objects, but in the willing self-sacrifice made by friends who love him (the exception, of course, is Mundungus, hence Mad Eye's death). We begin the golden references with the Polyjuice Potion "Essence of Harry" that these volunteer shades-of-Harry drink; it is golden, potable gold, and, if Hermione is to be trusted, tasty.

This is to be expected. Harry is the subject/object of the alchemical work, the base metal becoming the *rebis*/Stone. By the beginning of the *rubedo*, the work is largely done (the *rubedo* is the revelation of the work accomplished in the previous white stage). The white peacocks at Malfoy Manor are a nod to the *albedo* we have left in *Prince* at the white sepulcher of Albus Dumbledore to enter the *rubedo*.

And "Essence of Harry" isn't the only golden piece of the first eight chapters. The socks he sorts at the Burrow have "golden balrushes," the book Ron gives him about witches is "solid gold," albeit figuratively speaking, and almost everything at the wedding is golden, including the tent poles, dance floor, band jackets, balloons, bells, and bridesmaids' dresses; Tonks even arrives as a blonde. Luna explains that her father came in his yellow robes because it is traditional to wear "sun colors to a wedding for luck."

As important as this solar flaring at the Wedding itself is the flame that comes spontaneously from Harry's wand that goes to autopilot when confronted with Voldemort.

> "As the pain from Harry's scar forced his eyes shut, his wand acted of its own accord. He felt it drag his hand around like some great magnet, saw a spurt of golden fire through his half-closed eyelids, heard a crack, and a scream of fury." (*Deathly Hallows*, Scholastic standard, page 61)

We don't learn Dumbledore's explanation for this until King's Cross (page 711), but we do see that something interior to Harry, as with the potion, is "golden" and very good – in this case, inner virtue capable of defeating Lord Voldemort.

But Harry is by no means a finished work. He learns in the second chapter that there are reasons to doubt the identity he has taken on as a "Dumbledore Man," and these reasons are not about his unworthiness, but Dumbledore's. Harry reads "Dogbreath" Doge's tribute to his friend and hero, Albus Dumbledore, in *The Daily Prophet* — and then, in the same rag, reads strong hints from Rita Skeeter that Doge left out important and not-so-flattering facts from his eulogy. The pattern repeats itself at the Wedding when Harry meets Elphias Doge in person, who exhorts him to "let nothing tarnish your memories of Albus Dumbledore." But Auntie Muriel shares every nasty thing she has ever heard about the late Hogwarts Headmaster. Harry's faith in the deceased is effectively cracked, if not yet broken.

We see signs, too, that the "quarreling couple" of Ron and Hermione, who represent alchemical sulphur and mercury respectively in the series, will soon again be at loggerheads. Hermione hugs Ron on his return to the camping tent, but is startled to hear the man she loves has more than acquitted himself by escaping from the Death Eaters. "'Always the tone of surprise,' [Ron] said a little grumpily, breaking free [of Hermione]" (page 76). Hermione offers this exact retort at the wedding when Ron marvels at her beauty (page 142). If Harry is going to have to exorcise his doubts and "struggle to believe," his traveling companions are already prepped to create the necessary friction and catalytic reaction for this transformation.

Whatever the differences between Ron and Hermione, Bill and Fleur's wedding does take place, an important Anglo-Franco alliance in a book with such heavy allegorical undertones of the war against Nazi totalitarianism. And the new alliance gets its Dunkirk before the honeymoon has even begun. Kingsley's Patronus announces the death of the Minister of the magic, the first red man death, and the *rubedo* proper begins.

The *Nigredo* in Deathly Hallows

The principal events of the black stage in the finale, stretching from Ch. 9, "A Place to Hide," through Ch. 18, "The Life and Lies of Albus Dumbledore," are:

* The escape from the wedding by the Trio and their finding sanctuary in the House of Black
* Professor Severus Snape becomes Hogwarts Headmaster
* The Ministry of Magic under Pius Thicknesse, Voldemort Stooge, becomes a literal and figurative sewer
* The Trio become a Duo and experience Division and Doubt and near Despair in the Wilderness ['Thief' to 'Silver Doe' (14-18)]
* Harry and Hermione spend Christmas Eve in the Godric's Hallow Graveyard and at Bathilda Bagshot's house with Nagini and the Dark Lord
* Harry's wand, his faith in Dumbledore and his destiny are broken, all seemingly irreparably, as the *nigredo* closes in "The Life and Lies of Albus Dumbledore"

These are the depressing chapters of *Deathly Hallows* that many fans complained dragged on too long. I confess that, reading these chapters aloud to my three youngest children, I worried that the finale was going to be another book like *Phoenix*, the *nigredo* of the entire series. But, as the black stage of the last book, these chapters accomplish the work they need to and, relatively quickly, in order to make the transformations of the last two stages of the book important and credible.

For those of you haven't (yet) read *Unlocking Harry Potter: Five Keys for the Serious Reader* (and your excuse again is what?) in the black, initial stage, "the body of the impure metal, the matter for the Stone, or the old, outmoded state of being is killed, putrefied, and dissolved into the original substance of creation, the *prima materia*, in order that it may be renovated and reborn in a new form" (Abraham, *Dictionary*, page 135). The *nigredo* is the stage of dissolution and loss of defining characteristics or identity. Harry in *Half-Blood Prince* all but shouts down the Minister of Magic's requests for help or just cooperation with chest-pounding statements of allegiance to Albus Dumbledore. In Chapters 9 to 18 of *Deathly Hallows*, we see Harry disavow this allegiance.

It isn't a pretty process. These chapters are quite painful, in fact, to get through.

First, Ron departs, moved by jealousy, disappointment, and hunger for food and action. In each of the Potter novels that the Quarreling Couple actually split up during the action because of their disagreements (*Prisoner* and *Goblet*), this split serves as Harry's "dark night." *Deathly Hallows* is no different. Being abandoned by his oldest and closest friend in the winter of his need almost disables Harry and sends him to his beginnings at Godric's Hollow, in search of the truth.

This journey, undertaken in desperation by Harry and Hermione, has been the the book's most misinterpreted chapter because of the presence of Christian scripture in the Graveyard. It is anything but a "faith experience." They are, after all, entering into a "Hollow," a small valley between mountains but quite literally, an "emptiness." Godric's Hollow, as you might expect from the name, is where Harry begins to grapple with his break from Dumbledore, the man who has been the closest thing to spiritual authority in his life, if not a stand-in here for God.

Harry and Hermione go to Godric's Hollow on Christmas Eve. Through the magic of Polyjuice Potion, they appear to be middle-aged Muggles when not under Harry's Invisibility Cloak. Hermione takes Harry to the graveyard next to the church in which the faithful are singing carols at the Christmas service. They find three headstones of interest: the marker of Ignotus Peverell with the Deathly Hallows sign, the Dumbledore family memorial inscribed with "Where your treasure is, there will your heart be also" (Matthew 6:21) inscribed, and the Potter tombstone, on which they read "The last enemy that shall be destroyed is death" (1 Corinthians 15:26).

The lights have gone out in the church and "the darkness and the silence seemed to become, all of a sudden, much deeper." When

Hermione finds the Potter plot at last, she calls to Harry "out of the blackness." Harry feels "the same sensation he had had right after Dumbledore had died, a grief that actually weighed on his heart and lungs." He reads St. Paul's words from 1 Corinthians about the victory over death and finds no solace in them. Just the opposite. He is horrified and says as much. "Isn't that a Death Eater idea? Why is that there?"

Hermione interprets it for him. "It doesn't mean defeating death in the way the Death Eaters mean it, Harry," said Hermione. It means... you know... living beyond death. Living after death."

And this is what many Christian readers miss in this chapter. Harry *rejects* this meaning and possibility as "empty words." In their excitement about the evidence that Ms. Rowling is indeed a Christian, too many readers neglect to notice that these citations are in the *nigredo* of the book. Harry's response to scripture is *to reject it*.

> "But they were not living, thought Harry. They were gone. The empty words could not disguise the fact that his parents' moldering remains lay beneath snow and stone, indifferent, unknowing." Harry, in fact, in his near-despair, comes "close to wishing... that he was sleeping under the snow with them" ("Godric's Hollow," pages 328-329).

And things only get worse. They are suckered into a visit to Bathilda Bagshot's home, in which Bathilda has been decomposing while animated by Nagini, Lord Voldemort's Horcrux and familiar. They escape only a second before the Dark Lord's arrival, but Harry "sees" what Voldemort experiences and recalls on his return to Godric's Hollow.

"Voldemort screamed with rage, a scream that mingled with the girl's, that echoed across the dark gardens over the church bells ringing in Christmas Day..." (page 342). Harry finally sees the events of his parents' murder on Halloween so many years ago. He snaps out of this Horcrux-enabled nightmare in the forest tent with Hermione, where he learns that his Holly and Phoenix feather wand has been broken in the fight with Nagini and cannot be repaired.

Harry then reads "The Greater Good" chapter in Rita Skeeter's *The Life and Lies of Albus Dumbledore*. Harry learns that his mentor and master had once planned with Grindelwald "to conquer Muggles by force" and that he had neglected his little sister who had consequently died. Even before this, we see:

And his fury at Dumbledore broke over him now like lava, scorching him inside, wiping out every other feeling. Out of sheer desperation they had talked themselves into believing ... that it was all part of some secret path laid out for them by Dumbledore; but there was no map, no plan. Dumbledore had left them to grope in the darkness, to wrestle with unknown and undreamed-of-terrors, alone and unaided: Nothing was explained, nothing was given freely. ("Life and Lies of Albus Dumbledore," page 351).

After reading 'The Greater Good,' he explodes:

"Look what he asked of me, Hermione! Risk your life, Harry! And again! And again! And don't expect me to explain everyting, just trust me blindly, trust that I know what I'm doing, trust me even though I don't trust you! Never the whole truth! Never!"...

"I don't know who he loved, Hermione, but it was never me. This isn't love, the mess he's left me in" ("Life and Lies of Albus Dumbledore," page 362).

Here we have reached the nadir of the *nigredo*. Harry's faith like his Holly wand lies broken (but not discarded) in the darkness and despair when the church lights have gone out and, as C.S. Lewis writes in *The Lion , the Witch and the Wardrobe*: "it is always winter and never Christmas." As I'll explain in Chapter 3, Ms. Rowling sets her *nigredo*, *albedo*, and *rubedo* in the settings of Christmas, Theophany, and Passion Week so that her alchemical artistry mesh with Christian symbolism. It is not the birth of the Messiah she marks in her Christmas *nigredo*, therefore, but the world's darkness before His coming.

There are hints of the coming *albedo* in the graveyard snow and marble tombstones (the placement of the scripture on these glowing white markers is not accidental). But the color and tones of the *nigredo* Chapters, 9-18 in *Deathly Hallows*, are black and dark, spare and isolated. From the House of Black and the Statue of Black Stone ("Magic is Might") in the Ministry "sewer" to the forest shadows, night watches, and pitch-black night in the graveyard, church lights extinguished, Harry's faith and idea of himself as a Dumbledore man are broken. His faith is not discarded, but it is a near thing. Only his tears on the brilliant white marble and wreath of Christmas roses remind us there is a light that will shine in the darkness that will not be put out.

The A*lbedo* of Deathly Hallows

The *albedo* or white stage in *Deathly Hallows* begins with "The Silver Doe" (Ch. 19), the central and pivotal point in the book, and continues through Harry's return to Hogwarts and "The Sacking of Severus Snape" (Ch. 30). The "bleed" from black to white is relatively short, beginning with the snow and marble headstones in the Godric's Hallow graveyard. The transition from white to red begins as early as Dobby's red funeral mound with an engraved white stone (Ch. 24). *Deathly Hallows' albedo* is the longest part of the Great Work's final cycle and the heart of Ms. Rowling's alchemical artistry in the finale.

A quick review here of alchemical basics: alchemy as a spiritual work follows the revealed traditions in being a three part task. The *nigredo* or dissolution stage is the work of "renunciation" or "repentance." It is preparatory to the work of "purification" and "illumination" that in alchemy is done in the second, so-called "white" stage," the *albedo*. Alchemy represents spiritual accomplishment or perfection in its *rubedo* or "red stage."

"The *albedo* occurs after the blackened matter, the putrefied body of the Stone has been washed to whiteness by the mercurial waters or fire" (Abraham, *Dictionary*, page 4). This is the stage of purification and the transformation of the subject, already broken down into *prima materia*, into the *rebis* or Philosopher's Stone. This work, though, is hidden; the accomplishments of the white stage are revealed in the drama of the red finale.

To understand the *albedo*, it helps to know that the Latin root of "*albedo*" and the Headmaster's given name, 'Albus,' means both "white" and "resplendent." There's a hint of "luminescent" or "brilliant" that is, not coincidentally, reflected in our use of the word "brilliant" to mean "really flashy or bright" and "really smart." Aberforth calls his brother "Mr. Brilliant," in fact (page 565), and Albus describes his younger self as "brilliant" in King's Cross (page 715). We think of smart people like Dumbledore as "enlightened," and "purification unto illumination" perhaps best describes the "albification" process.

Titus Burckhardt explains why gold is one product of alchemy in terms of light:

> Gold itself, which outwardly represents the fruit of the work, appears as an opaque body become luminous, or as a light

become solid. Transposed into the human and spiritual order, gold is bodily consciousness transmuted into spirit or spirit fixed in the body. (Burckhardt, *Mirror of the Intellect*, page 132).

Gold is "light become solid" and the alchemist is "spirit become human" via his purification and enlightenment. The stages of the work can be understood in terms of light as well as color. As Burckhardt writes: "Black is the absence of color and light. White is purity; it is undivided light – light not broken down into colors. Red is the epitome of colors, its zenith and its point of greatest intensity" (Burckhardt, *Alchemy*, page 182).

The three colors can be seen as metallurgical steps: dissolution or "blackening," distillation and purification or "bleaching," and recongealing or "reddening." I remember these steps by thinking of the sun at day's end. As the sun sets, the sky darkens and I become less focused; my ego self dissolves into sleep. In the night, there is reflected light, sun on the moon, which illumines my supraconscious self in secret. At dawn, in the light of day, I am re-membered and different because of my purifying rest in the lunar light.

Waking up is important but I am re-born, in a way, every morning because of my rest in the darkness. Which is not a bad summary of the alchemical work. The recongealing or perfection of the human person in the *rubedo* or red stage is really only a revelation of the re-newing, purifying transformation that took place in the dark. Throw in a full moon and a long bath in that white stage at night, and you have a snapshot of the predominant white stage imagery and meaning.

This second step, the *albedo*, is represented in literature with the color white, the silver element or color, with light, especially the light at night (the moon or 'Luna' frequently plays a part), and with water. These elements are used as backdrops and props to story events of purification, illumination, and reconciliation or healing. Again, think of a prophetic dream or insight while lying in bed under the moon after a long bath when recovering from a shattering day; that's an *albedo*. No one will know about it until it is revealed in the light and through the events of the coming day, but that change in the moonlight is the greater part of the Great Work.

The Story Events in the twelve "white" chapters are:

- The Silver Doe: Ron's return, his "baptism," and his

destroying the Locket Horcrux;

- The Adventure of the Lovegood Ziggurat: The trio learn the legend of the Deathly Hallows;

- A Trip to Malfoy Manor: Captured! But the trio are saved by Dobby, who returns – and dies;

- Shell Cottage: Harry buries Dobby, makes a decision in the grave, and works a plan;

- Invasion of Gringotts: The trio and Griphook liberate the Cup and a Dragon;

- A Dip in the Lake and trip to Hogsmeade: Meeting Aberforth, the last test of faith; and

- The Return to Hogwarts: Harry's trips to the Room of Requirement and Ravenclaw Common Room

Just as the *nigredo* is a hot and dry work for the most part and "black" or dark throughout, the *albedo* or white work is about "ablution" or cleansing by water and white or light. The sense of the *albedo* is renewal and purification. Ms. Rowling hits us over the head with all of these qualities from Chapter 19, "The Silver Doe," to Chapter 30, "The Sacking of Severus Snape."

In the adventure with the silver doe and the Locket Horcrux in the Forest of Dean, Ron finds his friends by using Albus' gift to him – the "deluminator," a light-gadget. He and Harry are in a forest covered with snow, both white and wet. They both take a bath in the forest pool and Ron is purified and illumined by destroying the Horcrux (described and explained in the next chapter) The trio reunite and, if Hermione does not warm up to Ron immediately, the trio's reconciliation means the *nigredo* is over.

They then travel to Luna's home and, presto, though Luna is offstage (appropriately, we're told she's down by the river), we learn the most important information possible: the story of the three Hallows. Illumination!

After the trio's escape from the Ziggurat, they debate Horcruxes versus Hallows. Ron, though, is finally able to tune in the Potterwatch program on his wireless. You probably could have helped him guess the password: "Albus" (page 438). Lee Jordan is broadcasting, but with the alias "River," fitting both because of its water reference and due to the River Jordan, most notable for being where Jesus of Nazareth was baptized.

But the name taboo snares them; the good guys are dragged by Greyback to Malfoy Manor, guarded by "a ghostly white shape" (page 455) over their heads, in the form of an "albino peacock"! Quick-thinking Hermione had transformed Harry's face to disguise him with a spell featuring "a burst of white light" (page 446), but to little avail. They wind up in the Manor's dungeon with – who else? – Luna. Ron uses his deluminator again to bring light into darkness. Pettigrew, sent by Malfoy to investigate the sound created by Dobby's disapparating, is taken aback by the light – and strangled by his own pitiless silver arm.

Miraculously, everyone escapes, though Dobby dies. They find refuge where? By the sea, at Bill Weasley's Shell Cottage. Harry digs a grave in the darkness and is enlightened (more on that to come). He marks Dobby's grave next to the sea, of course, with a large white stone (page 481). Bill's house walls are painted a peculiar shade: they're described as "light-colored" (page 482). Voldemort walks on the lakeshore at Hogwarts to the "white marble tomb" which, of course, he enters to take the Death Stick from Albus' incorrupt, "translucent" hands (page 501).

While the trio and Griphook plan the raid on Gringotts in the "light cottage" (page 504), Remus Lupin appears, "white-faced," "his graying hair windswept" (page 514), with the news of Teddy Lupin's birth. (Mr. Ollivander had arrived at the Order's safe-house, Aunt Muriel's, with her "moonstone and diamond" tiara, page 512.)

We leave the seaside for an incognito trip to "snowy-white Gringotts" (page 528) in Diagon Alley. The invaders go up the marble steps to the silver inner doors and gain entry to "the vast marble hall of the bank" (pages 529-30). The good guys and Griphook manage to get into the bank's carts and tracks, but their disguises are revealed by "the Thief's Downfall," a waterfall that "washes away all enchantment, all magical concealment" (page 534).

The dragon? He is described as "pale and flaky," "its eyes were milkily pink" (page 535). After rescuing the Cup-Horcrux, the blind dragon by the underground lake is their means of escape. The liberated dragon flies them well north to land on a "coppery" colored lake in the mountains, water it had "divined" "by the flashes of reflected sunlight." Our three friends, of course, take a refreshing dip to cool their burns (and escape the dragon).

And so at last we get to Hogsmeade and Hogwarts. Before re-entering the school, though, we have to learn the great Albus' painful secrets as recounted by his brother before the picture of Ariane, a blonde girl dressed, not surprisingly, in white (page 569). Are we done with silver, white, wet, milk, snow, washings, dunkings, and illumination? No way.

First, Aberforth's name is a water reference: "*Aber* in Scottish place names means 'confluence' or 'river mouth,' so it could mean the location of Edinburgh-- at the mouth of the river Forth."[13] Next, this is a great truth-telling and clearing of the record about Albus, the white, before his sister in white. If you don't think, this is an *albedo* climax, check out the trio's responses to the river mouth's effluence:

> [Aberforth's] voice broke on the last word and he dropped down into the nearest chair. Hermione's face was **wet with tears**, and Ron was **almost as pale** as Aberforth. Harry felt nothing but revulsion. He wished he had not heard it, wished that he could **wash his mind clean** of it. (page 567, my emphases)

That would be three white stage references, four if you include pale Aberforth, in a single, short paragraph. It must be time to be moving onto the *rubedo*, which, in fact, does happen after a trip into the Room of Requirement, a grand reunion, and Harry's trip with the Queen of the Night (and *albedo*), Luna, to the Ravenclaw common room.

And those are the *surface* references. In the next chapter, I'll discuss how Ms. Rowling uses the alchemical stages in tandem with three Christian holiday echoes to open up the meaning of those holy days in a path of spiritual transformation. Before moving on to the *rubedo* of this book, though, I wanted to note two things about the *albedo* of *Deathly Hallows*.

The references in these chapters are not only of the "sense" of the alchemical stage – wet, white, illuminating, reconciling, etc. – they are of specific hermetic images from the tradition that are important. The silver doe, for instance, is Snape's Patronus and a part of the *albedo* woof and warp in being silver, in being part of the Forest of Dean snow scene, and, we learn eventually, in its being a Lily Evans echo ('lily' like 'luna' is an *albedo topos*). It is also the alchemical *cervus fugitives* or "escaping deer" of the alchemical work.

"The fleeing deer or hart symbolizes Mercurius in his role as the intermediary soul which unites the body and spirit of the Stone"

(Abraham, *Dictionary*, page 52). Harry, Hermione, and Ron, as discussed in *How Harry Cast His Spell*, are a soul-faculty triptych, "spirit, mind, and body." Ms. Rowling, in her depiction of the reunion of "spirit" and "body," – Harry and Ron – uses the tradition's detailed image to deliver this message and wraps it up with Arthurian and Christian touches (the sword, the baptism, the exorcism) that buttress the alchemical meaning. This isn't just using nice touches of pale color and cleansing moisture; this is the thrust of her artistic effort, however subliminal.

The transformation that Harry experiences in the work's white stage, revealed in the crisis at the end of the novel, is his decision to believe in Dumbledore. He makes this decision in Dobby's grave, a grave he initiates and digs by spade himself (no magic) at night by the sea. So what?

Well, it's the biggest decision in the book and I'll explain that in the next chapter, too. Here, though, in the "just alchemy" chapter, I'm obliged to note that the grave is an alchemical image. Again, Lyndy Abraham:

> **grave** the alchemists vessel during the *nigredo*, when the matter of the Stone, the united sulphur (male) and argent vive (female) undergoes death, dissolution and puterfaction. Other names for the vessel at this stage are the tomb, coffin, sepulchre, tumulus, prison and ark, Rutland's *Lexicon* calls the vessel the 'Sepulchre and Tomb' and 'Grave, Churchyard, because the Stone lies hidden there' (413,323). Ripley wrote of burying male sulphur and female argent vive in a grave: 'Therefore at the begynnyng [of Puterfaction] our Stonys thou take,/And bery ech on wyth other wythin ther Grave' (TCB, 150). Emblem 6 of Mylius's *Philosophia reformata* shows the dead bodies of the united lovers in the coffin as vessel (see fig. 10).

The emblem of the lovers and the tomb occurs as a three-dimensional tableau in Shakespeare's *Romeo and Juliet*. Juliet, already secretly married to Romeo, begs her mother to 'Delay this marriage for a month, a week,/ Or if you do not, make the bridal bed/ In that dim monument where Tybalt lies' (3.5.199-201), Indeed, Romeo and Juliet finally do unite in Tybalt's tomb after Romeo obtains poison from an apothecary whose shop is adorned with alchemical insignia (5.1.40-4;5.3.101-20).

In alchemy the souls of the dead bodies, sometimes depicted as one hermaphrodite body, are released and fly to the top of the alembic, leaving the blackened, putrefied bodies to be washed

> **and purified so that they become the white foliated earth of
> the *albedo*. This earth (or cleansed body) is then pure enough
> to reunite with the soul (or united soul/spirit), and from this
> union the philosopher's stone is born.** (my emphasis)

> Thus the vessel which is the tomb of death is also the womb of
> new life, of generation (see **generation**). John Dunne equates the
> grave and the alembic in the 'Elegy on the Lady Marckham'; 'So
> at this grave, her limbeck, which refines/ The diamonds, rubies,
> sapphires, pearls and mines' (lines 23-4), and in 'A Nocturnal
> upon s. Lucy's Day' he wrote: 'I, by love's limbeck, and the grave/
> Of all, that's nothing' (lines 21-2) [*Dictionary of Alchemical
> Imagery*, pages 90-91]

I give you the full definition from the best of nine alchemical image
reference books I own to show I'm not making this stuff up. As used by
poets like Shakespeare and Donne, the grave is the alchemist's vessel
in which the *nigredo* events take place as well as the critical work of
the purifying stage. Harry enters the grave willingly, personally, and
sacrificially (no magic, this is for Dobby, his savior). He goes in a
confused, shattered young man of doubts; he rises from the alembic by
the sea *knowing* what he must do:

> In the darkness, with nothing but the sound of his own breath
> and the rushing sea to keep him company, the things that had
> happened in the Malfoys' returned to him, the things he had
> heard came back to him, and understanding blossomed in the
> darkness (The Wandmaker, page 479)

We learn when he speaks with Aberforth that his time in the grave
had set his path, the path of trust and belief, that would lead him against
all odds to victory over the Dark Lord:

> He had made his choice as he dug Dobby's grave, he had decided
> to continue along the winding, dangerous path indicated for
> him by Albus Dumbledore, to accept that he had not been told
> everything that he wanted to know, but simply to trust. (The
> Missing Mirror, page 563)

C. S. Lewis has Prof. Ransom in the *albedo* novel of his *Space Trilogy*
fly from earth to Venus and back in a white coffin. Same idea, same
medieval imagination, same hermetic, subliminal detail.

Beyond the depth of the artistry, I need to put the marker down that this *change* in Harry from skeptic to determined believer is not immediately obvious but it is the conscious choice that when played out in the crisis of the *rubedo* and its several revelations is the substance and greater part of Harry's ability to vanquish the Dark Lord. I explain in the next chapter how the Godric's Hollow nightmare/*nigredo*/nadir is a Christmas Eve snapshot; how Ron's baptism and illumination are an echo of Theophany (Christ's baptism), and how the story's climax, the *rubedo* in the last six chapters, is in many ways Harry's 'Passion narrative' of Holy Week and Easter.

The *real* Easter, though, on the calendar in the story falls at the time and perhaps the day (page 575) Harry goes into Dobby's grave and rises from it with his decision to trust and to believe in Dumbledore, his Horcrux mission, and in his friends. His resurrection after King's Cross and seeming death in the Forbidden Forest is only the *rubedo* revelation of the victory won in the white stage alembic at Easter.

The *albedo* of *Deathly Hallows*, beyond the wet, white, and enlightening references, then, is about how:

- The *cervus fugitivus* and shared baptism and purification of Ron and Harry renew the quest

- Harry's doubts about Dumbledore are dissolved by the heroic faith of Dobby and Harry's willing entrance into the grave – and –

- Harry chooses to believe in his mission and to trust his mentor and his friends

The *rubedo*

And having learned all that, we come at last to the subject of this chapter, the *rubedo* or red stage of *Deathly Hallows* the book and of the *Harry Potter* epic taken as a whole. To explore this aspect of literary alchemy properly, let's begin with some clarification of what a *rubedo* is, how it shows itself in literary alchemy so we know what to be looking for, and then a look at the last chapters of *Deathly Hallows* to see how they succeed or fail to complete the single alchemical cycle of Harry's last year as well as the Great Work of Harry's seven year transformation.

To understand the last step in alchemy, the red stage, we really have to have a good grasp of what the alchemist is after in metallurgical and spiritual terms. In a nutshell, "resolution of contraries" is what it's all about. To understand that, though, means learning a little traditional cosmology and metaphysics. Put your geek hat on and your boots; this is heavy plowing for a few paragraphs!

The world view of the alchemist is that there is an Absolute God that is transcendent or "totally Other." In Christian language, this is "God the Father." The Supreme Reality is also immanent because Its very perfection or absoluteness means It includes an aspect of Infinitude, which in spatial language that is not descriptive, includes an idea of extension. Non-Being or Other, because infinite, includes Being, which in turn creates existent beings.

Every aspect and element of this creation, consequently, no matter how ephemeral or close to eternal is marked by the signature polarity sans division in the Supreme Reality that is both Transcendent and Immanent. God's being unknowable and unknown in Its essence or Non-being and God's being closer to us than our heartbeat and existence, is the cause of the polarity in all things: the night/day, contraction/expansion, male/female, hot/cold, near/far, summer/winter, early/late, yin/yang, and Gryffindor/Slytherin apposition we see all around us in myriad quality-pairs.

If you ask the man on the street (and I'm not recommending you do this) what alchemy is all about, most folks will say "changing lead into gold" or just "gold." That's not quite right. The alchemist is trying to create the Philosopher's Stone, from which he can draw the Elixir of Life or Dragon's Blood. This effluent, if drunk, keeps the alchemist alive for as long as he keeps drinking it, and, if poured on any other substance, turns that material into gold. The most visible end product, of course, is gold, which if understood correctly is explanation in itself of why the alchemical work is about "resolving contraries."

In the traditional view of the alchemist, remember, the created world is an image of its Unknowable Creator in being a balance or imbalance of contrary tendencies, call them "male" and "female." Our polarized existence reflects God's being simultaneously and as a unicity both within and outside creation (panentheism). Those things that are "most like" this Reality are a fixed balance or resolution of the contrary masculine and feminine principles, which resolution is a unity and peace that reflects in time and space God's unicity.

The alchemist wants to be able to change lead into gold through his Philosopher's Stone. This is possible because "the true essence of lead is gold" (Burckhardt, *Alchemy*, page 72-73). The male and female tendencies, yang and yin, in esoteric metallurgy are called alchemical sulphur and alchemical quicksilver or mercury. Lead is an imbalance of these tendencies; Gold is their perfect, luminous resolution.

> sulphur, the original masculine power, and quicksilver, the original feminine power, both strive towards the wholeness of their one and eternal prototype. The latter is at the same time the reason for their opposition and for their mutual attraction – just as the masculine and feminine natures long for the integrality of the human state, and as a result of this seek both to separate from one another, and to unite with one another. By means of their physical union both try to re-establish the image of their common eternal prototype. This is the marriage of man and woman, sulphur and quicksilver, Spirit and soul.
>
> In the mineral domain it is gold that is born of the perfect union of the two generative principles. Gold is the true product of metallic generation. *Every other metal is either a premature birth or abortion*, an imperfect gold, and, in this way of looking at things, the alchemical work is nothing more than a midwife or helper, which art offers nature so that the latter can perfectly ripen the fruit whose maturation was being hindered by certain temporal circumstances. (Burckhardt, *Alchemy*, pages 125-126; my emphasis)

Gold, "solid light," is what matter is *supposed to be*. The alchemist, using the reagents and catalysts sulphur and mercury ("the quarreling couple" of antagonistic complements), work to restore or accelerate the change of lead to its proper and natural splendor as gold.

He does this, as we've seen, by working to create a Philosopher's Stone, the "run-off" of which will create gold or life by affecting a material or person with the transformations the alchemist worked in its substance to create the Stone. In the first of the three stages of transformation, what is called the *nigredo*, he strips away the non-essential qualities of the substance. In the second stage, the *albedo*, he washes or "whitens" the substance, which as discussed above, is its hidden illumination. The stone is produced in the second stage but it is white and can only change substances into silver.

The *rubedo* or third step is "the reddening of the white matter of the stone at the final stage of the opus alchymicum" (Abraham, *Dictionary*, 174). In the *nigredo*, all form, color, and light are taken from the substance to reduce it to blackened "prime matter." In the *albedo*, a light like the moon's reflected colorless light is evident in the white stone produced. In the *rubedo*, the contraries are resolved, the white stage's accomplishments are revealed, and the Stone becomes red; "red is the epitome of colors, its zenith and its point of greatest intensity" (Burckhardt, *Alchemy*, page 182). Imagine the lunar light shining through a prism to reveal all colors and especially their epitome, red.

The *rubedo*, then, the last step in creating the Philosopher's Stone, is the stage in which the *albedo* illumination is perfected and revealed in the red Philosopher's Stone. The sympathetic process of creating the Stone, a resolution of the sulphur/mercury complementary antagonistic qualities, resolves the Spirit/soul contraries in the alchemist so that he returns to Edenic perfection and purity. This resolution of male/female contraries is often represented as a *"rebis,"* Latin for "thing-twice," or a hermetic androgyn, a hermaphrodite. The Stone, in being the "death" of male and female contraries, is sometimes called the "Philosophical Orphan" because its "parents" died at its birth.

Literary *rubedo*

Whew. If you made it through that, you're made of good stuff. The rest is easy. Having made it through Alchemy Boot Camp, the next step, the literary version of the *rubedo*, namely, how story-tellers and poets use alchemy in their tales and verses, is a piece of cake. You just have to pick up on what to look for.

Like metallurgical and esoteric alchemy, the last step will be about revelations, resolutions, and red-productions, even "reproductions" or reproducing. It's the climax of the story in which all loose ends and conflicts come to a head and to a close. In an alchemical climax, though, you need to be looking especially for:

- The wedding of a Red King and White Queen;

- The revelation of concealed identities and changes in character;

- The resolution of enmity, contraries, and antagonism; and

- The production of a Philosopher's Stone or one of the many story symbols for it.

If you're struggling with this, just think "Shakespeare." How many Shakespeare plays *don't* end this way? Capulets and Montagues united, twins finding each other, women playing the parts of men revealing themselves and their loves, a Shrew revealed to be sweet Kate. As bald as Ms. Rowling is in her alchemical display, she is only following the Bard's lead in four-element accents and hermetic storytelling.

As we lay out the contraries being resolved in the *Deathly Hallows* storyline and the series narrative as well, think *"rebis,"* – in whom are these contraries being resolved? That person or those people will have died to their personal concerns and become a sacrifice of sorts, just as the Stone and Orphan are born in the death of the quarreling couple.

And the red? I like to think of the story *rubedo* as a crucible in which all the story elements are brought to a red heat and boil. This makes sense to me because the "resolution" we're looking for can only come from union or conflict, neither of which is an easy process. A "union of opposites," say, in physical congress, the beast of two backs is "resolution" we can call "love," even "life." In Elizabethan language, though, this sexual union was also a figurative "death" because both male and female identities are lost in the union.

That's easier to see in "resolution by combat" or strife. Here the conflict and contrariness make an exciting, fighting ending with the face-offs, sword or wand fighting, blood, death, and re-birth, winner and loser, as consequences. In war, we call the resolution of contraries "peace."

With those ideas in mind, then, let's look at *Deathly Hallows'* last chapters as that book's *rubedo* and then at *Deathly Hallows* as the *rubedo* book of the Harry Potter series.

The *Rubedo of Deathly Hallows*

Deathly Hallows' finale comes in Chapters 30-36 and the book's Epilogue. A quick synopsis of the principal events of these chapters will be a helpful review:

- Battle of Hogwarts: Snape is sacked soon after Harry's return and the War is on. Riddle wants Potter and attacks Hogwarts; Harry searches for the remaining Horcruxes and the means to destroy them.

- Horcrux Search and Destroy: While the battle rages and the Room of Requirement burns, Hermione and Ron destroy the Cup-

Horcrux, and Crabbe and Goyle conjure Fiendfyre to finish off the Diadem-Horcrux.

• Body Count: It's not a bloodless battle. Fred Weasley, Colin Creevey, Nymphadora Tonks, and Remus Lupin (and more than 50 other witches and wizards) die to buy Harry time to complete his mission.

• The Death and Memories of Severus Snape: The Potions Master and Harry's great nemesis dies – and the memories he pours out in death include instructions from Dumbledore for Harry.

• The Forest Again: Harry walks to his death in the company of departed family and mentors to destroy the Scar-Horcrux.

• King's Cross: Harry has the first of two Dumbledore Denouements in *Deathly Hallows* in a 'place' he thinks is like King's Cross Station.

• The Flaw in the Plan: Harry returns to life and triumphs over the Dark Lord. The story ends with Harry renouncing the Hallows in the Headmaster's Office.

• Epilogue: Harry speaks with his son Albus Severus at the more familiar King's Cross Station, 19 years after the Dark Lord's defeat.

For these chapters and Epilogue to be a proper finish to the book's alchemical work as a self-contained three-step cycle, we should find a wedding, a Stone or *rebis*, and both revelation and resolution. We do.

The *albedo* illumination Harry experiences in Dobby's grave at Easter is revealed both in the Calvary and Paschal experiences he has in the Forest (see the next chapter) and his regained capacity for trust.

You recall that Lupin, after the misadventure in getting Harry out of Privet Drive, chastises him for not stunning Stan Shunpike and for insisting on trusting his friends. Lupin was not alone in assuming that one member of the Order had betrayed Harry, intentionally or unintentionally. Harry's response is denial: "We've got to trust each other. I trust all of you. I don't think anyone in this room would ever sell me to Voldemort" (Page 80).

Harry loses this faith, however, in his fellows, his mission, and especially in his mentor, Albus Dumbledore, after a few months on the run. By the end of his reading of *The Life and Lies* at *nigredo*'s depths,

Harry interprets Dumbledore's lack of trust in him as reason to suspect there was no love involved, either.

> "Look what he asked from me, Hermione! Risk your life, Harry! And again! And again! And don't expect me to explain everything, just trust me blindly, trust that I know what I'm doing; trust me even though I don't trust you! Never the whole truth! Never!... I don't know who he loved, Hermione, but it was never me." (page 362)

And then Dobby dies to save him. Harry thinks of Dumbledore three different times while burying Dobby and comes out of the grave, as we have seen, having made the decision to do as he was told – Horcruxes, not Hallows (pages 479-482). He keeps to this decision even when confronted by Aberforth's revelations about his brother's failings:

> [Harry] had made his choice while he dug Dobby's grave; he had decided to continue along the winding, dangerous path indicated for him by Albus Dumbledore, to accept that he had not been told everything that he wanted to know, but simply to trust. (page 563)

When Harry arrives in the castle, though, he is surrounded by Dumbledore's Army wanting to help him. He initially refuses their help, but Ron and Hermione think this is a mistake. Harry, having put aside doubt, has to trust his friends as well:

> Harry thought fast.... Was he turning into Dumbledore, keeping his secrets clutched to his chest, afraid to trust? But Dumbledore had trusted Snape, and where had that led? To murder at the top of the highest tower...(page 583)

He struggles and then he trusts. And his faith and sharing the burden make his pursuit of the final Horcruxes possible and successful. The DA, Order, Quidditch Team, and Hogwarts faculty with friends from Ravenclaw, Hufflepuff, and Gryffindor keep the Death Eaters and monsters sufficiently engaged so the trio are able to destroy the Cup and Diadem-Horcruxes. When they begin to hunt Nagini, these friends even save Harry, Ron, and Hermione from the Dementors (page 649).

We can contrast Harry's position on trust, not only with Dumbledore (who apologizes explicitly on this count at King's Cross: "Can you forgive me for not trusting you?" page 713), but also with the Dark Lord. None of the Death Eaters know what objects the Horcruxes are, where they are kept, or why Voldemort is murderous when he learns one has been destroyed (page 549). Like Dumbledore, he even keeps Severus Snape, his most valuable lieutenant, in the dark:

> To tell Snape why the boy might return would be foolish, of course, it had been a grave mistake to trust Bellatrix and Malfoy: Didn't their stupidity and carelessness prove how unwise it was ever to trust? (page 551)

Of course, if he had befriended and trusted the Malfoys, Narcissa would have certainly betrayed Harry when she was forced to see if he was dead or alive in the Forbidden Forest. Harry had entered the grave willingly at Easter and risen from the psychological death of going-it-alone. And the difference was revealed and played out in the *rubedo*.

The book begins with a wedding. Is there one at the end, too? In a sense. After Voldemort had died, and his body taken out of the hall:

> McGonagall had replaced the House tables, but nobody was sitting according to House anymore: All were jumbled together, teachers and pupils, ghosts and parents, centaurs and house-elves, and Firenze lay recovering in a corner, and Grawp peered in through a smashed window, and people were throwing food into his laughing mouth. (page 745)

We see the contraries and set-identities of House, magical species, parent, teacher, even the living and dead, put aside in the aftermath of this great conflict and Harry's victory over the Dark Lord.

I think we can see this sort of resolution, too, in the solving of this specific Harry Potter adventure's mystery, "What are the Deathly Hallows? How can Harry defeat the Elder Wand?" Harry, iconic Gryffindor Champion, defeats the Dark Lord with the wand of Draco Malfoy, his Slytherin nemesis, the wand that had disarmed Albus Dumbledore. Lord Voldemort had ordered Draco to kill the Headmaster, and, it turns out, that wand had mastered Albus. A Slytherin wand in the hands of a Gryffindor hero closes the great divide of the Wizarding World and at Hogwarts. In that wedding (and the peace, love, and life it represents), Voldemort didn't stand a chance.

So we have a revelation and resolution significant enough, I think, it could be called a wedding (if not a marriage). The only thing left on the *Deathly Hallows rubedo* list is a Philosopher's Stone or *rebis*. Harry certainly qualifies as one of those.

The *rebis*, what I called a "Hogwarts hermaphrodite" in *Unlocking Harry Potter*, isn't both a man and a woman simultaneously, but the resolution of masculine and feminine tendencies in one person. The signature of this achievement is a semi-divine passionlessness or *apathia*, in which state personal advantage is not the guide. The person is ruled instead by love and charity, even the will to sacrifice. It is not the addition of one quality and one more complementary quality, giving the *rebis* two natures, but the unity of complements creating a self-transcendent nature out of imbalance.

This selflessness, with the Expelliarmus Charm, is Harry's signature. It's "what he does" when the going gets tough and the hard decisions are made - in *every single book*:

- In *Philosopher's Stone*, it is his *not* wanting the Stone for his own purposes that allows him to remove it from the Mirror of Erised.

- In *Chamber*, he risks everything to save his best friend's sister "miles beneath Hogwarts."

- In *Prisoner*, he prevents the murder of the man who betrayed his parents to Voldemort by stepping between him and his would be executioners.

- In *Goblet*, Harry tries to rescue all four underwater hostages – and tells Cedric he will share the Tournament Cup.

- In *Phoenix*, Voldemort uses Harry's "saving-people-thing" to lure him all the way from Hogwarts into a Department of Mysteries trap.

- In *Half-Blood Prince*, he goes with Dumbledore to the Cave in search of the Locket-Horcrux, but not until he has returned to the Gryffindor Common Room to give his Felix Felicis potion to the friends he thinks will need it.

And *Deathly Hallows* is no exception. Three times we see Harry forsake taking invaluable things for their own sake, as he did the Philosopher's Stone as an eleven-year-old. He doesn't want to steal Gringott's treasure, which causes Griphook to remark, "If there was a wizard of whom I would believe that they did not seek personal gain, it would be you, Harry Potter" (page 488). The goblin had been won over by the respect and protection Harry had demonstrated and given to him and Dobby at Malfoy Manor and Shell Cottage.

Then Harry wins over the Gray Lady with a similar show of indifference about personal gain in finding the Ravenclaw Diadem-Horcrux. She rebuffs his requests for information, with scolding comments about his seeking greater knowledge with it until he says, ("fiercely") – "Haven't I just told you, I'm not interested in wearing it!" She spills her Brothers Grimm story about the Bloody Baron in the face of this passionate apathy (page 615).

And, most important, Harry does not pursue either the Resurrection Stone or the Wand of Destiny. And when he inherits two Hallows and wins the other in combat, he keeps only the family heirloom, thereby forsaking unimaginable power and advantage, even the "mastery of death."

Why? How?

Dumbledore, who is a master alchemist remember, is a kindred spirit. He set the Mirror of Erised up in Harry's first adventure so that only selflessness and indifference to personal gain could unlock it. The Headmaster also destroyed the Philosopher's Stone after consulting with Nicolas Flamel and, in that, threw away something like personal immortality.

This like-minded, if flawed hero explains to Harry at King's Cross that he did what he could to delay Harry's learning about the Hallows lest he be tempted and fall (as Dumbledore did). The Headmaster tells Harry that his success in resisting the tug to "get the Elder wand!" and become the "master of death" back in Dobby's grave means:

> You are the true master of death, because the true master does
> not seek to run away from Death. He accepts that he must die,
> and understands that there are far, far worse things in the living
> world than dying (page 721)

The master of death trusts, obeys and believes in greater realities than himself – sufficiently enough to die sacrificially for them. This is, of course, exactly what Harry does in "The Forest Again" and it is his willing self-sacrifice which saves his life, destroys the Scar-Horcrux, and all but insures Voldemort's defeat (more on this in the next chapter).

Harry is the *rebis* and our *Deathly Hallows rubedo* checklist is complete.

Deathly Hallows as *Rubedo* of the Seven Book Series

If you've read either *Unlocking Harry Potter* or *How Harry Cast His Spell*, you know that alchemy is a seven-cycle series of these three stage cycles and that Harry's seven-year education is really his alchemical transformation. Every year he goes through a blackening, a bleaching, and a crucible rubification that turns him into his opposite. The first four years he merely gained in character and in confidence through these experiences. Beginning in *Order of the Phoenix*, he prepared for his final transformation and test with Voldemort.

In brief, *Phoenix* was Harry's *nigredo* novel. Though it had three steps like the others, the book as a whole was about stripping all the inessential identity tags from him ("great Quidditch player," "Ron & Hermione leader," "son of a great guy," "happy at Hogwarts," etc.) to leave him with only his destiny at the end. This "black book" featured Sirius Black, took place in parts at the House of Black, and sadly, ended with the death of Black.

Half-Blood Prince was Harry's *albedo* novel, and, as you'd guess, it was about Harry's purification and illumination. He spends a lot of time in tutorials with Albus, with special emphasis on learning about Horcruxes, and the Dark Lord and how he thinks. Albus, the white and resplendent, also sadly dies at the end of the white book and stage.

We must expect, consequently, that *Deathly Hallows*, as the final book and following the *nigredo* and *albedo Harry Potter* books, would be the *rubedo* novel for the series as a whole. If it has a revelation of something that took place in the white work of the series, namely, *Half-Blood Prince*, the previous book, an alchemical wedding, and the production of a Stone or *rebis*, we can say the book has met or exceeded expectations.

Deathly Hallows doesn't lack for revelations! Certainly we learn what really happened on the Astronomy Tower in *Half-Blood Prince* as well as the backstory of Dumbledore's something-like-assisted-suicide there. And in the Pensieve, the *Deathly Hallows* reader also learns the Severus Snape story, the agony of his unrequited love, and his unbroken remorse for being the cause of his true love's death (if only the Bloody Baron had told him his story!). From Aberforth, Rita Skeeter, and Dogbreath Doge, and, ultimately, from Albus Dumbledore himself, we learn the "greatest wizard of the age" had not only a spotted history but also a penchant for playing Machiavelli with people's lives.

As discussed in Chapter 1, learning the perspectives and background of both beloved mentor and despised enemy allows Harry to admire and assimilate more from each (the light *and* the dark) than he did when both were one-dimensional caricatures. More on this in a second. Let's get to the wedding!

Or should I say "weddings"? *Deathly Hallows* first wedding announcement is given by Lord Voldemort who tries to shame Bellatrix with the news that her niece Nymphadora had married a werewolf. They are marked for death there and, as usual, Ms. Rowling paid off the markers she put down in chapter one at story's end.

The real alchemical wedding, of the Red King and the White Queen, is the marriage of choleric Bill Weasley and phlegmatic Fleur Delacour, which introduces the alchemical work of *Deathly Hallows*. This sign of the *rubedo* leaves little doubt about the alchemical meaning of this book.

I would add to this list of alchemical weddings Ron and Hermione's nuptials. (Harry and Ginny's marriage is an Arthurian set-piece rather than anything especially esoteric). But Ron and Hermione's wedding *is* alchemical and a big *rubedo* moment because of their roles as the "Quarreling Couple" in the books, even though their actual wedding doesn't take place until years after the Battle of Hogwarts.

Ronald Bilius Weasley is marked by both his red hair, gender, passionate nature, and middle name as choleric sulphur, representing the masculine pole of existence. Hermione's initials, Hg, are the Periodic Table symbol for mercury; her first name is the feminine for "Hermes" the Greek equivalent in the Olympian pantheon for "mercury," and alchemical mercury represents the feminine, intellective aspect of creation. Did I mention her parents are dentists? How many mercury cues do we need?

Ron and Hermione are the story symbols of the reagents working on Harry in each book for his alchemical transformation. He is pretty tired of their back-and-forth nastiness at times but he isn't really himself in these adventures without at least one by his side. Ron and Hermione begin *Deathly Hallows* as a couple, but one with issues (their mutual "always the surprise" comments before Bill and Fleur's wedding). Ron's departure from the trio amounts to a trial separation and she does not greet his return in the Forest of Dean with anything like affection.

The couple has to resolve their differences, though, sometime in the *rubedo* if the Philosopher's Stone is to be produced. Ron wins her over completely in the Battle of Hogwarts by speaking a little Parseltongue in the bathroom and declaring that the house-elves need to be protected. When Hermione drops her Basilisk teeth and embraces Ron, the story is effectively over and Voldemort vanquished. Harry felt there was still a war going on, but according to formula, at the moment of Ron and Hermione's snogging, he was already the resolution of contraries, a *rebis* or Philosopher's Stone.

Which brings us back to Harry as a Gryffindor/Slytherin *rebis*. In the Epilogue we learn Harry has named his second son, the one with Lily's eyes, "Albus Severus Potter." Harry's son should have been called "Albus Severus Potter, *Jr.*," for two reasons.

First, Harry is the conjunction of Gryffindor and Slytherin natures since his first Sorting, but especially in *Chamber*. The Scar-Horcrux, no doubt, had something to do with this duality or inner polarity. But certainly Harry, after learning the Snape/Dumbledore secrets in the last chapters of *Deathly Hallows* and dying to the Voldemort within him, takes on their best qualities. It is "Albus Severus Potter, Sr.," who dispatches the Dark Lord in the Great Hall.

And, those initials: ASP! The boy was obviously meant for Slytherin. If the Harry Potter story is really a three-generation epic about bridging the Gryffindor/Slytherin divide, Ms. Rowling is pointing to the ASP child, Rose Weasley, and Scorpius Malfoy to complete the work that might have been done in Harry's parent's generation.

Sirius Black, from a Slytherin family embraced Gryffindor, and Lily Evans, a Gryffindor, was good friends with Severus Snape of Slytherin House. The pieces were in place, but none of the players were equal to their parts, with predictably tragic results. Perhaps the reason behind Harry's Scar/Horcrux was the need for a Gryffindor/Slytherin *rebis*... We'd have to ask Firenze.

Albus Severus Potter, though – the ASP of the Epilogue, is almost certainly a Slytherin. Ms. Rowling points to this in his initials, his conversation with Harry, and in his friendship with Rose and probable friendship with Scorpius. The Rose is an alchemical symbol for the Philosopher's Stone (no surprise that she is the child of the Quarreling Couple!) and her relationships with the ASP and Scorpius point to reconciliation at long last between the progeny of Salazar Slytherin and Godric Gryffindor.

Conclusion

You want more?

How about Fred dying instead of George? This is almost certainly to satisfy the colored-death formula of the last three books of the series (that's fRED, called "Rodent" on 'PotterWatch by host 'River' Jordan, both because of the rodent/weasel joke and because "rot," pronounced "road" is the German word for "red")

And Teddy Lupin being the Philosophical Orphan of the adventure?

Did you catch the alchemical note in the first sentence of the Epilogue? "The morning of the first of September was crisp and as golden as an apple." Maybe the "gold" there was enough to clue you in, or the hat-tip to the garden in Lewis' *The Magician's Nephew*. If not, read this entry from *The Dictionary of alchemical Imagery* for 'Hesperides:'

> Hesperides: the place or garden in which the philosopher's stone is found. The mythological Hesperian gardens were a favorite symbol in alchemy, because they contained a tree that grew golden apples. The image of the golden apples was used by the alchemists to symbolize gold and the philosopher's stone.... This image relates to the popular alchemical symbol which compares the philosopher's stone to the growth of the philosophical tree and the production of golden fruit. (Abraham, *Dictionary*, page 101)

As I said back in the beginning, these are subtle, subliminal touches and formulaic structures. They are well below the surface reading, buttress that meaning, and create a complementary and more profound one. Each time I read *Deathly Hallows*, more of the author's hermetic artistry surfaces. And I marvel at the layering and the dove-tailing of (1) her surface postmodern message about tolerance, diversity, and making heroic choices to confront evil, (2) the thrust of her symbolism and pointers to traditional faith just beneath this narrative line, and (3) the hermetic framework and accents that speak, a la, Shakespeare, to the perfection or divinization of hero and reader. [The three layers of Ms. Rowling's story symbolism is the subject of chapters 6 and 7.]

Ms. Rowling told her readers in 1998 that alchemy helped her "to set the parameters and establish the stories' internal logic." *Deathly Hallows*, the series finale and its best-seller, is the *rubedo* of the seven-book alchemical work and an alchemical cycle all of its own. In your efforts to understand Ms. Rowling's books and their popularity, I encourage you to use this chapter to jump-start your study of her use of alchemy. None of it jumps up at the reader (with the exception of the first book's title!) but, like effective advertising, thoughtful stage setting, and in the best writing (to paraphrase C. S. Lewis), the messages planted beneath our conscious minds are the ones that penetrate most deeply.

Endnotes

1   Peter Hitchens, 'This is the Most Dangerous Author in Britain,' *The Mail on Sunday*, 27 January 2002, p.63; http://home.wlv.ac.uk/~bu1895/hitchens.htm

2   Lev Grossman. "J.K. Rowling Hogwarts And All," *Time Magazine*, 17 July, 2005; http://www.accio-quote.org/articles/2005/0705-time-grossman.htm

3   http://thehogshead.org/2007/11/21/around-the-common-room-34/#comment-271580; the video link can be found here: http://www.youtube.com/watch?v=ZyQjr1YL0zg

4   http://www.medialit.org/reading_room/article50.html

5   http://skeptoid.com/episodes/4063

6   http://www.ibiblio.org/pub/electronic-publications/stay-free/archives/22/subliminal-advertising.html

7   http://touchstonemag.com/archives/article.php?id=20-10-022-f

8   Grossman, op. cit.

9   C.S. Lewis, *The Literary Impact of The Authorised Version*. The Ethel M. Wood Lecture delivered before the University of London on 20 March 1950. London: The Athlone Press, 1950. pg. 22; http://www.biblicalstudies.org.uk/pdf/kjv_lewis.pdf

10   http://www.accio-quote.org/articles/1998/1298-herald-simpson.html

11   Titus Burckhardt, *Alchemy* (Penguin, 1971) page 149

12   "So I'm told repeatedly. The two groups of people who are constantly thanking me are wiccans (white witches) and boarding schools. And really, don't thank me. I'm not with either of them. **New ageism leaves me completely cold,** and Jessie would never go to boarding school. I went to a comprehensive." Hattenstone, Simon. "Harry, Jessica and me," *The Guardian*, July 8, 2000; http://www.accio-quote.org/articles/2000/0700-guardian-hattenstone.htm

13   The Akashic Record, 'A' ; http://m5p.com/~pravn/hp/a.html

Chapter 3

Choosing to Believe

The Christian Content of
Harry Potter and the Deathly Hallows

Ms. Rowling twice told reporters in 2000 that the seventh novel in the series would answer questions about her faith raised by 'The Controversy' over the use of magic in the books. On July 13, 2000, she told CBC *News World*:

> *E: You do believe in God.*
>
> *JK: Yeah. Yeah.*
>
> *E: In magic and...*
>
> *JK: Magic in the sense in which it happens in my books, no, I don't believe. I don't believe in that. No. No. This is so frustrating. Again, there is so much I would like to say, and* **come back when I've written book seven. But then maybe you won't need to even say it 'cause you'll have found it out anyway. You'll have read it***. (emphasis mine)* [1]

On October 26, 2000, a reporter from The *Vancouver Sun* published another *bon mot* from Ms. Rowling about the end of the series and her faith:

> *Harry, of course, is able to battle supernatural evil with supernatural forces of his own, and Rowling is quite clear that she doesn't personally believe in that kind of magic — "not at all." Is* **she a Christian?**
>
> **"Yes, I am," she says.** *"Which seems to offend the religious right far worse than if I said I thought there was no God. Every time I've been asked if I believe in God, I've said yes, because I do, but no one ever really has gone any more deeply into it than that, and I*

*have to say that does suit me, because **if I talk too freely about
that I think the intelligent reader, whether 10 or 60, will be
able to guess what's coming in the books.***" (emphasis mine) [2]

'The Controversy' today is restricted to individual parishes and
overwrought individuals but, in the year 2000, every article written
about Harry Potter seemed to include mention of Ms. Rowling's
Cinderella story and discussion of Christian objections to the books. In
this context, Ms. Rowling was asked about her faith that year. Culture
warriors claimed the Harry Potter novels were "a gateway to the occult."
The author was caught in a frustrating bind—discussing her Christian
faith would reveal the ending, yet the ending would make pointless
questions about her beliefs and the occult. "Because you'll have found it
out anyway. You'll have read it."

Well, we've read it now. What does *Deathly Hallows* tell its readers,
if anything, about Ms. Rowling's beliefs?

Without straining to hear or turning up the volume, *Deathly
Hallows* clearly tells us three things Ms. Rowling believes:

1. Religious Belief is an Essential Struggle and a Choice;
2. Materialism, the Occult, and New Age faiths are Poor Choices; and
3. Ms. Rowling is a "Christian Who Writes" and an "unconventional Non-Conformist."

Let's start with the "struggle to believe."

Ms. Rowling has compared her own faith to that of Catholic
author, Graham Greene: *"Like Greene, my faith is sometimes about if
my faith will return. It's important to me."*[3] Even more recently, in her
post-*Deathly Hallows* interviews on MSNBC with Meredith Vieira, she
expanded on this idea:

> *Meredith Vieira: Harry's also referred to as the chosen one. So are
> there religious–*
>
> *J.K. Rowling: Well, there– there clearly is a religious– undertone.
> And– it's always been difficult to talk about that because until
> we reached Book Seven, views of what happens after death and
> so on, it would give away a lot of what was coming. So ... yes, **my
> belief and my struggling with religious belief and so on I think
> is quite apparent in this book**.*
>
> *Meredith Vieira: And what is the struggle?*

J.K. Rowling: **Well my struggle really is to keep believing.**
(emphasis mine)[4]

So you sometimes think I must be "making things up" contrary to what Ms. Rowling may have said in interviews? It just ain't so. Let's review, though, lest I fuel any suspicions you have, what Ms. Rowling has told us herself, speaking as the author, before looking at *Deathly Hallows* and confirming or denying what she has told us to look for.

   * She has told us she is a Christian.
   * She has said the last book would answer reporters' questions about what she believes.
   * She has said if she answered those questions herself, "intelligent readers" would know the series' ending.
   * She said her faith is important to her and that she "sometimes" waits for her faith to return.
   * She said last month that her struggle is to keep believing and her "struggling with religious belief and so on" is "quite evident" in *Deathly Hallows*.

Turning to the text of *Harry Potter and the Deathly Hallows*, the only character who "struggles to believe" is Harry himself. He's also the only character who shares Ms. Rowling's birthday and her green eyes. And Ms. Rowling seems to be upfront about this subject-author connection:

Lukas, 9: Is Harry Potter based on anyone that you know?

JKR: No, Harry is entirely imaginary. Erm, so I suppose that must mean that he comes from me a bit as well. [5]

Ellen Smyth wrote[6] that the struggle to believe in the book was relatively transparent: "Harry represents Jo while Dumbledore represents God. Throughout this novel, Harry struggles to trust Dumbledore while that devilish Rita Skeeter continually plants seeds of doubt." Louise M. Freeman, Ph.D, Psychology Professor at Mary Baldwin College, wrote[7] that "Dumbledore could instead, or additionally, represent the church as an institution."

Let's assume from Ms. Rowling's comments that her "struggling with religious belief and so on" is "quite evident" in *Deathly Hallows* in the shape of Harry's struggle to believe in the late Professor Albus Dumbledore. Ms. Smyth and Dr. Freeman argue persuasively for a religious undertone that borders on allegory, equating Dumbledore and God or the Church. I think this is a challenging theory throwing light on the series' conclusion, but I suspect it falls apart in King's Cross when Harry Meets Dumbledore again.

Harry is a "Dumbledore man through and through" at the end of *Half-Blood Prince*. Yet, after the first chapters of *Deathly Hallows*, faced with contradictory evidence, his faith in his mentor, in Dumbledore's virtue, and Dumbledore's mission for Harry to defeat Voldemort is broken. I'll assume for the sake of this discussion that Dumbledore, inasmuch as he "stands for" anything allegorical, represents the object of "religious belief and so on," be it God, the Church, or a specific spiritual guide or confessor. Harry is not the book's author, per se, or exclusively, but an Everyman figure in a heroic, comic morality play. Call him "the Seeker" like his angry Gryffindor Quidditch teammates did in *Philosopher's Stone*.

Deathly Hallows, looked at as an exercise or "struggle to believe," has three parts that parallel the alchemical black, white and red stages of the Great Work. Harry begins the book convinced he will never see Dumbledore again; he abandons his faith more and more through the first eighteen chapters (culminating in *The Life and Lies of Albus Dumbledore*). He then chooses to believe in Dumbledore, though he lacks sure knowledge to substantiate this faith and trust, and then overcomes his internal demon and external foes because of this choice.

Curious as it might seem, Harry's thoughts in the book's second chapter suggest that he doesn't believe in an afterlife. Luna believes the voices she heard beyond the Veil confirm that she will see her dead loved ones again. Harry, though clearly speaking about the impossibility of seeing Dumbledore again on *this side* of the Veil, as clearly does not think as Luna does about death:

"A flash of brightest blue. Harry froze, his cut finger slipping on the jagged edge of the mirror again.... He had imagined it, there was no other explanation; imagined it, because he had been thinking of his dead headmaster. If anything was certain, it was that the bright blue eyes of Albus Dumbledore would never pierce him again" (In Memoriam, page 29). Dumbledore is dead, Harry thinks, and that's that. By story's end, of course, Harry has seen Dumbledore again "face to face," with the transformation of his beliefs from beginning to end largely forgotten.

But it is quite a trip. Harry moves from beliefs protecting him from his grief for the Headmaster he cannot contact, to doubting in his mentor's goodness and denial that Dumbledore loved him, to reconsidering what he believes. Ms. Rowling uses two characters to represent "unexamined belief" and "unexamined disbelief," who both undermine Harry's faith in Dumbledore, because Harry wants his belief to be based on the truth, not reflex opinion.

The two characters are Elphias Doge and Rita Skeeter. Their contradictory testimony is the focus of Chapter Two, "In Memoriam," in which we read Doge's eulogy for his friend Albus and an interview with Rita Skeeter about her new book, 'The Life and Lies of Albus Dumbledore.' We see the pair again at 'The Wedding,' Chapter Eight, where Harry listens to an argument between Doge and a Skeeter advocate, Auntie Muriel. Ron's Aunt pretty much wipes the floor with Dogbreath, to whose every objection she has a pointed answer, often with damning testimony from witnesses. As the *nigredo* begins in Chapter Nine, Harry's child-like faith in the Headmaster, his surety that "help will always come to those who ask for it," is on the rocks.

What is most interesting in the Doge/Muriel exchange is the way Ms. Rowling frames Harry's struggle. She makes the matter of choice, a key theme in the books, a theme, ironically and intentionally born of Dumbledore's explicit teaching on this subject in *Chamber of Secrets*.

> "'Don't believe a word of it!" said Doge at once. 'Not a word, Harry! Let nothing tarnish your memories of Albus Dumbledore!'
>
> Harry looked into Doge's earnest, pained face and felt, not reassured, but frustrated. Did Doge really think it was that easy, that Harry could simply *choose* not to believe? Didn't Doge understand Harry's need to be sure, to know *everything*?" (The Wedding, pages 152-153, emphasis on "choose" and "everything" in original)

Ms. Rowling draws our attention to choice and belief again in Chapter Ten, "Kreacher's Tale," when Harry and Hermione argue about whether to believe like Doge or join the Skeeter skeptics like Auntie Muriel:

> "'Harry, do you really think you'll get the truth from a malicious old woman like Muriel, or from Rita Skeeter? How can you believe them? You knew Dumbledore!'
>
> 'I thought I did,' he muttered.
>
> 'But you know how much truth there was in everything Rita

wrote about you! Doge is right, how can you let these people tarnish your memories of Dumbledore?'

He looked away, trying not to betray the resentment he felt. There it was again: Choose what to believe. He wanted the truth. Why was everybody so determined that he should not get it?'" (*Hallows*, "Kreacher's Tale,'" p. 185)

In his meeting with Doge, Harry asks himself how Doge could think Harry could "choose not to believe" Auntie Muriel's nastiness about Dumbledore. With Hermione, he reframes the question into a choice whether to believe the "for-" or "against-Dumbledore" advocates without demonstrative proof or sure evidence from either side. He has his positive experience and he is learning what Dumbledore never shared with him; if the two contradict as obviously as his experience and these reports do, how is the Seeker to choose to believe one way or the other and maintain his sanity? In Harry's mind, "choosing" your beliefs is a little like "choosing" what you see and hear, namely, the mark of an idiot. You believe 'what is true' or, at least, 'what can be perceived by the senses,' not 'what you want to believe.'

Dumbledore may have left him clueless about important things but he didn't leave him without an important teaching about choice. "It is our choices, Harry, that show what we truly are, far more than our abilities." Ms. Rowling has said this end of *Chamber* scene and doctrine is a critical point in the books.[8] I think we all understood it in the context of what she was saying about prejudice and choice trumping birthright. If what we believe about what we cannot know for sure comes down to personal choice, though, as Harry says, Dumbledore's teaching about choice is resoundingly relevant. "What we choose to believe" about subjects lacking demonstrations or refutations will "show what we truly are."

Before Harry makes his conscious choice either way, he throws off his "acquired, not chosen" Dumbledore Man beliefs (Life and Lies of Albus Dumbledore, p. 351). He reaches bottom after reading "The Greater Good" chapter in Skeeter's *Life and Lies* book (Life and Lies of Albus Dumbledore, p. 362).

No longer a Dumbledore Man, Harry and Hermione apparate under cover to The Forest of Dean. Harry feels "as though he was recuperating from some brief but severe illness" (page 364). And then the light begins to shine in the darkness:

A bright silver light appeared right ahead of him, moving through the trees. Whatever the source, it was moving soundlessly. The light seemed simply to drift toward him.

He jumped to his feet, his voice frozen in his throat, and raised Hermione's wand. He screwed up his eyes as the light became blinding, the trees in front of it pitch black in silhouette, and still the thing came closer....

And then the source of the light stepped out from behind an oak. It was a silver white doe, moon-bright and dazzling, picking her way over the ground, still silent, and leaving no hoofprints in the fine powdering of snow. She stepped toward him, her beautiful head with its wide, long-lashed eyes held high.

Harry stared at the creature, filled with wonder, not at her strangeness, but her inexplicable familiarity. He felt that he had been waiting for her to come, but that he had forgotten, until this moment, that they had arranged to meet. His impulse to shout for Hermione, which had been so strong a moment ago, had gone. He knew, he would have staked his life on it, that she had come for him, and him alone (The Silver Doe, pp. 365-366).

Is this Gouge's *Little White Horse*? Wordsworth's White Doe? Sort of. It is certainly the *Cervus Fugitivus* of literary alchemy, as discussed in chapter 2. Abraham in *The Dictionary of Alchemical Imagery* explains "the fleeing deer or hart symbolizes Mercurius in his role as the intermediary soul which unites the body and spirit of the Stone" (Abraham, *Dictionary*, p. 52). In what I think is the most successful sewing of a tapestry of alchemical, Arthurian, and Christian threads in Ms. Rowling's seven books, Harry and Ron pull the Sword from the baptismal pool and Ron is purified and rejoined to the triptych of mind, body, and spirit because he and Harry followed the silver doe.

The critical thing to grasp here, beyond the alchemical symbolism, is that Harry, without beliefs or pronounced disbelief, but with broken faith and wand secure near his heart, knows the silver doe is there *for him.* "Caution murmured it could be a trick, a lure, a trap. But instinct, overwhelming instinct, told him that this was not Dark Magic. He set off in pursuit" (The Silver Doe, p. 366).

We know from Snape's memory that the silver doe is his Patronus, the Patronus of Lily Evans Potter. Harry's immediate, intuitive identification with this icon without the need of proof and his instinctive decision- making throughout the chapter (going into the pool after the

Sword of Gryffindor, having Ron destroy the Horcrux, etc.) speaks to a cardiac rather than a cranial intelligence guiding Harry. Remus Lupin understands Harry as well as any man but Dumbledore:

> "Romulus, do you maintain, as you have every time you've appeared on our program, that Harry Potter is still alive?"
>
> "I do," said Lupin firmly. "There is no doubt at all in my mind that his death would be proclaimed as widely as possible by the Death Eaters if it had happened, because it would strike a deadly blow at the morale of those resisting the new regime. 'The Boy Who Lived' remains a symbol of everything for which we are fighting: the triumph of good, the power of innocence, the need to keep resisting."
>
> A mixture of gratitude and shame welled up in Harry. Had Lupin forgiven him, then, for the terrible things he had said when they had last met?
>
> "And what would you say to Harry if you knew he was listening, Romulus?"
>
> "I'd tell him we're all with him in spirit ," said Lupin, then hesitated slightly, "And I'd tell him to follow his instincts, which are good and nearly always right." (*Hallows*, "The Deathly Hallows," p. 441)

Dumbledore called this cardiac intelligence not "instincts" or "intuition" but "love." Harry's heart, though, was darkened by his confusion of "Dumbledore Man" beliefs and Thinking Person disbelief. Having passed through the Nigredo and having been stripped of this muddle, he begins to see with the eye of the heart. And he makes the choice to believe.

It isn't an easy thing and it is only in the context of the temptation of the Deathly Hallows and Dobby's heroic death that Harry makes this choice. Xenophilius Lovegood has told them the story of the Three Brothers from *Beadle the Bard* and Harry has figured out what the three Hallows are, that he has two of them and Voldemort is after the third. It is in his excitement about this last point that he breaks the name taboo and is taken to Malfoy Manor. Harry asks Aberforth's eye (that he thinks is Albus,' see Chapter 5, "The Seeing Eye") for help and Harry's disciple, Dobby the house-elf, arrives.

Dobby's heroic efforts save the trio, Griphook, Dean Thomas, Luna, and Ollivander. But it's his death that saves Harry. Dobby's life and death are, with Neville's heroic resistance while waiting for Harry's return, the two examples of Christian discipleship in *Deathly Hallows*.[9]

Dobby? The Vladimir Putin[10] look-alike comic-effect figure of the stories? Yep.

Dobby is a slave in the House of Bad Faith (Mal-foy). He hears about 'The Boy Who Lived,' a savior who had delivered his people from the Dark Lord. When he learns the Malfoys are plotting against Harry Potter in *Chamber of Secrets*, Dobby resolves against all convention and house-elf obedience to serve his true Master. This sacrificial, loving, and often very funny service results in Harry freeing Dobby from his Malfoy masters and Dobby's greater love for Harry Potter.

In *Deathly Hallows*, Dobby is called on to save Harry and his friends. He returns to the place of his worst nightmares, the House of Malfoy, to demonstrate his freedom and fidelity to his savior. Not very surprisingly, this exercise results in Dobby's dying to save his friends and, most especially, Harry. He dies in Harry's arms near Shell Cottage with his beloved Harry Potter's name as his last words.

Allegorical? I think so. Just plug in "Christ" for "Harry Potter" in the above story and you have a story-form version of the Christian Everyman, slave to passions and misconceptions, liberated by a child's belief in the Messiah, and a growth in love that imitates at life's end the sacrificial and unrestricted love of his Savior. Certainly Dobby's faith in and sacrifice for him knocks Harry off his feet.

Harry's intelligence is arational for the most part which serves him well in the Cloud of Unknowing. To his credit, he "gets" the meaning of Dobby's Christian example in choice, belief, obedience, and sacrifice. The Malfoy Manor, the place of Dobby's servitude, the place from which his faith in Harry Potter freed him, had to be the last place Dobby wanted to go, but go he did. Dobby is comic relief for much of the books but it is his death and his example that cause something of a faith-chrysalis in Harry.

Harry goes underground. He experiences a revelation. And he makes a choice. Believe in Dumbledore; forsake the Deathly Hallows temptation and get the Horcruxes as instructed.

> "Grief, it seemed, drove Voldemort out... though Dumbledore, of course, would have said that it was love....
>
> In the darkness, with nothing but the sound of his own breath

and the rushing sea to keep him company, the things that had happened in the Malfoys' returned to him, the things he had heard came back to him, and understanding blossomed in the darkness...." (page 479)

"I'm going to wash," Harry told Bill looking down at his hands still covered with mud and Dobby's blood. "Then I'll need to see [Ollivander and Griphook], straight away." He walked into the little kitchen, to the basin beneath a window overlooking the sea. Dawn was breaking over the horizon, shell pink and faintly gold, as he washed, again following the train of thought that had come to him in the dark garden...

Dobby would never be able to tell them who had sent him to the cellar, but Harry knew what he had seen. A piercing blue eye had looked out of the mirror fragment, and then help had come. Help will always be given at Hogwarts to those who ask for it.

Harry dried his hands, impervious to the beauty of the scene outside the window and to the murmuring of the others in the sitting room. He looked out over the ocean and felt closer, this dawn, than ever before, closer to the heart of it all.

And still his scar prickled, and he knew that Voldemort was getting there too. Harry understood and yet did not understand. His instinct was telling him one thing, his brain quite another. The Dumbledore in Harry's head smiled, surveying Harry over the tips of his fingers, pressed together as if in prayer.

You gave Ron the Deluminator...You understood him...You gave him a way back...

And you understood Wormtail too...You knew there was a bit of regret there, somewhere...

And if you knew them...What did you know about me, Dumbledore?

Am I meant to know but not to seek? Did you know how hard I'd feel that? Is that why you made it this difficult? So I'd have time to work that out?

Harry stood quite still, eyes glazed, watching the place where a bright gold ray of dazzling sun was rising over the horizon ("The Wandmaker," pp. 483-484).

And then in the golden pink (yes, white to red, like the stones on the grave, the transition to rebedo . . .) of dawn, Harry makes his decision.

He knows, but doesn't seek the Deathly Hallows. He chooses to believe in Dumbledore and in the mission assigned him:

> Harry hesitated. He knew what hung on his decision. There was hardly any time left; now was the moment to decide: Horcruxes or Hallows?
>
> "Griphook," Harry said. "I'll speak to Griphook first."
>
> His heart was racing as if he had been sprinting and had just cleared an enormous obstacle. ("The Wandmaker," p. 484).

Harry has made the leap of faith, not in ignorance but with knowledge of his choices and how he might proceed to defeat Lord Voldemort. He chooses Dumbledore's designated path and the story is over in large part. With this choice, Harry "has shown what he truly is," to paraphrase the Headmaster, and victory over Voldemort, if not a done deal, is before us.

That Harry has made a choice and is consciously committed to it, is revisited in his conversation with Albus' shadowy brother Aberforth, who, unlike Rita Skeeter, knows the Headmaster's faults as intimately as a second self. But even Aberforth does not sway Harry from the choice he made underground by the sea:

> "Harry kept quiet. He did not want to express the doubts and uncertainties about Dumbledore that had riddled him for months now. He had made his choice as he dug Dobby's grave, he had decided to continue along the winding, dangerous path indicated for him by Albus Dumbledore, to accept that he had not been told everything that he wanted to know, but simply to trust. He had no desire to doubt again; he did not want to hear anything that would deflect him from his purpose" ("The Missing Mirror," p. 563).

Ms. Rowling has said her "struggling with religious beliefs and so on" are "quite evident" in *Deathly Hallows*. And they are. But this is not the struggle of a skeptic or of a school child who is beginning to re-examine mechanically-held beliefs. This is the agony of the agnostic who knows that there is no knowing for certain rationally, but that not believing has consequences; belief, in many ways, is always a choice. Seeing what happens to those who choose not to believe or, to use another word with which Ms. Rowling contrasts Harry and Voldemort, those who choose not to trust, Harry chooses to believe and to trust.

And it is this choice that makes all the difference.

So, if Harry is Everyman and a seeker after truth, the moral of the story, if you will, is to believe. But what is Dumbledore representing in this morality play? God? The Church?

Listen to Dumbledore in King's Cross:

> "'Can you forgive me,' he said. 'Can you forgive me for not trusting you? Harry, I only feared that you would fail as I have failed. I only dreaded that you would make my mistakes. I crave your pardon. Harry, I have known for some time now, that you are the better man'" ("King's Cross," p. 713).

That's a pretty rough speech for God to make or the Church. I'd almost prefer a Freudian psychological interpretation with the Headmaster "old man" representing the super-ego. But I think "loving authority" or "spiritual director," even "Father" is as good.[We'll revisit this subject in chapters 5 and 6.]

Ms. Rowling non-didactically, but in a not especially opaque fashion, delivers on her promises about the seventh book. We see in the story of Harry's transformation from Dumbledore Man to Dumbledore denier to Dumbledore's better (even his confessor), the trials and consequences of the struggle to believe. "Religious Belief is a Struggle and a Choice," she tells us in story form, and "It is Essential to Believe in order to Overcome both Internal Failings and External Enemies."

Without Harry's choice in the grave, Voldemort's soul-piece wins the battle for Harry and the world as well. And, perhaps as important, in hearing Dumbledore's confession and request for forgiveness and redemption, we see that "Spiritual Authorities are Fallen People with Tragedies and Failings of their own." Their failings are not reason to choose disbelief or the temptations of worldly power.

Deathly Hallows seems to tell us (and as Ms. Rowling has told us it means) that her religious beliefs are hard-won, a day-to-day choice and, if she is like Harry and his belief or trust in Dumbledore, this choice is critical in understanding the sort of person she is and is becoming. In *Deathly Hallows*, Harry's decision to believe in Dumbledore -- in the face of all the reasons and evidence fostering his doubts and disbelief -- is what makes him successful in cleansing himself of the Voldemort Horcrux and defeating the Dark Lord, despite the Elder Wand. Ms. Rowling elegantly and seamlessly ties together in *Deathly Hallows* what we have learned about choice in the previous six books with Harry's "struggle to believe."

Deathly Hallows, then, is an argument *for* the choice of religious belief. Harry recognizes in Dobby's example that those who believe are different – and better – than those who do not (think Auntie Muriel, Rita Skeeter, Lord Voldemort...). But, if Ms. Rowling in *Deathly Hallows* is making an argument for religious belief, however difficult the struggle to choose to believe, what *specific* recommendations does she make about this belief, if any? Equally important, in the context of Ms. Rowling's 2000 interview comments suggesting the last book would answer objections about the series' supposed occult elements, how does *Deathly Hallows* answer her Christian critics concerned about Harry Potter as a gateway to the occult?

What Are We To Struggle To Believe?

Stated baldly, Ms. Rowling, both in her interviews and in *Deathly Hallows*, makes a case against secularism, Occultism, and what she calls "New Age-ism." Her endorsement of "belief" versus "disbelief" is not a blanket endorsement of any or all beliefs; in the story line of *Deathly Hallows*, Ms. Rowling gives particularly strong rebukes to beliefs without God, beliefs embracing power and individual gain rather than transformation, and beliefs that are just about "knowing better." Ms. Rowling's critics who claim her books are soft on the occult, and who assert that *Harry Potter* is an invitation to New Age, amorphous, or insubstantial beliefs, have not read or understood *Deathly Hallows*.

The Muggles featured in the stories are Harry's Aunt, Uncle, and cousin, all of whom are only concerned about their material wealth, the perception of others about their status and "normalcy," and their comfort. In *Deathly Hallows*, Ms. Rowling gives a spectrum of possibilities about the "redeemability" of such people. Uncle Vernon, the businessman? Totally lost and unable to see beyond the restricted area of vision defined by his prejudices and ignorance. Aunt Petunia? She wants to say a kind word at Harry's farewell, but finds herself unequal to even right sentiment.

Only Dudley, who has faced Dementors with Harry (and under their influence seen himself as he really is), is able to escape from the meanness and spiritual barrenness of his upbringing. He startles Harry at their farewell by his earnest, if still very awkward, expression of good will. Ms. Rowling suggests the only hope is with the children, the intended audience of her artistry.

What does Ms. Rowling want to share with these children? What should they struggle to believe in, if just more toys and computer games aren't the *summum bonum* of human existence? Well, witchcraft and the New Age aren't what she is promoting.

Ms. Rowling hasn't minced words about the witchcraft controversy that led to some schools banning her books from class. Those who read her books and see an advertisement for real-world sorcery just aren't very good readers:

> **"I truly am bemused that anyone who has read the books could think that I am a proponent of the occult in any serious way,"** she says. "I don't believe in witchcraft, in the sense that they're talking about, at all.
>
> "I'm certainly not a witch myself," she says with a laugh, "and you would be surprised how many otherwise intelligent people have asked me that question." (emphasis added)[11]

And the so-called New Age and "every person for themselves" spirituality?

> "So I'm told repeatedly. The two groups of people who are constantly thanking me are wiccans (white witches) and boarding schools. And really, don't thank me. I'm not with either of them. **New ageism leaves me completely cold,** and Jessie would never go to boarding school. I went to a comprehensive." (emphasis added)[12]

So she says in interviews. *Deathly Hallows*, though, confirms her disdain for the occult and New Age, as we can see in her treatment of Horcruxes and the Deathly Hallows.

Horcruxes and Deathly Hallows:
Occult Magic, Idolatry, and the Vanity of the New Age

Lord Voldemort's pursuit of individual immortality through murder and dark magic is certainly a pointer to "secret knowledge" or so called gnostic spirituality. As much as occultists claim a secret way, an esoteric wisdom that elevates them above the empty exoterism of the common herd, Ms. Rowling, both in her depiction of the astrologer centaurs in *Deathly Hallows'* Forbidden Forest and in the Dark Lord's means of salvation, terms their path mistaken, even evil and inhuman. "Occult" comes from the Latin word *occultus* meaning "secret, hidden." *Harry Potter* does not make an argument for private spirituality or secret wisdom.

The Horcruxes, too, are, in a sense worse than "occult objects." As discussed in Chapters 5 and 6, the act of creating a Horcrux – the murder of a person and the deposition of soul into a physical object – is also an act of idolatry and self-love much like materialists make. Most of us don't fall to the temptations of occult practice or worship more serious than looking up our birthdays in newspaper astrology columns. I suspect, however, that we all have invested soul fragments in things that we own, or in ideas of ourselves in which we have secretly hope to live forever in one form or another. Ms. Rowling, in making the Horcrux the focus of her Evil One stand-in and Harry's shadow-self, is pointing to this idolatry – and to private means to immortality – as a failing and "spirituality" we must understand as a greater danger to us than occult groups.

Harry's big temptation was never to learn how to make a Horcrux and ensure his personal immortality. The decision which is the turning point of the whole book, as discussed above, is Harry's choice to not pursue the Elder Wand to complete the set of Deathly Hallows, but to destroy Voldemort's Horcruxes in obedience to Dumbledore's instructions. After Harry's sacrificial death, Dumbledore tells him at King's Cross that in being equal to the temptation of the Hallows, he was a "much better man" than the Headmaster. We can tell Dumbledore isn't kidding because *he* wasn't equal to the temptation of the Hallows. In fact, the three greatest wizards of the series – Gellert Grindelwald, Albus Dumbledore, and Lord Voldemort, each fall, consequent to their fascination with the power of the three magical objects the legendary Peverell brothers received from Death: the Elder Wand, the Resurrection Stone, and the Invisibility Cloak. The tales about the Hallows concluded that the witch or wizard who possessed all three would be the "Master of Death" and undefeatable.

The great wizards, consequently, pursue the "Wand of Destiny" and the other Hallows, just as Hitler pursued the "Spear of Destiny": for occult power and individual gain in the name of the "Greater Good." Fascination with the Hallows was what brought Dumbledore and Grindelwald together – and what led to Ariana's accidental death and Dumbledore's decision never to pursue personal or political power.

His death, however, despite this resolution, was largely a consequence of his excitement and momentary regression to his childish error upon discovering the Resurrection Stone in one of Lord Voldemort's Horcruxes. The Peverell ring had been cursed and only Severus' genius with the Stoppered Death potion prevents the Headmaster's immediate demise.

Ms. Rowling isn't offering the Way of the Occult to her readers as anything but a path to spiritual and physical death. Even the relatively comic treatment of New Age seekers in her books also makes their private preoccupation and parlor-game-spirituality seem a dead-end.

Sybill Trelawney, Divinations teacher at Hogwarts, though she is right more often than her critics like to acknowledge (and the vehicle of otherworldly prophecy at least twice), is always presented as a self-important and pathetic looney-tune. Dumbledore suggests once or twice that she only is kept on at Hogwarts as an act of charity – and to protect her from Lord Voldemort and his search for the exact wording of the original prophecy. She has her student admirers (all female and as bizarre as their mentor) but the disdain with which she is treated by Umbridge, McGonagall, and Hermione Granger marks her as a New Age nut.

She barely enters into the story of the Deathly Hallows. It is from Xenophilius Lovegood that Harry, Hermione, and Ron learn the meaning of the Deathly Hallows "triangular eye" (see Chapter 6) – and to him the children's fairy tale as recorded by Beadle the Bard is fact, not fantasy. Xenophilius, it turns out, "seeks" the Hallows as a New Age believer practices numerology, astrology, and tarot card reading, which is to say, as a path to his individual enlightenment.

Lovegood, though a comic figure like Professor Trelawney, is anything but "hallowed" by his beliefs and pretense. Super "seeker" that he pretends to be, and champion of the absurd and countercultural, when push comes to shove, his principles are revealed to be empty posturing. Sybill at least fights for the right in the Battle of Hogwarts. Xenophilius ("friend of the strange," by the way) delays Harry, Ron, and Hermione when they come to his ziggurat tower, in the hope he'll be able to trade them for his daughter, whom the Death Eaters have taken prisoner to ensure his silence and obedience.

His New Age foppery gave him the principles and package of Peter Pettigrew.

Ms. Rowling in her public statements and stories, then, tells us that religious belief "is important to me" and that she "struggles to believe" and make the choice to believe. She does not, however, think all religious beliefs are edifying or equal. Far from it. She presents secularism, occultism, and New Age-ism as "spiritual paths" that darken the heart and diminish the characters of the people who choose to follow them. A large part of Harry's achievement in *Deathly Hallows* is in his deciding on the path of trust and obedience, rather than the way of personal power and occult enlightenment.

So What Does Ms. Rowling Struggle to Believe?

Ms. Rowling's largely successful struggle to believe, if Harry's spiritual journey in *Deathly Hallows* is taken alongside her own confession of faith, is all about her life as a disciple of Christ. This last novel is certainly not an in-your-face altar call or "witnessing"; it is, nonetheless, a story so saturated in specifically Christian points of reference and meaning that to deny them is to miss a large, perhaps even the greater, part of the transcendent meaning of the books.

Most notably, the book's three alchemical parts – its black, white, and red sequencing – in which Harry is broken down, illumined, and triumphant, are told in the sequence of the three principal Christian feasts that parallel these three stages in chronological sequence. By examining the chapters of *Deathly Hallows* in which Harry "celebrates" the holy days and meaning of Christmas, Theophany, and Easter, his final spiritual chrysalis and transformation into a "little Christ" is, as Ms. Rowling has herself said of the stories' Christian content, "obvious."[13] If you have the book handy, the chapters we will be looking at are Chapters 16 and 17, "Godric's Hollow" and "Bathilda's Secret" (Christmas eve); Chapter 19, "The Silver Doe" (Theophany or the baptism of Christ) and Chapters 34, 35, and 36, "The Forest Again", "King's Cross", and "The Flaw in the Plan" (the Crucifixion, Harrowing of Hell, and Resurrection of Christ).

Christmas Eve at Godric's Hollow

Harry and Hermione resolve in Chapter 16 to go to Godric's Hollow to see if Dumbledore had not hidden the sword of Godric Gryffindor there with the aged Bethilda Bagshot. They arrive in the small village as Polyjuiced, middle-aged Muggles and discover the village is largely a magical memorial to the Potters, whose deaths to save The Boy Who

Lived saved the wizarding world from Voldemort. The Muggle war memorial changes into a statue of the Potter family as the two pass by. The Potter home is marked with a sign saying it has been left unchanged "as a monument to the Potters and as a reminder of the violence that tore apart their family" (*Hallows*, "Bathilda's Secret," pp. 332-333). The sign is covered with graffiti from magical tourists expressing their love for and faith in Harry.

This last really lifts Harry's spirits because the adventure in Godric's Hollow is undertaken almost in desperation, and certainly in the depths of Harry's spiritual winter and doubt. The trio had been broken in the previous chapter when Ron Weasley departed in anger and disgust over their meager rations and inability to find and destroy Horcruxes. Harry's camping trip with Hermione alone, thereafter, is very miserable, at least until they agree to venture to Godric's Hollow, as they have no plan beyond evading capture.

After seeing the villagers with their presents on the way to the Godric's Hollow church, the Polyjuiced couple realize it is Christmas Eve. They decide to go to the church as well, when Hermione sees a graveyard behind it in the light from the windows. "They'll be in there, won't they? Your mum and dad?" (*Hallows*, "Godric's Hollow", p. 323).

The first gravestone Harry stumbles upon is the Dumbledore family marker over the graves of Kendra and Ariana, Aberforth's and Albus' mother and little sister. "Upon the frozen, lichen spotted granite" are carved the words "Where your treasure is, there will your heart be also," without the notation that this from Matthew 6:21, the Sermon on the Mount (*Hallows*, "Godric's Hollow", p. 325). Harry is convinced that Albus must have chosen these words, but their meaning escapes him and he feels only bitterness about all the things the Headmaster never told him.

They find the grave of Ignotus Peverell with the Deathly Hallows symbol, before Hermione stumbles on the Potter tombstone. Its inscription, "The last enemy that shall be destroyed is death," from 1 Corinthians 15:26, also leaves Harry frustrated and angry.

> "'The last enemy that shall be destroyed is death'..." A horrible idea came to him, and with it a kind of panic. "Isn't it a Death Eater idea? Why is that there?"
>
> "It doesn't mean defeating death in the way the Death

Eaters mean it, Harry," said Hermione, her voice gentle. It means... you know... living beyond death. Living after death."

But they were not living, thought Harry. They were gone. The empty words could not disguise the fact that his parents' moldering remains lay beneath snow and stone, indifferent, unknowing. (*Hallows*, "Godric's Hollow," p. 328)

Hermione leaves a wreath of Christmas roses at the grave as Harry weeps in denial of the scriptural message he has read. The lights in the church have gone out as, seemingly, they have in Harry's heart as well.

And then things go horribly dark. They meet what they believe is Bathilda Bagshot and she takes Hansel and Gretal to her home. But this is only the snake-animated corpse of the former author of *History of Magic*; "she" is a Voldemort trap and a nightmare of Gothic horror. His snake, Nagini, bursts from Bethilda's body and attacks! Harry and Hermione barely Disapparate in time before the Dark Lord arrives. He isn't happy as Christmas Day arrives: "Voldemort screamed with rage, a scream that mingled with the girl's, that echoed across the dark gardens over the church bells ringing in Christmas Day..." (*Hallows*, "Bathilda's Secret", p. 342).

Harry's Christmas gift from the Lord Thingy? A trip down memory lane that Harry shares through their Horcrux mind-link. Voldemort remembers the Potter murders on Halloween, 1981, and Harry learns at last the grisly details of his parents' execution and sacrifice. As bad, when he revives in the tent, he learns his Holly and Phoenix feather wand was irreparably broken in the fight with Nagini. After reading the Skeeter book they had picked up at Bathilda Bagshot's home, *The Life and Lies of Albus Dumbledore*, Harry tells Hermione that he believes the Headmaster never loved him and, because of his secretiveness, is responsible for the mess they are in.

Christian Undertones in *Deathly Hallows* Christmas Chapters

This is, without doubt, the lowest of the several nadirs and *nigredos* in all the Potter novels. What does this despair, trial, and feelings of abandonment have to do with the Nativity of Christ with which they coincide? Why does Ms. Rowling have the darkest of Harry's dark nights of the soul take place on Christmas Eve, of all times, when the light came into the world which darkness has never comprehended (John 1:5)?

First, we have to see that Harry and Hermione's adventure is supposed to remind the reader of the Christmas story. A couple in disguise travel to the man's ancestral home. They have no place to stay and they have a great secret they cannot share with anyone. In case you miss the parallel with Mary and Joseph coming to Bethlehem, Joseph's family origin and point of taxation, Ms. Rowling puts a Holy Family crèche of sorts in the village center with baby Harry, sans scar, and his loving mother and father. That it is actually Christmas Eve, and the action of the first half of their visit takes place in the light shining through stained glass windows in a church graveyard, while carolers sing inside, just drives the obvious home.

But Christmas is a time of great cheer and hope. So why the darkness of Harry's Christmas Eve, with the despair he feels at his parents' grave, his desperate struggle with Nagini, and the doubts he has about Dumbledore's love and care for him? Ms. Rowling uses Nativity (and, specifically, the night before Nativity) as the occasion of Harry's *nigredo* because of the darkness of World before the advent of the Word or Logos as Jesus of Nazareth, the light of the world.

Nagini's gothic-nightmare attack on Harry and Hermione from within the Bagshot corpse, then, represents, as does the whole Godric's Hollow story, the reason for the incarnation of Christ, namely, the Evil One's dominance in the world before Nativity. Nagini's failed attack parallels the plotting of the Serpent-Devil to destroy the Christ child through Herod. The retelling of the story of The Boy Who Lived as the bells of the church toll in Christmas day with Voldemort's screams, are retellings of the Nativity and the Holy Family's escape into Egypt despite the slaughter of the innocents.

It isn't a tit-for-tat allegory, of course. But the parallels are strong enough for us to somewhat experience the pre-Christ darkness of the world in Harry's doubts about the love and covenant with his mentor (here, I think, with Dumbledore meant to be understood as God). We also get, too, the hope of Christians in the dead of winter and the depth of darkness; in the coming of their Savior as a child who will escape and eventually be victorious over the Prince of the World. Harry's holly wand, with its Christmas association, *is* broken and only held together by the feather of the Resurrection Bird. But, however much he disavows God/Dumbledore, Harry keeps the remnants of his faith in the bag next to his heart. He clings to his broken faith through the *nigredo*.

Theophany in The Forest of Dean: *The Silver Doe*

Fortunately, Harry (and the reader along for the ride) doesn't have to wait long for some light to shine into his darkness. In the very next chapter, The Silver Doe, Ron returns, he and Harry find the Sword of Gryffindor, Ron destroys the Horcux necklace and the trio are reunited, even if Hermione doesn't welcome Ron with backflips.

We discussed Harry's encounter with and trust in Severus' Doe Patronus above as an act of faith. Let's look at where the *Cervus Fugitivus* takes him and this chapter's details. The chapter is evidently one of Ms. Rowling's favorites because she chose to read it to her Carnegie Hall audience during her Open Book Tour through the US and Canada after the publication of *Deathly Hallows*. Its seamless combination of alchemical symbols, Arthurian legend, and traditional Christian content, as I've said, makes "The Silver Doe" perhaps the finest single chapter in the seven novels and the best example of Ms. Rowling's peculiar genius and artistry.

In a nutshell, the Doe Patronus leads Harry to a frozen pool in the Forest of Dean. Harry sees the Sword of Gryffindor in the pool and resolves to do the heroic Gryffindor thing and get it. Stripping himself down to his underwear and the Horcrux necklace, he breaks the ice and enters the pool's freezing waters. Incredibly, the Horcrux attacks him: "the chain of the Horcrux had tightened and was slowly constricting his windpipe" *(Hallows*, "The Silver Doe," p. 370).

Ron, *deus/amicus ex machina*, appears out of nowhere and rescues Harry from the pool and the attack-necklace. He also retrieves the Sword from the icy pool. After a brief catch-up, Harry tells Ron he must be the one to destroy the Horcrux and Ron, well aware that the Horcrux affects him more strongly and perversely than the others, reluctantly agrees.

Ron was right to hesitate. He destroys the Locket Horcrux with the Sword, but only after the soul fragment of the Dark Lord reveals all of Ron's poisonous doubts about the love of his mother, Hermione, and even Harry, his best mate, in odious fashion. Harry embraces and encourages him before they return to the tent and Ron explains to Harry and the hysterically angry Hermione where he has been and his Deluminator-driven return.

Christian Undertones in "The Silver Doe"

I don't think many readers struggle with understanding the Christmas Eve scenes in Godric's Hollow as Harry's *nigredo* and a snapshot of the world before Christ's Nativity. We all know the story well, and the *Harry Potter* version is fairly explicit in its Christmas references. The Christian content of "The Silver Doe", however, is relatively opaque because we're not as familiar with the event from the life of Christ being depicted here, or what Ms. Rowling is after in this chapter. Let's start, then, with the alchemical and Arthurian meanings to get at the spiritual heart of this dense chapter.

Alchemically, the *albedo* or "white" and "cleansing" (ablutionary) stage follows the *nigredo* or black breakdown phase. Except for the ending in the warm tent, "The Silver Doe" takes place completely outdoors in the white snow of day and features a frozen pool into which both Harry and Ron enter against all common sense or instinct for self-preservation. The doe as alchemical *cervus*, as discussed above, represents the joining of body and spirit and, in this chapter that turns on ritual cleansing with water and confrontation of one's darkest doubts, we see Ron and Harry reconciled.

The central Arthurian element is the drawing of the sword, both from stone at the pool's bottom and from the water itself. In this we have echoes of Arthur's demonstrating his lineage with Uther Pendragon; Arthur pulls the sword from the stone and receives Excalibur from the Lady of the Lake after his sword is broken in battle with King Pellinor. Harry remembers the meaning of the Sword of Gryffindor in "The Silver Doe" when he sees the sword at the bottom of the pool:

> What was it, Harry asked himself... that Dumbledore had told him the last time he had retrieved the sword? *Only a true Gryffindor could have pulled* that *out of the hat*. And what were the qualities that defined a Gryffindor? A small voice inside Harry's head answered him: *Their daring, nerve, and chivalry set Gryffindors apart* (*Hallows*, "The Silver Doe", p. 368).

The little voice is the voice of the Sorting Hat who sang about the Four Houses and their peculiar qualities in *Philosopher's Stone* (*Stone*, "The Sorting Hat", p. 118). We learned in *Goblet of Fire* (*Goblet*, 'The Tri-Wizard Tournament'12, p. 176) that the Sorting Hat was Godric Gryffindor's hat, enchanted with "some brains" by the Four Founders. "Gryffindor," you'll recall, means "golden griffin" and is a pointer to

Christ. Harry and Ron, by pulling the sword from the pool with selfless and sacrificial acts, demonstrate that they're both "mental," as Ron puts it, and also "true Gryffindors." Ron saves Harry's life much like symbols of Christ do at the end of the first six books, a salvific event that Harry notes five times before chapter's end.

Which leads us to the spiritual meaning and specifically Christian content of the chapter. It is a retelling of Christ's baptism in the River Jordan, with Ron's enlightenment experiences illustrating what this Christian event means for the believer.

The baptism of Christ, "Theophany" in the Eastern Orthodox tradition (meaning "the appearance of God") and "Epiphany" in the West, is not celebrated with school closings, decorated trees and store sales after Thanksgiving, so many people know little about it. In "ranking" holy days, however, the traditional Church considers Theophany the biggest feast on the Christian calendar, with the exceptions of Pascha ('Easter') and Pentecost.

What was the big deal? Christ submits to baptism by John the Baptist (though the Baptist feels he should be baptized by Christ, cf., Matthew 3:14) to "fulfill all righteousness" (Matthew 3:15 KJV). And when John baptizes Jesus, "the heavens were opened unto him, and he saw the Spirit of God descending like a dove, and lighting upon him: And lo a voice from heaven, saying This is my beloved son in whom I am well pleased" (Matthew 3: 16-17 KJV; Luke 3:21-23). God reveals Himself at the baptism of Christ in the Jordan as a holy Trinity: Christ as Son, the Father in the voice from heaven proclaiming His pleasure, and the Holy Spirit in the form of a dove. Theophany is the feast above all others except Christ's Resurrection and the 'birthday' of the Church at Pentecost because it's the revelation of God as He is, that is to say, in His three *hypostases* or "persons."

Harry's immersion and Ron's enlightenment does not include a Trinitarian moment, alas, but it does show what baptism means in a Christian's life, while closely paralleling the Gospel account. Let's look at it again.

First, Harry, the Chosen One, is the Christ figure of the piece. He has already demonstrated he's a "true Gryffindor" in *The Chamber of Secrets* and has little to prove here. Like Jesus, he only enters the pool to "fulfill all righteousness," that is, to do what a Gryffindor must do. When I spoke with good friend and Pepperdine English Professor James

Thomas about this at the *Prophecy 2007* Harry Potter Conference in Toronto, he said we know this is the case because we have "Ron the Baptist" there to do the deed. It's Ron who pulls Harry from the water and retrieves the Sword from the pool's bottom.

At this point, though, it's Harry who takes charge, telling Ron he must be the one to use the Sword to destroy the Horcrux. It's Harry who opens the Horcrux, who stands by shouting encouragement and instruction during Ron's psychological scourging, and who embraces and lifts Ron up after his shattering victory over his inner demons. True, Ron played the part of John the Baptist in the pool, and of Harry's savior in removing the Horcrux that was strangling Harry. But Harry is Ron's master through his illumination.

Baptism comes from the Greek word meaning "immersion" and there's some dispute among Christian groups over whether a "baptism" must be a complete dunking. Certainly the word can be used as a washing or ritual ablution (cf., Luke 11:38); St. Paul's understanding seems to leave little doubt that the mystery of baptism involves submersion as a burial of sorts (cf, Romans 6:2-13, Colossians 2:12-13). Either way, in *The Silver Doe*, Ron and Harry are fully immersed and ritually cleansed by their sacrificial time in the pool.

Ron's experience is the most important, because his symbolic baptism and liberation afterward, from the demons darkening his heart, is an enlightenment or "illumination." Traditional Christians use the word *photismos* or "illumination" for baptism (after St. Clement, *Paedagogus* 1.6).

> The sanctification that comes with the Spirit's descent in baptism bestows illumination and perfection, making illumination the immediate effect of baptism, which leads in turn to adoption, perfection, and ultimately, immortality. Indeed, [to Clement] baptism is the 'one grace' of illumination and the illumination we receive is knowledge (*gnosis*). Clement comes close here to suggesting that a virtual infusion of knowledge accompanies baptism (*The Divine Sense: The Intellect in Patristic Theology*, A. N. Williams, Cambridge University Press, 2007, p. 72).

Ron explains to Harry and Hermione in the tent that he was only able to find them because of Dumbledore's gift to him, the Deluminator. He describes his experience with its light, after he had clicked it, in response to hearing Hermione use his name Christmas morning:

Ron raised his empty hand and pointed in front of him, his eyes focused on something neither Harry nor Hermione could see.

"It was a ball of light, kind of pulsing, and bluish, like that light you get around a Portkey, you know?... I knew this was it," said Ron. "I grabbed my stuff and packed it, then I put on my rucksack and went out into the garden.

"The little ball of light was hovering there, waiting for me, and when I came out it bobbed along a bit and I followed it behind the shed and then it... well, it went inside me."

"Sorry?" said Harry, sure that he had not heard correctly.

"It sort of floated toward me," said Ron, illustrating the movement with his free index finger, "right to my chest, and then – it just went straight through. It was here," he touched a point close to his heart. "I could feel it, it was hot. And once it was inside me I knew what I was supposed to do. I knew it would take me where I needed to go. So I Disapparated and came out on the side of a hill. There was snow everywhere...." (*Hallows*, "The Silver Doe", p. 385)

Now the sequence here is not exactly like a Christian baptism experience, but all the elements of illumination or *photismos* in Christ via the Holy Spirit are here. Step by step:

Ron departs from the fellowship of his vocation – and immediately repents and feels remorse about his betrayal. He is ensnared (by "Snatchers") and is unable to find his way back on his own. He waits, consequently, and listens for his name to be called. On the day Christ comes into the world, he hears his name and follows the light that has appeared to him. This light enters his heart and illumines him; he knows what he is "supposed to do." He finds Harry at the pool of icy water and enters it to save the life of his betrayed friend. Consequent to this willing, sacrificial immersion or baptism, Harry, who recognizes Ron as a true Gryffindor, guides Ron in completing his purification – by using the power of the Golden Griffin to reveal, confront, and slay his personal demons. This exorcism, post-illumination, completes Ron's initiation and purification; Ron provisionally re-enters the fellowship, a soul tryptich which is once again a trinity.

The usual sequence of the path to traditional baptism is repentance, acceptance of Christ as savior, instruction as a catechumen, tonsuring, exorcism, and three-fold immersion in the name of the Trinity, which leads to illumination of the darkened intellect or *nous*, the so-called eye of the heart. Ms. Rowling jumbles this order, of course, in weaving her alchemical, Arthurian, and Christian tapestry which illustrates the event of Theophany and the meaning of baptism or initiation in the life of a believer.

I cannot remember, however, any artist ever attempting anything as grand as this in English literature and pulling it off without "waking the sleeping dragons" of skepticism. The Silver Doe, as a work of "literary baptism," initiates readers into a universal path to illumination, using the symbols and rites specific to her faith and literary traditions. It is simultaneously engaging, challenging, even inspiring – and, I would argue, one of the finest and most effective short pieces of writing of the last hundred years.

The Forest Again

Ms. Rowling may have chosen to read "The Silver Doe" to her Carnegie Hall audience in late 2007, but it isn't the most meaningful chapter of *Deathly Hallows* to her. That honor is reserved for the chapter describing Harry in the Garden of Gethsemane, carrying his cross, and at Calvary in Chapter 34, "The Forest Again." As she says:

> *Kristy:* What was your favorite scene to write in *Deathly Hallows*?
>
> *J.K. Rowling:* Chapter 34: "The Forest Again."[14]
>
> *JKR:* I really, really, really cried after writing Chapter 34, which is where Harry walks back into the forest for what he thinks will be the last time. Because I had to live that with Harry and feel the weight of his disillusionment and his fear because he believes he's being sent to his death by Dumbledore who he thought wanted to keep him alive. So that was massively moving to me to write.[15]

And --

> Meredith Viera: Overall, the loss of which character brought you to tears?
>
> JKR: Definitely the passage that I found hardest to write of all of them in all seven books and the one that made me cry the most is Chapter 34 in this one. But that was-- and that was partly because of the content-and partly because it had been planned for so long and been roughed out for so long. And to write the

definitive version felt like a-- a huge climax.

MV: And can you tell us what was in 34?

ROWLING: It's when Harry sets off into the forest. Again. So that's my favorite passage of this book. And it's the part that when I finished writing, I didn't cry as I was writing, but when I finished writing, I had enormous explosion of emotion and I cried and cried and cried.[16]

Most of the meaning of "The Forest Again" is caught up in Harry's sacrifice of self, and it's a truckload of spiritual content, no doubt about it. The author herself has admitted repeatedly that even writing the chapter was a cathartic event. Before unpacking this meaning, though, let's take a second look at the chapter title, "The Forest Again."

The curious thing about the title is the word "again." Harry hasn't been in the Forbidden Forest in all of *Deathly Hallows*. He's had quite a few adventures there, of course. Firenze rescues him from Quirrell/Voldemort in the Forest in *Philosopher's Stone*, and Mr. Weasley's magical Ford Anglia rescues him and Ron from Aragog's Acromantula cove in *Chamber of Secrets*. In *Prisoner of Azkaban*, Harry is beside the lake when attacked by Dementors (the movie features an exciting battle between a werewolf and hippogriff in the Forest, which isn't in the book). In *Goblet of Fire*, Barty Crouch, Sr.'s son kills him at the Forest's edge and, in *Order of the Phoenix*, Grawp is in residence there, inspiring Hermione's diversion luring Professor Umbridge into her downfall/contretemps with the Centaurs.

In *Half-Blood Prince* and *Deathly Hallows*, Harry doesn't go into the Forbidden Forest. The hint in the chapter title, though, leads us to believe Harry's trip into the Forest is a repeat or echo of previous incidents. From the story-line, I'd guess it was Firenze or car rescues; Harry does eventually escape in Chapter 36 of *Hallows*, but his trip out cannot be really called a rescue, and the action of "The Forest Again" is largely in the Acromantula clearing Harry and Ron found by following the spiders in *Chamber*.

But I don't think Ms. Rowling is referring to her own storyline, however important I think the Forest of Dean chapter, "The Silver Doe," really is. I think "The Forest Again" is a pointer to the beginning of Dante's *Divine Comedy*, because the trial Harry begins in "The Forest Again" parallels Dante's three part spiritual odyssey that begins in a dark wood.

Chapter 33 in *Deathly Hallows*, "The Prince's Tale", links Dante and Severus Snape, because each book or cantica of the *The Divine Comedy* is 33 cantos. Chapter 34, largely the story of Harry's walk into the woods to sacrifice himself so as to defeat the Horcrux within him and the enemy outside him, is Ms. Rowling's fictional depiction of "Holy Friday." The link with the *Divine Comedy* is that Dante's journey through Inferno, Purgatorio, and Paradiso, begins with his waking in the woods on Holy Friday in the year 1300:

1   Midway in the journey of our life
2   I came to myself in a dark wood,
3   for the straight way was lost.

4   Ah, how hard it is to tell
5   the nature of that wood, savage, dense and harsh –
6   the very thought of it renews my fear!

7   It is so bitter death is hardly more so.
8   But to set forth the good I found
9   I will recount the other things I saw.[17]

Dante's walk in the woods to God ends at Easter in Paradise, much as Harry's agony ends when Sun rises in the Great Hall ceiling at his conquest of Voldemort. The title, "The Forest Again," is Ms. Rowling's hat-tip to the agony of Dante, the first and greatest Christian Everyman and spiritual pilgrim, and a pointer to the meaning of Harry's trip to Calvary via the Forbidden Forest in *Deathly Hallows*.

A review of this chapter's events, in sequence:

Harry wakes up on the floor of Dumbledore's office after his trip through Severus Snape's memories in *The Prince's Tale*. He has learned he has a scar-Horcrux and that the Headmaster's Machiavellian plan, all along, was to have Harry destroy Horcruxes, and then sacrifice himself to Voldemort when he is the last link the Dark Lord has to life. Harry accepts his destiny as Horcrux and the need to sacrifice himself to defeat Voldemort.

Under the Invisibility Cloak, Harry makes his way to the Forest and his fate. He reveals himself only once, to Neville – his faithful disciple, the only friend who never doubted Harry would return and who, in this faith, acted all year as Harry might have. After having given Neville instructions to kill Nagini if he has the chance, Harry returns to the concealment of his Cloak and reaches the edge of the Forest.

Harry opens the *"I open at the close"* inheritance-Snitch with the words, "I am about to die." The Resurrection Stone brings him Lily, James, Remus, and Sirius, "less substantial than living bodies, but much more than ghosts," something like "memory made nearly solid" (*Hallows*, "*The Forest Again*", p. 699). His parents, his god-father, and his favorite teacher accompany him through the Forest, "[acting] like Patronuses to him" (*Hallows*, "*The Forest Again*", p. 700).

Harry meets Death Eaters Dolohov and Yaxley, who are searching for him. He follows them into Voldemort's camp where he takes off his Cloak, stuffs it and his wand into his robes, and deliberately drops the Resurrection Stone. His ghostly family vanishes. He draws the Dark Lord's attention and is killed without making a move of resistance. As Sirius had told him at the edge of the Forest, dying was "quicker and easier than falling asleep" (*Hallows*, "*The Forest Again*", p. 699).

Spiritual Freight and Christian Content of "The Forest Again"

"The Forest Again" is simultaneously a retelling of the Crucifixion and a story of the death of a Christian Everyman. Harry's choices, and successful struggle to believe, have transformed him into a transparency of the God-man in Whom he believes, in his own story of dying to himself. The Passion narrative here, first, and then "Harry as Everyman."

Harry has Garden of Gethsemane desires and chooses to act in obedience as savior: The Christ, the night before his death on the Cross, doesn't sleep like a babe. He sweats blood and prays "O my Father, if it be possible, let this cup pass from me: nevertheless not as I will, but as thou wilt" (Matthew 26:39). He embraces the necessity of conformity to the Divine Will, but it's no party cup from which He will be drinking. Similarly, Harry hesitates at the abyss when he reaches the Forest:

> A swarm of dementors was gliding amongst the trees; he could feel their chill, and he was sure he would not be able to pass safely through it. He had no strength left for a Patronus. He could no longer conceal his own trembling. It was not, after all, so easy to die. Every second he breathed, the smell of the grass, the cool air on his face, was so precious. To think that people had years and years, time to waste, so much time it dragged, and he was clinging to each second. At the same time he thought that he would not be able to go on, and

knew that he must. The long game was ended, the Snitch had been caught, it was time to leave the air.... (*Hallows*, "*The Forest Again*", p. 698)

Harry walks the Via Dolorosa, stumbles, and is helped by Lily, his mother: The *Via Dolorosa*, "Street of Sorrows," is an actual avenue in Jerusalem, along which Christians believe their Savior carried His cross to Golgotha or Calvary. Christ fell under the weight of the cross as many as three times in different places along the Via Dolorosa, according to tradition, because of his having been tortured the previous night. He's comforted by His mother, Veronica and the grieving women (Luke 23: 27); his cross is borne at least part of the way by Simon the Cyrenian (Luke 23:26).

Harry's mother, who appears with James, Remus, and Sirius, when Harry opens the Snitch and turns the Resurrection Stone "over in his hand three times" (*Hallows*, "*The Forest Again*", p. 698), is also a great comfort to Harry on his walk to his Place of the Skull.

Harry looked at his mother.

"Stay close to me," he said quietly.

And he set off. The dementors chill did not overcome him; he passed through it with his companions, and they acted like Patronuses to him.... he stumbled and slipped toward the end of his life, toward Voldemort." (*Hallows*, '*The Forest Again*', pp. 700-701).

Harry dies sacrificially and without resistance to defeat the Dark Lord, as Christus Victor died on the Cross: When Christ is betrayed and His disciples begin to fight, He rebukes them, saying:

Then said Jesus unto him, Put up again thy sword into his place: for all they that take the sword shall perish with the sword. Thinkest thou that I cannot now pray to my Father, and he shall presently give me more than twelve legions of angels? But how then shall the scriptures be fulfilled, that thus it must be? (Matthew 26:52-54)

Christ goes to His Crucifixion in this same spirit, as a lamb to the slaughter. Harry learns, via Severus' memories in the Pensieve, that Dumbledore believed Harry must die and "Voldemort himself must do it, Severus. That is essential" (*Hallows*, "The Prince's Tale," p. 686). Consequently, Harry doesn't make any attempt to defend himself when he reveals himself to the Dark Lord in the Forest clearing: "his hands were sweating as he pulled off the Invisibility Cloak and stuffed it beneath his robes with his wand. He did not want to be tempted to fight" (*Hallows*, "*The Forest Again*," p. 703). Harry dies as a willing sacrifice.

To non-Christians, this may seem tiresome. After *Deathly Hallows* was published, one Jewish reader told me that she'd said a prayer when she bought it, that, "if nothing else, the story not become some kind of Christian allegory with Harry as Jesus." You may be surprised to hear she thought *Deathly Hallows* was anything but a gospel re-write with the Death Eaters standing in as Jews yelling, "Crucify Him!" She thought the book was undeniably Christian, yet sufficiently universal for her to find it spiritually satisfying.

This is a critical point in understanding the popularity of Harry Potter. It is "undeniably Christian," that is, loaded with specific Christian symbolism and meaning from the author's faith and literary traditions, "yet sufficiently universal to be spiritually satisfying to anyone." This last explains both the popularity of *Harry Potter* novels and, at least as important, the tenacity and pervasiveness of Christianity despite millennia of persecution and attacks. There is no such thing as a specifically "Christian truth"; what is true in the Christian revelation is truth, period.

Christians survived the Soviet holocaust, despite the loss of 60 million believers to the Communists, by clinging to this sustaining truth. They endured five centuries of Muslim occupation and dhimmitude in the Balkans for the same reason; apostatizing from their faith would have meant denying the answers to human questions they had empirical evidence were answers that were true and worked.

Of course, not everyone embraces these truths; the specific forms in which they come wrapped may not match the psychological locks with which they have been fit by their culture. Or the power of spiritual immunization many people have received is sufficient to reject anything labeled "Christian." The popularity of *Harry Potter*, despite its "obvious" Christian content and pervasive Christian symbolism, demonstrates an important point. Even without "the Christian label" or, better, with the label "rejected by Christians everywhere," the truth within the Christian tradition is spiritually satisfying to everyone. *It answers universal questions about what it means to be human. It works.*

I confess to wondering what non-Christians, or those who make denying anything perceptibly Christian the focus of their spiritual life, make of scenes in the *Harry Potter* novels like Harry putting the Golden Snitch/Resurrection Stone to his lips and opening it with the words, "I am about to die" (*Hallows*, "*The Forest Again*", p. 698). This is essentially a picture of Harry communing and drawing strength from this Mystery or sacrament to carry on into the Forest and face his death.

I doubt they see the specifically Christian content, buried as it is in the Snitch's alchemical symbolism and the obscurity of the Christian reference to nonsacramental readers. And Harry's sacrifice with its clear echoes of Christ's march to Calvary? Just as Christ's sacrifice is an example to all people of what a human life is all about, so is Harry's. The Gospel passage in which Christ tells his disciples:

> And when he had called the people unto him with his disciples also, he said unto them, Whosoever will come after me, let him deny himself, and take up his cross, and follow me. For whosoever will save his life shall lose it; but whosoever shall lose his life for my sake and the gospel's, the same shall save it. **For what shall it profit a man, if he shall gain the whole world, and lose his own soul?** (Mark 8:34-6 KJV; emphasis added)

Nonbelievers may gag on the exclusive claim that only people dying "for my sake" are saved, but would anyone deny the truth that a man's soul is more valuable to him than gaining a world he can't take with him? Not *Harry Potter* readers, it seems. They identify and cheer Harry's decision to die to save his friends. Like the alchemists, they, even if they do not know the Bible verse citation, also see in this story a restatement of the truths revealed in scripture:

> Verily, verily, I say unto you, Except a corn of wheat fall into the ground and die, it abideth alone: but if it die, it bringeth forth much fruit. [John 12:24 KJV; cf., Thou fool, that which thou sowest is not quickened, except it die (1 Corinthians 15:36 KJV)]
>
> Greater love hath no man than this, that a man lay down his life for his friends. (John 15:13 KJV)

And Harry's trip into the Forest in the company of Lily, James, Sirius, and Remus? Yes, it's a parallel story of the Stations of the Cross. It's also, though, a restatement of the universal hope we have, in St. Paul's words, of being "compassed about with so great a cloud of witnesses," those who have successfully completed the spiritual test set before us:

> Wherefore seeing we also are compassed about with so great a
> cloud of witnesses, let us lay aside every weight, and the sin which
> doth so easily beset us, and let us run with patience the race that
> is set before us, Looking unto Jesus the author and finisher of
> our faith; who for the joy that was set before him endured the
> cross, despising the shame, and is set down at the right hand of
> the throne of God. (Hebrews 12:1-2 KJV)

Ms. Rowling, being a Christian and a writer in the English tradition, inevitably tells Harry's story in language resonant with the Passion gospels. As those narratives reflect transcendent reality and human truths, they touch the hearts of all human beings without hardened hearts and Christ-o-phobia.

From Calvary, then, to King's Cross!

Chapter 35: King's Cross

Ms. Rowling has been asked about Harry's afterlife experience at King's Cross quite a few times:

> *Elisabeth: In the chapter of King's Cross, are they behind the
> Veil or in some world between the real world and the Veil?
> J.K. Rowling: You can make up your own mind on this, but I think
> that Harry entered a kind of limbo between life and death....*
>
> ---
>
> *Katie B: Why was Kings Cross the place Harry went to when he died?
> J.K. Rowling: For many reasons. The name works rather well, and
> it has been established in the books as the gateway between two
> worlds, and Harry would associate it with moving on between two
> worlds (don't forget that it is Harry's image we see, not necessarily
> what is really there)....*
>
> *Jon: Since Voldemort was afraid of death, did he choose to be a ghost?
> If so, where does he haunt or is this not possible due to his Horcruxes?
> J.K. Rowling: No, he is not a ghost. He is forced to exist in the
> stunted form we witnessed in King's Cross.* [18]

Personally, I just love the answer to the question, "Why King's Cross?" "The name works rather well." After a chapter on Harry's sacrificial death, yes, the name does "work rather well" – and you have to admire Ms. Rowling's reticence in spelling it out for Katie B. [See chapters 5 and 6 for the explanation of the meaning beyond Calvary for "King's Cross," the reason Dumbledore laughs when Harry tells him the place is "like King's Cross."]

But what do we learn at Harry's mystical King's Cross station and what does it mean?

Events of King's Cross

Harry wakes up naked in a misty palace or train station, with a suffering Voldemort soul fragment squealing nearby. Harry thinks he wants some clothes and his desire is instantly accomplished. He meets Dumbledore – just as the proven Dumbledore Denouement formula says we should at this point – and Harry learns from the departed Headmaster that he is *not* dead yet, but sustained in the world by means of his connection with his mother's sacrifice and blood in Lord Voldemort's new body.

Dumbledore has become positively voluble in death; Harry learns Hallows lore and the Headmaster's story, from Grindelwald and Ariana, to his incapacity to wield power, and what he and Voldemort have in common (the desire to be "Masters of death"). He apologizes to Harry for his secretiveness and foolishness; he confesses knowing for some time that Harry is the better man.

He explains, too, that Harry is the "worthy possessor of the Hallows" and "the true master of death, because the true master does not seek to run away from Death. He accepts that he must die, and understands that there are far, far worse things in the living world than dying" (*Hallows*, "King's Cross", pp. 720-721). Harry decides to return after Dumbledore tells him "by returning, you may ensure that fewer souls are maimed, fewer families are torn apart" (*Hallows*, "King's Cross", p. 722). Harry seeks some assurance that this conversation has been real and not just a hallucination or dream in his head; Dumbledore departs while saying, "of course it is happening inside your head, Harry, but why on earth should that mean that it is not real?" (*Hallows*, "King's Cross", p. 723).

Christian echoes and Spiritual meaning of King's Cross

The action in King's Cross is all consequent to Harry's sacrifice and seeming death in "The Forest Again", but the title "works well" because it points on one level to Christ's Sacrifice at Calvary on the Cross as "King of the Jews" (cf., Mark 15:26). This meaning is not allegorical or two-dimensional. We learn from Dumbledore that, because Harry died willingly and without resistance, Voldemort's curse in the previous chapter has killed only that soul fragment Harry had been carrying in his forehead since becoming the Chosen One.

Harry, consequently, is not a fictional messiah or Jesus-double as much as he is an Everyman figure. He has died to the evil within him; freed from this very real burden, he can, to risk using Christian language, be "born again." Not unlike Ron's confrontation with the Necklace Horcrux in "The Silver Doe", Harry had to stare down and die to the worst part of himself – and choose this death even though he couldn't know it wouldn't mean the death of his own soul as well. Again, Mark 8:35: "whosoever will save his life shall lose it; but whosoever shall lose his life for my sake and the gospel's, the same shall save it."

Harry survives but only, once again, because of "the bond of blood" he has with the person whose sacrificial death long ago saved him from the Dark Lord. The Christian echo here rings out; Harry's choice to die only resulted in his "victory over death" (here, as "master of death") because of his communion and shared life with a savior via that savior's blood. This is, to risk stating the obvious, the "bond of blood" that scandalized Jesus' followers in his time (John 6:53-66), and, perhaps, still scandalizes believers in some denominations not celebrating the Eucharist as their focus of public worship.

> Then Jesus said unto them, Verily, verily, I say unto you, Except ye eat the flesh of the Son of man, and drink his blood, ye have no life in you. Whoso eateth my flesh, and drinketh my blood, hath eternal life; and I will raise him up at the last day. For my flesh is meat indeed, and my blood is drink indeed. He that eateth my flesh, and drinketh my blood, dwelleth in me, and I in him. As the living Father hath sent me, and I live by the Father: so he that eateth me, even he shall live by me. (John 6:52-57)

Harry is saved by sacrificial death and blood just as Christians are saved by Christ's sacrifice and Blood. This doesn't offend Potter readers, I think, because Harry is not drinking blood of any kind (as Voldemort drinks the Unicorn's blood unworthily and unto damnation in *Philosopher's Stone*). And the focus of the story is Harry's willingness, his choice to die, which brings the salvific power of Lily's sacrifice into play.

All of us wanting to change "the man in the mirror" recognize this difficult first step – choosing to change, to even let part of one's identity die – as the foundation of spiritual transformation. Whatever graces are available to us in our spiritual traditions, we have to prepare the ground for them or they will fall and not take root (cf., the Parable of the Sower, Matthew 13:3-23; the Sower does not plow the field).

Harry's time in netherworld has its Christian equivalent or parallel in Christ's breaking the gates and the "harrowing" of Hell between his Crucifixion and Resurrection. Harry's perfected body in his limbo afterlife? The perfection of the Saints after judgment. Harry's decision to return once again reflects Christ's decision to drink the bitter cup, to die, and to rise again. The victory over the Evil One, the Prince of the World, was not complete at Christ's death on the Cross; that was won at His Resurrection and His preparing His disciples for the advent of the Holy Spirit at Pentecost.

Harry is not especially excited about leaving the "warm and light and peaceful" way-station; "he knew that he was heading back to pain and the fear of more loss." Dumbledore assures him, though, saying, "I know this, Harry, that you have less to fear from returning here than [Voldemort] does" (*Hallows*, "King's Cross", p. 722).

Voldemort's agony is vividly shown as a "small, naked child, curled on the ground, its skin raw and rough, flayed looking, and it lay shuddering under a seat where it had been left, unwanted, stuffed out of sight, struggling for breath" (*Hallows*, "King's Cross", p. 707). Harry thinks he ought to help it but can't get over his revulsion. Dumbledore assures him "you cannot help" and directs him to seats well away from the suffering, whimpering, trembling soul fragment.

This is perhaps the most difficult part of Ms. Rowling's picture of the world behind visible reality [see Chapter 5] and it is, again, just perhaps her greatest accomplishment. The righteous who have tried to embody love and die to themselves are in something like paradise where their slightest wish is granted – except for the ability to help those who chose the path of ego, personal advantage, and self-advancement. They're judged by their own deeds, taking the form of their soul's capacity for love at death. In Voldemort's soul fragment we see the irreparable condition of souls unprepared for eternal life.

Christ tells the same story in the Parable of Lazarus and the Rich Man in hell. The Rich Man begs Abraham for help only to learn "between us and you there is a great gulf fixed: so that they which would pass from hence to you cannot; neither can they pass to us, that would come from thence" (Luke 16:26). The Rich Man asks that a messenger be sent from the dead to tell his brothers what to do to avoid the torments awaiting them. Abraham says quite simply that this will not help: "If they hear not Moses and the prophets, neither will they be persuaded, though one rose from the dead" (Luke 16:31).

I wrote above that Ms. Rowling's retelling of this parable with Voldemort's suffering and inconsolable soul fragment was perhaps her "greatest accomplishment." I think this because, if there is one message that postmodern readers do not, perhaps cannot hear, it's that they will be judged in an afterlife for their thoughts, words, and deeds. Ms. Rowling in King's Cross presents this "judgment" in such a way that it seems anything but the work of an angry God. Rather, our condition in eternity will be the consequence of our choices and our capacity for love – and there will be no helping those who enter God's Glory with atrophied spirits and darkened hearts. She portrays transcendent justice without a juridical, anthropomorphic "heavy" Who is only the servant of the greater god, Necessity.

In the last chapter, Harry does try to help Lord Voldemort and learns that Abraham was right; "neither will they be persuaded, though one rose from the dead."

Chapter 36: The Flaw in the Plan

Ms. Rowling doesn't want her readers to think of Harry as an Aslan or cardboard-Jesus:

> *J.K. Rowling*: Harry is not, and never has been, a saint. Like Snape, he is flawed and mortal. Harry's faults are primarily anger and occasional arrogance.[19]

Such thinking is inevitable, though, because, as she says, the Christian symbolism of the books is "obvious," and Harry will be remembered largely as a "Christ symbol." I think this is an unfortunate simplification of meaning to transparent allegory -- x standing for y-- and ultimately a misunderstanding which will obscure why the books are so popular. No one I know loves the books and rereads them because "Harry is Jesus." A quick review of the last chapter and a longer look at its larger meaning [see Chapters 5 and 6] will help explain what drives

Pottermania and why simplifying this meaning is to miss the power of the books entirely.

Harry returns from King's Cross to the Forbidden Forest to find that Voldemort was laid out by the killing curse, too. The Dark Lord rises and Harry plays possum. Voldemort wants to know for sure that the Chosen One is dead; Narcissa Malfoy is pressed into action. She realizes Harry is alive and asks him if Draco is alive. When Harry says that he is, Narcissa's "nails pierced him" and she declares him dead.

The Dark Lord decides he must desecrate the dead and hits Harry's supposedly lifeless body with the Unforgiveable Cruciatus Curse by which he throws Harry in the air three times. Remarkably, "the pain he expected did not come" (*Hallows*, "The Flaw in the Plan", p. 727). In fact, throughout the chapter, the Dark Lord seems unable to hurt Harry or curse his enemies effectively, even to silence them for any period of time.

Hagrid carries Harry out of the Forest, an echo of his carrying baby Harry out of the destroyed Potter home. This time, alas, Hagrid believes Harry is dead, and weeps and rages in alternation. Voldemort presents Harry's corpse to Harry's followers in Hogwarts and offers them terms of surrender.

Neville, the loyal disciple, confronts Voldemort to get at Nagini, and, because of his "need and valor" (*Hallows*, "The Prince's Tale", p. 689), Neville is able to pull the Sword of Gryffindor from the flaming Sorting Hat the Dark Lord had placed on his head to punish him.

> With a single stroke Neville sliced off the great snake's head, which spun high into the air, gleaming in the light flooding from the entrance hall, and Voldemort's mouth was open in a scream of fury that nobody could hear, and the snake's body thudded to the ground at his feet – (*Hallows*, "The Flaw in the Plan", p. 733)

Chaos erupts as the giants, thestrals, centaurs, Buckbeak, and a host of families and Hogsmeade citizens join the fray. Harry chooses this moment to cover himself in the Invisibility Cloak to disappear and attack, mostly to defend his friends with protective spells. The battle moves into the Great Hall on a tide of combatants, including the house-elves of Hogwarts under Kreacher's leadership.

The battle is reduced to two duels: Bellatrix Lestrange against Molly Weasley and the feature battle between Harry Potter and Lord Voldemort. Molly defeats Bellatrix with the killing curse and Harry reveals himself to the furious Dark Lord after shielding Molly Weasley from his rage.

And Harry tries to save the soul of Lord Voldemort.

He explains first how his self-sacrifice in the Forest has protected his friends; "I've done what my mother did." Then he dares to call Voldemort by his given name and tutor him about Dumbledore's death on the Tower, Severus Snape's love for Lily and loyalty to Dumbledore and, finally, about the Dark Lord's need for remorse.

> "[B]efore you try to kill me, I'd advise you to think about what you've done.... Think and try for some remorse, Riddle...."
>
> "What is this?"
>
> Of all the things that Harry had said to him, beyond any revelation or taunt, nothing had shocked Voldemort like this. Harry saw his pupils contract to thin slits, saw the skin around his eyes whiten.
>
> "It's your one last chance," said Harry,"it's all you've got left....I've seen what you'll be otherwise.... Be a man... Try... Try for some remorse...."(*Hallows*, "The Flaw in the Plan", p. 742).

This is beyond Voldemort's capacity to understand or act upon. So Harry explains that he is the master of the Elder Wand because he disarmed the previous master, Draco Malfoy, during the escape from Malfoy Manor. (Draco had disarmed Dumbledore on the Tower which made him, unknown to Draco and his family, the Elder Wand's sovereign.)

As dawn breaks over the enchanted ceiling of the Great Hall, Voldemort hurls the death curse and Harry responds with his signature disarming spell. Harry is right; the Elder Wand refuses to harm its master and the killing curse rebounds to destroy the Dark Lord.

The story ends with Harry, Ron, and Hermione in the Headmaster's office. Harry asks Dumbledore's portrait for his advice about the Hallows. Harry asks if it's wise to leave the Resurrection Stone in the Forest, but keep his Invisibility Cloak. Dumbledore applauds both ideas. Harry then renounces the Elder Wand and, after repairing his holly and phoenix feather wand (which Hermione had broken in their Christmas Eve escape), he pledges to put the Wand of Destiny back in Dumbledore's tomb. Close curtain. *Exeunt omnes.*

Christian Echoes and Spiritual Meaning of The Flaw in the Plan

You want Passion narrative and other biblical parallels and allusions? Step right up.

- Narcissa's nails "pierce Harry's flesh" and she announces his death ~ Crucifixion Of Christ with nails to the Cross and His Burial in the Tomb

- Voldemort desecrates Harry's body with the Cruciatus Curse ~ Another Crucifixion reference, on the fly, for anyone who missed the first five or six

- Hagrid carries Harry's body from the Forest ~ a picture like Michaelangelo's *Pieta*, a reference to the women who come to the Tomb to care for Christ's body

- The Dark Lord's Incapacity to hurt Harry or his friends ~ Christ's sacrifice has broken the Devil's power over humanity

- Harry's disappearance under the Invisibility Cloak at Hagrid's feet ~ the Empty Tomb discovered by the women and their announcement of same to the Apostles

- Neville's decapitation of Nagini as Harry comes to life ~ the victory over the Garden's serpent at Christ's Resurrection

- Harry's use of a blackthorn wand and victory over Voldemort using a hawthorn wand ~ *Christus Victor* via Crown of Thorns and Cross, not through individual triumph in arms

- Harry's urging Voldemort to "feel some remorse" and sharing with him all he knows about the Elder Wand ~ Christ as the Truth waiting for the repentance of all sinners

- Harry's rejection of the Elder Wand and Resurrection Stone ~ Christian victory via Christ's Resurrection over the temptations of power and the fear of death

Reading that list, you almost have to suspect Ms. Rowling wanted to just bury her Christian critics in an ending so transparently biblical, and about the Crucifixion and Resurrection, they might blush and apologize. If that was her hope, it didn't work out that way.

With all these not-so-subtle parallels and echoes, though, aren't we supposed to think of Harry as Jesus? Isn't his return from King's Cross meant to be one more Hogwarts formulaic end-story Resurrection, this time with Harry as a symbol of Christ himself rather than needing a

Phoenix, Stag or some other Christ symbol to fill that role?

Yes. And no.

Yes, the parallels and allusions are all right there: "the Cross, the Nails, the Spear and Death." Firenze the Centaur is lanced in the side and lies wounded in the Great Hall during the Battle of Hogwarts as an image of the Christ pierced on the Cross. Ms. Rowling's faith and the tradition in which she writes make what already leaps from the page undeniable; a Buddhist or a Sufi couldn't have written "The Flaw in the Plan," even as an exercise in Christian storytelling. This is the work of a Christian who knows how to use images from scripture and symbols of the English fantasy literature tradition with subtlety, and quite openly, as her story dictates.

I worry, though, that "Harry as Jesus" rather misses the point. If Harry is anyone's real-world double written into story, I suspect, as I wrote at the beginning of this chapter, he is Ms. Rowling's stand-in. They share the same birthday, eye color and lost mother, and Ms. Rowling said there's quite a bit of her rolled into Harry. Her "struggle to believe," she's said, is evident in *Deathly Hallows* – and the only character who struggles to believe is Harry himself.

And "Harry = Jesus" can't explain the popularity of the books; if anything, it makes the popularity of *Deathly Hallows,* and the other books to which it is a fitting finale, rather mysterious. It's pretty hard to suspend disbelief sufficiently that one can identify with the Jesus cardboard cut-out and experience the catharsis alongside Christ on the Cross at the same time.

The solution is simple. Ms. Rowling's Harry is no saint – and no Jesus, either. Harry, like Ms. Rowling, struggles to believe and to overcome doubts about spiritual realities. He struggles, but, by the force of the example of people (and one house-elf) who believe and those who do not, he chooses the path of obedience, love, and sacrifice. The result is that Harry becomes a Christian Everyman, who dies not as a savior for the whole world, but who dies with respect to his own interior evil or sin – the Scar Horcrux, his own corrupted soul fragment.

Harry's final transformation and victory over the evil within and without, not surprisingly, has strong echoes with the sacrifice and obedience of Christ in the Garden of Gethsemane and on Golgotha. Not because Harry is an allegorical Christ, but because his choices must be the same as the Christ's.

Harry is a hero with human doubts, failings, and temptations, with which every reader can identify, and, frankly, has identified with. The consequence of Harry's victory over the Scar Horcrux he carried, and his internal triumph at King's Cross (no less real for taking part in his head), is his defeat of Lord Voldemort, who represents the very real external foe whose power was broken on the Cross.

Reading *Harry Potter and the Deathly Hallows* as an allegory is tempting. But the story's power and meaning are lost by interpreting an alchemical and spiritual drama with universal human meaning as a denominational tract (especially for postmodern readers with doubts). Readers around the world love this book, and the series which it closes in spectacular fashion, because it encourages them and also challenges them to make hard, sacrificial, loving choices to overcome the Voldemort on the inside to get at the Voldemort on the outside.

And the first, hardest and most important choice for many – to include, it seems, Ms. Rowling – is to believe in God. This choice means, if Harry's experience is our guide, enduring the agonies of the *nigredo* and the world before Nativity, the purification and illumination of baptism into Christ's death and Resurrection, and the crucible of dying to our fallen nature and confronting this evil in the world as well.

If we choose to do this, because we accept it as both our design and destiny as essentially spiritual beings, we won't become Jesus; we will, however, have some hope of being fully human and experience some measure of the love, freedom, and joy available to us through the disciplines, graces, and sacrifices of an orthodox spiritual tradition.

Conclusions

Deathly Hallows, then, is a spectacular spiritual finish to the *Harry Potter* series with "obvious" Christian content and edifying universal meaning. It's the destination to which the six previous books' literary alchemy, hero's journeys, doppelgangers and traditional symbolism pointed and foreshadowed. Harry's decision in Dobby's grave to feel his remorse and the love that heals a splintered soul, and to choose to believe despite his doubts, leads to his triumphs over the little bit of the Dark Lord within him and the very real extension of this internal evil in the "real world." Ms. Rowling delivered on her several promises in the year 2000 that the last book of the series would answer all questions about her faith "because you will have read" the answers in that story.

We learned in *Deathly Hallows* that the choice to believe, including its struggle with doubts, is the first and most important choice for human beings to make. All spiritual choices are not equal; Ms. Rowling in *Deathly Hallows* rejects the idolatry of materialism, the egotism and power-lust of occult belief and the superficial profundity of the New Age. By casting her alchemical stages in Harry's last adventure around and in the image of the Christian holy days of Nativity, Theophany, and the Resurrection of Christ, she points to an orthodox belief in Christ as a valid path to spiritual transformation and fully human life, without evangelizing or excluding other faiths as somehow invalid.

We learned, too, about the power of this inclusive spiritual artistry. In all her books, Ms. Rowling uses Christian images, symbols, themes, and meaning which, of course, have special resonance with her Christian readers. But the author in interviews denies evangelical intention and proselytizing purpose.[20] However, for those readers who aren't Christians (even those immunized against anything with a Christian label) she uses traditional items from her faith and the English 'Greats.' And because she uses them with such a light hand, their universal and transcendent spiritual freight are delivered without negative feeling or suspicion on the skeptical reader's part. It's this freight that is the meaning driving Potter-mania. *Harry Potter*, simply put, satisfies on an imaginative level the human need for religious, mythic, or spiritual experience. Ms. Rowling, as postmodern Christian artist, satisfies this need like no other living writer.

Endnotes

1   "J.K. Rowling Interview," *CBCNewsWorld: Hot Type*, July 13, 2000; http://www.accio-quote.org/articles/2000/0700-hottype-solomon.htm

2   Wyman, Max. " 'You can lead a fool to a book but you can't make them think': Author has frank words for the religious right," *The Vancouver Sun* (British Columbia), October 26, 2000; http://www.accio-quote.org/articles/2000/1000-vancouversun-wyman.htm

3   Stephen McGinty, *The Scotsman*, January 2006, 'Life After Harry'; http://news.scotsman.com/jkrowlingharrypotter/Life-after-Harry.2741104.jp

4   Vieira, Meredith. "JK Rowling One-On-One: Part One." *Today Show (NBC)* , 26 July 2007; http://www.accio-quote.org/articles/2007/0726-today-vieira1.html

5   Op. cit.

6   http://hogwartsprofessor.com/?p=144#comment-12490

7   http://hogwartsprofessor.com/?p=144#comment-12706

8   Anelli, Melissa and Emerson Spartz. "The Leaky Cauldron and MuggleNet interview Joanne Kathleen Rowling: Part One," *The Leaky Cauldron*, 16 July 2005; http://www.accio-quote.org/articles/2005/0705-tlc_mugglenet-anelli-1.htm

9   Ms. Deborah M. Chan ("Arabella Figg") at the HogPro boards first pointed out that Dobby is the model Christian of the series. See http://hogwartsprofessor.com/?p=134#comment-11760

10 www.atimes.com/atimes/Central_Asia/EA29Ag01.html,   http://news.bbc.co.uk/cbbcnews/hi/world/newsid_2693000/2693711.stm

11 Woods, Audrey. "Harry Potter and the Magic Key of J.K. Rowling," Associated Press, 6 July 2000; http://www.accio-quote.org/articles/2000/0700-ap-woods.html

12 Hattenstone, Simon. "Harry, Jessica and me," *The Guardian*, July 8, 2000; http://www.accio-quote.org/articles/2000/0700-guardian-hattenstone.htm

13 'Harry Potter' Author J.K. Rowling Opens Up About Books' Christian Imagery:'They almost epitomize the whole series,' she says of the scripture Harry reads in Godric's Hollow, Shawn Adler: http://www.mtv.com/news/articles/1572107/20071017/index.jhtml, http://hogwartsprofessor.com/?p=196

14 *Bloomsbury Chat, 29 July 07;* http://www.bloomsbury.com/jkrevent/

15 Vieira, Meredith. "Harry Potter: The Final Chapter" *Dateline (NBC)*

, 29 July 2007; http://www.accio-quote.org/articles/2007/0729-dateline-vieira.html

16 Vieira, Meredith. "JK Rowling One-On-One: Part One." *Today Show (NBC)* , 26 July 2007; http://www.accio-quote.org/articles/2007/0726-today-vieira1.html

17 *Inferno*, Canto I, 1-9, translation courtesy Princeton Dante Project; http://etcweb.princeton.edu/dante/pdp/

18 Bloomsbury Chat, op. cit.

19 Bloomsbury Chat, op. cit.

20 www.time.com/time/specials/2007/personoftheyear/article/0,28804,1690753_1695388_1695436,00.html; See also the Runcie documentary: 'A Year in the Life,' http://hogwartsprofessor.com/?p=311

"It turns out that Rowling, like her hero, is a Seeker. She talks about having a great religious curiosity, going back to childhood. "No one in my family was a believer. But I was very drawn to faith, even while doubting," she says. "I certainly had this need for something that I wasn't getting at home, so I was the one who went out looking for religion." As a girl, she would go to church by herself. She still attends regularly, and her children were all christened. Her Christian defenders always thought her faith shined through her stories. One called the books the "greatest evangelistic opportunity the church has ever missed." But Rowling notes that there was always another side to the holy war. "At least as much as they've been attacked from a theological point of view," she says, the books "have been lauded and taken into pulpit, and most interesting and satisfying for me, it's been by several different faiths." The values in the books, she observes, are by no means exclusively Christian, and she is wary of appearing to promote one faith over another rather than inviting people to explore and struggle with the hard questions.

Rowling's religious agenda is very clear: she does not have one. "I did not set out to convert anyone to Christianity. I wasn't trying to do what C. S. Lewis did. It is perfectly possible to live a very moral life without a belief in God, and I think it's perfectly possible to live a life peppered with ill-doing and believe in God." And now she climbs into a pulpit of her own, and you can tell how much this all matters to her, if it weren't already clear from her 4,100-page treatise on tolerance. "I'm opposed to fundamentalism in any form," she says. "And that includes in my own religion."

Chapter 4

Snape's Green-Eyed Girl

Dante, Renaissance Florence, and the Death of the Potions Master

There have been *Harry Potter* conferences and conventions in Orlando, Las Vegas, Philadelphia, LA, London, Toronto, Ottawa, Chicago, even Hudson, Ohio, and Appleton, Wisconsin. I have heard of other big gatherings in Dallas, Salem, New Orleans, Copenhagen, and Reading (UK). The city that should have been first to host anything to do with *Harry Potter*, though, is Florence, Italy. Not because 'Firenze' is the Italian name for 'Florence.' *Harry Potter* readers and scholars need to meet in Florence because Dante is the soul of Ms. Rowling's epic about love and death.

Maybe Italy is too far. There are nine states in the US alone that have at least one city or town named 'Florence.' I recommend the one in Massachusetts so The Dante Society in America[1] can sponsor part of the conference or at least give a prize for the best Dante-Rowling talk given. It's time we wake up to the enormity of Ms. Rowling's Florence fetish and talk about it at length. This chapter's purpose is just to begin that conversation.

The best I can do here, given the breadth and depth of the topic (we're talking Dante here!), is open the conversation about the ways the Florentine Bard has influenced Ms. Rowling's *Harry Potter* epic. I don't think it's disputable that there *is* an influence here. The depth of it will probably be a subject of Fandom and Ivory Tower speculation for as long as serious readers reread Dante and Rowling (put this in the file labeled "until the Lord comes").

Even in a quick survey, though, you'll learn why Lily's eyes are green, what Snape accomplishes by looking into Harry's eyes in the Shrieking

Shack and what the "white rose" (Albus/Rose) on the Epilogue train platform is all about. I think Dante's *Divine Comedy* may be the neglected super-source for the Christian hermeticism, architecture, and many plot points of the *Harry Potter* books.

If that seems like a stretch to you, let's start out with what are "reasonable observer" objections to the possibility of this influence. Here are three reasons to discount or be skeptical about a Dantean echo in Ms. Rowling's work:

(1) A word search for "Dante"[2] at the Accio Quote treasury of most every interview Ms. Rowling has given since 1997 yields ***nothing***. It's safe to assume Ms. Rowling hasn't mentioned Dante as an influence in any interviews in which she's been asked what books and writers shaped her work, which is to say almost every interview of the past decade.

(2) If there are any hat-tips to Dante in the names or places of the seven novels, beyond the nod to Florence in "Firenze," they are sufficiently obscure to have escaped me.

(3) Dante's faith is not an implicit part of his work readers must hunt for between the lines and in his choice of symbols; the Commedia is as oblique or obscure a Christian work as Chartres Cathedral or the Tridentine Mass (i.e., if you don't understand that it's Christian, start to finish, you don't know the first and defining thing about it).

Despite these reasons for skepticism, there are significant indications we will explore here which all suggest that Dante's influence is heavy in *Harry Potter*, as great an influence perhaps on Ms. Rowling as the alchemical dramatist's, the Narnian's, and even Jane Austen's.

Here are the topics discussed below to open our conversation about Dante and Rowling:

- Ms. Rowling's abundant pointers in her books to Renaissance Florence;

- The importance of Lily's green eyes to Severus Snape; and

- The meeting of Albus Potter and Rose Weasley in the Epilogue.

Along the way, I hope to touch on the hermetic and Christian content of both *The Divine Comedy* and *Harry Potter*, the three tiered structure of both works and trinitarian elements in each, and note the writers through whom Ms. Rowling shares a taste for Dante and through whom she may have acquired this taste. First, though, a trip to Florence.

Florence and Renaissance Italy in Harry Potter

When discussing months ago the possibility that the real Prince in the Harry Potter books was Machiavelli's *Prince*, I argued that one of the compelling elements of Ms. Rowling's work in support of this possibility was all the references to Florence in her novels. To review:

•   The "good" centaur in the *Harry Potter* books is named "Firenze." Firenze is the Italian word for the city of Florence, arguably the center and heart of the 15th century renaissance of arts and sciences in Northern Italy. Firenze the Centaur is an accomplished astrologer and, unlike the herd in the Forbidden Forest, believes his art does not reveal what *must* come to pass so everyone should step aside and "let it happen." Firenze argues with Bane and others what is essentially the humanist "free will" position of Albus Dumbledore that "what is foretold" reveals the playing field of choice. (Friends of Narnia will see Ms. Rowling's tip of the hat here to Roonwit the Centaur's final words in *The Last Battle*.)

•   Maybe you don't like Firenze or the Centaurs. How about Buckbeak the Hippogriff? Ms. Rowling lifts this magical animal right out of Ariosto's early 16th century epic *Orlando Furioso*, which is in many ways the completion of Matteo Boiardo's *Orlando Innamorato* of the late 15th century. Both writers are from Emilio and Ferrara. Hippogriffs are the heroic steeds of Italian Renaissance fantasy epic.

•   Ms. Rowling said in 1997 that "To invent this wizard world I've learned a ridiculous amount about alchemy...to set the parameters and establish the stories' internal logic." If you've read *Unlocking Harry Potter: Five Keys for the Serious Reader* (and if you haven't, you really should), you understand at no little depth how literary alchemy is the skeleton on which Ms. Rowling has built her stories. This is a pointer to Florence and the Renaissance because alchemy, as a hermetic art, owes its Western rebirth (or better, "second wind") to Ficino's 15th century translation at the direction and expense of the Medici of Hermes Trismegistus. Alchemy is a cornerstone of Renaissance magic.

•   How big a part of Harry Potter would you say "memory" is? Go ahead and pull out the incarnate memory 'Tom Riddle, Jr.'

plays in *Chamber of Secrets*, 'Snape's Worst Memory' from *Order of the Phoenix*, the Time Turner from *Prisoner of Azkaban*, and the Pensieve lessons and experiences in *Goblet of Fire* and *Half-Blood Prince*. Memory is a huge piece of Ms. Rowling's magical pie and, yes, this reflects its importance in Renaissance magic. Frances Yates, the author of the magisterial *Giordano Bruno and the Hermetic Tradition* (University of Chicago Press, 1964), thought memory was so important in understanding the magic of Bruno — and Shakespeare — that she wrote another book, *The Art of Memory* (University of Chicago Press, 1966), to detail the astrological and cabalistic elements of Renaissance memory systems. Dumbledore remarks at Harry's first sorting feast that music is "a magic beyond all we do here." I suspect memory, rather than being "beyond" Hogwarts magic, is at the heart of it.

•   The Italian Renaissance is largely about the relations between the **four** Principal Cities of the Peninsula: Florence, Naples, Venice, and Milan. Their inability to get along, or even cooperate in shared emergencies, leads to their subjection to France (Charles VIII, Louis XII) and Spain (Ferdinand of Aragon). "Four rivals in division being vulnerable to takeover"– sound familiar? I suspect, too, that one of the spurs to Ms. Rowling's creation of Quidditch as experienced at Hogwarts was the *Palio di Siena*. Though now a competition between 17 different sections of the city, these passionate horse races, according to Titus Birckhardt in his book on Siena, were originally between the principal four quarters of the city.

•   And, while that mention of Titus Burckhardt is still fresh, two notes. Is it odd that this Swiss author of the best book on alchemy in print was born in Florence and wrote at length about Siena? And that, to University historians at least, the name "Burckhardt" means *Jakob* Burckhardt, the author of *The Civilization of the Renaissance in Italy*, and great uncle of Titus? What I wouldn't give for a peek at Ms. Rowling's bookshelf. I'm guessing that her copy of Titus Burckhardt's *Alchemy* is the one with the Hagrid Hermaphrodite on a dragon straddling a Golden Snitch. And that this book sits right next to Frances Yates' books on Renaissance magic and Jacob Burckhardt's *The Civilization of the Renaissance in Italy*.

- There's more. All the references in the *Harry Potter* books to specific stars (Sirius, Regulus, etc.) and the importance of astrology, both in Divinations and with the Centaurs, are pointers again to Renaissance memory-based magic, in which astrology plays a huge part. The Tarot? Again, whether you're talking about their origins as playing cards or their occult usage, you wind up in 15th century Italy (specifically, Milan). Remember Boiardo, the first *Orlando* epic poet? He wrote a poem on tarot cards as well.

Ms. Rowling's magical world, like it or not, is an echo of the hermetic magic and heroic literature of Renaissance Italy.

When I was first thinking about this pre-*Deathly Hallows*, I thought there might be a link between Severus and Machiavelli. It turns out there were connections between the Roman Emperor Severus that Machiavelli (who overcame Niger and Albinus to take power himself) engendering an Evil!Snape possibility. That possibility, of course, did not play out in *Deathly Hallows*. Instead we learned that, if any character was a Machiavellian figure, it was the lovable Headmaster who coolly calculated his own demise and was saving Harry only so he could be killed at *the right time*.

But could all the Florentine and Renaissance references be pointers to *Dante* instead of Machiavelli?

I think so.

First, *Harry Potter* is a literary work about a hero's personal transformation through a series of trials. Despite its themes concerning the judicious use of power, it isn't a political treatise wrapped in story. Its messages on power and trust, too, were anything but Machiavellian. It makes more sense that the Renaissance and Florentine highlighting everywhere in these books are nods to the greatest poet of Florence and Renaissance Italy and, many believe, of all World literature.

Second, Dante's Florence is a battlefield of warring houses, from the Guelphs and Ghibellines to the Franciscans and Dominicans, and, *The Divine Comedy*'s *Paradiso*, at least, is largely about the poet's seeing the otherworldly conjunction and resolution of these contraries. The central place of the conflict between the Gryffindors and Slytherins in Ms. Rowling's books is a clear echo of Dante's use of polarity ending in peace as preface to the Beatific Vision.

I'm the worst of Dante dilettantes. So you'll forgive me for sharing a theory peripheral to the little Dante scholarship I've read in the notes of several editions of the *The Divine Comedy* I've collected through the years. As important as all the historic references are in the *Commedia* — with notes explaining these people and Florentine parties almost always running to more pages than the poem text itself — it's still hard for me to believe Dante is writing an historico-political or even a theologico-political "gotcha" to celebrate his friends and patrons and diss his enemies.

It's fun to note the Margaret Thatcher and Tony Blair stand-ins in *Harry Potter*, too. But even if you have no idea about who those PMs are (and, clearly, the great majority of *Harry Potter* readers below the age of twenty – or readers in Japan, Chile, and Siberia – are largely unfamiliar with 20th century UK Prime Ministers), the book retains its meaning. Keith Olbermann can project his red state-blue state, Bush-bashing beliefs onto the Harry-Voldemort battle without "forcing the pieces" of the puzzle, but will he have found the reason explaining why the books are so popular in this supposed election year allegory?

Of course not. I think it's equally as silly to spend a lot of time with the historical personages and contraries in Dante's masterpiece (if, in *The Divine Comedy*, the figures are not just allegorical or possible representatives of ideas or types, but also the real-world men and women Dante knew or knew of). Why? Because, beyond understanding the outline of the historical person or situation represented, the reader will miss the heart of the exiled poet's meaning, which isn't an argument about the virtues and vices of specific partisan groups and individuals per se, but the virtues necessary and the vices detrimental to the transcendence of earthly duality and ascension to the Beatific Vision of God's glory. As much as Dante's work is "timeless" and "for all men," not just Florentines of the late Middle Ages, it is also about a real journey we're all taking in the dark wood and "forbidden forest."

This is the stuff and heart of hermetic artistry. God Himself is simultaneously Absolute (transcendent, other) and Infinite (immanent, within, everywhere). This polarity in the Godhead that is not duality, a 'That' neither Being nor Non-Being, is mirrored in His Creation brought into Being each moment from the silence of His Word. We are defined by polarity, from the working of our senses and thinking to the realities of male/female, night/day, and I/Thou.

Our lives, designed as we are for relationship, however, are about **the resolution of these contraries in love**, be it "health" in our peaceful relationship with our environment, or "life" consequent to our loving relationships with our fellow human beings, or "holiness" as we enjoy communion with God. We pursue, so much as we live by design rather than contrary to it, a life that, like God's simultaneously Absolute and Infinite reality, is love, peace, and life – all synonyms for the resolution of contraries.

Why do artists write poems, plays, and stories celebrating and illustrating this adventure rather than didactic treatises on this subject? Because the world of the discursive intellect is the realm of sophists (hence Plato's insistence in his Seventh Epistle that he had never written a word of philosophy) and, post-Enlightenment, of charcoal burners (the alchemists term for chemists) concerned only with measurable quantities and with reason divorced from the noetic. Jane Austen battles Hume through her novels, Blake takes on the Industrial Revolution in poems and paintings, and Lewis and Tolkien assault scientism and the cult of progress in their novels, each winning significant victories on the only battlefield that counts, the heart or cardiac intelligence of their readers.

Using Christian imagery and meaning in this battle to redirect hearts to their origin and end in the Absolute/Infinite Father is understandable. Why, though, is great literature adorned with all the astrological, alchemical, and cosmological trappings? Dante travels through the planetary spheres to reach the Empyrean before God's glory. Lewis' *Narnia* novels are built on an astrological architecture and his *Ransom* novels on alchemy. Ms. Rowling books and the woman herself tell us that the *Harry Potter* novels overflow with alchemy, the art of the soul's purification in conjunction with the resolution of contraries in metals. What's the reason for all the non-Biblical, even "occult" baggage in the writings of Chaucer, Shakespeare, Donne, Blake, Dickens, Hugo, Poe, Hawthorne, MacDonald, Yeats, Eliot, Lewis, Tolkien, and Rowling?

In brief, the "spagyric sciences" of astrology and alchemy (based as they both were on Four Element physics) reflect and pursue a metaphysics of harmony and communion with the still point, the defining origin of the dance of the elements ("Except for the point, the still point,/ There would be no dance, and there is only the dance." *Four Quartets: Burnt Norton*; cf., *Elizabethan World Picture*, Chapter 8, "The Cosmic Dance").

Astrology and alchemy were, in metaphor if not in substance (and only when pursued within a revealed tradition of Sacraments and Grace), the work of faith, namely, the crossing of an imaginary divide within Creator/Creation and return to the peace of the Father in Whom contraries of time/space, Being/NonBeing, Absolute/Infinite "are not."

Rene Guenon, in his *The Esoterism of Dante* (Sophia Perennis, 1996), reminds us that the poet urges his readers, first, "to search beneath the veil of my strange allegory" (*Inferno*, IX, 61-63) and that in *Convivio* (The Banquet), II:1, he says his poetry has diverse meanings and "they may be understood, and they must be explained in four senses."[3] In this, Dante follows the Angelic Doctor and traditional understanding of the four layers of text, especially scripture, to be the literal, allegorical, moral, and anagogical. About this last, the poet explains,

> *"The fourth sense is called anagogical, that is to say, beyond the senses; and this occurs when a scripture is expounded in a spiritual sense which, although it is true also in the literal sense, signifies by means of the things signified a part of the supernal things of eternal glory."*

Guenon writes that Dante today, however, is interpreted on three levels exclusively — the literal or poetic, the allegorical or "philosophical-theological hidden meaning," and the moral or the political or social. And, however profound the exegesis of the exoteric religious meaning at the level of allegory, the neglect of the anagogical or metaphysical means the kernel of the nut has not been revealed (*Esoterism*, p.2). Guenon then explores the Masonic and Hermetic parallels in the *Commedia* and concludes, incredible as it may seem, that Dante is describing an experience he had in reality, rather than just artfully synthesizing abstractions and theological positions with historical persons in story form. Guenon quotes Reghini:

> *It is natural that [critics fail to grasp Dante's depth], for to grasp and understand the allusions and the conventional and allegorical references, one must know the object of the allusion or allegory; in the present case this means an apprehension of the mystical experiences through which true initiation causes the myste and the epopte to pass. For anyone with some experience of this kind there can be no doubt about the existence in the Divine Comedy and the Aeneid, of a metaphysical esoteric allegory that simultaneously veils and unveils the successive phases through which the consciousness of the initiate passes in order to reach immortality (Esoterism of Dante, page 23).*

So what?

Remember Eliade's thesis about the religious function entertainments serve in a secular culture. In a normal or theocentric culture, entertainments and the greater arts serve a religious function. Not to supplant, but to foster religious practice. Entertainments are less to create a transcendent experience of sorts and foster a disposition for such things, than to deepen and further the longing for esoteric spiritual accomplishment within the exoteric forms and means of religious experience. Ms. Rowling's books are as popular as they are because their audience is starved for spiritual experience of any kind; her books, in their resurrection and alchemical imagery alone, provide a secondary, hermetic experience through the reader's identification with Harry. Dante is the greater artist, perhaps the greatest artist, not only because his poetry operates at a different depth than Ms. Rowling's (because of his experience) but because his audience is capable of a more profound experience and noetic understanding than the postmodern, secular reading public can imagine.

This notwithstanding, I'm half convinced that Ms. Rowling, perhaps through her reading of Eliot's *Four Quartets* with its Dante echoes, or of Charles Williams' *The Figure of Beatrice: A Study In Dante*, or of Dorothy Sayers' translation and commentary on *The Divine Comedy*, in her seven years of plotting these books, perhaps in her initial moment of inspiration, chose to write a Dante-esque novel with its four level of meanings. And, in this choice, born from her love of Dante and Florence of the Middle Ages and Renaissance, we have the necessity of the hermetic or alchemical backdrop and organization of her books.

But we'll need more than a "quarreling couple" and some throwaway references to an Italian city to make this Alighieri link seem more than the usual pastiche guesswork of Internet scholarship. What have we got in the *Harry Potter* novels that screams "Dante!"?

Here are three screamers that leapt up at me, with which I hope to open this discussion of Ms. Rowling's debt and allusions to Dante. I expect there are many more I've missed, if only because my knowledge and appreciation of Dante is so weak; I look forward to reading the correction and extension of my stumbling beginning here.

Severus Snape and Lily's Green Eyes

There are several *suggestions* of a link between Dante and Severus

Snape. Dante belonged nominally to the Guild of Medical Doctors and Apothecaries so, we're obliged to think of him as a physician or druggist, perhaps even a potions maker. The most popular images of Dante, via the drawings of Gustave Dore for *The Divine Comedy*, certainly look more like Severus[4] than any other Harry Potter character. But this is chaff.

The substantial connection between Severus and the Tuscan genius is in their unrequited or courtly love for green-eyed women and the meaning of this love, especially as connected with the eyes of their beloved.

Dante's green-eyed love is for Beatrice Portinari, a young woman with whom he fell in love on first sight when he was nine and she eight, whom he met only once more nine years later. She is the subject of his *La Vita Nuova* and his guide in the last cantos of *Purgatorio* and almost all of *Paradiso* (with Bernard). Dante's love for Beatrice was unknown to her during her short life and, as an example of love for a person acting as a stepping stone to spiritual love, knows no historical or literary equal.

Severus Snape's green-eyed love is Lily Evans. He also meets her when he is nine or ten if, unlike Dante and Beatrice, they become friends and Lily is well aware of him. Because of Severus' fascination with the Dark Arts, his companionship with young wizards hoping to be Death Eaters and his calling Lily a Mudblood during a humiliating fight with James Potter, Lily breaks with Severus. He continues to love her and, perversely, even hopes to win her affections after the Dark Lord kills James Potter and Lily's son Harry. But he pledges his life (*"Anything"*) to Dumbledore to protect her from Voldemort.

Pettigrew's betrayal results in the Potter parents' death despite the Fidelius Charm Dumbledore used to protect Harry's family. Dumbledore subsequently extracts from Severus a pledge to protect Harry Potter. Snape signs on in memory of Lily, and to ensure Lily's sacrifice to save her son was not in vain. Dumbledore wins this pledge from the grieving Snape by sharing a physiognomic point with the new Potions Master; the Boy Who Lived has his mother's eyes.

> *"Her boy survives," said Dumbledore.*
>
> *With a tiny jerk of his head, Snape seemed to flick off an irksome fly.*

"Her son lives. He has her eyes, precisely her eyes. You remember the shape and color of Lily Evans's eyes, I am sure?"

"DON'T!" bellowed Snape. "Gone... dead..."

"Is this remorse, Severus?"

"I wish... I wish I were dead...."

"And what use would that be to anyone? said Dumbledore coldly. "If you loved Lily Evans, if you truly loved her, then your way forward is clear."

(Deathly Hallows, Chapter 33, p. 678)

Hence the importance of Harry's eyes being just like his mother's. Their shape and color trigger remorse or grief in Severus, "what Dumbledore would call love," the agony makes him a great Occulomens and double agent, and the love moves him to sacrifice his public life to protect Lily's son, the prophesied vanquisher of Lord Voldemort. We see what value these eyes have to Snape in hindsight because of the many times he locks eyes with Harry in the first six books, but most especially in his Shrieking Shack final request at his death:

When the flask [of memories] was filled to the brim, and Snape looked as though there was no blood left in him, his grip on Harry's robe slackened.

"Look...at...me...." he whispered.

The green eyes found the black, but after a second, something in the depths of the dark pair seemed to vanish, leaving them fixed, blank, and empty. The hand holding Harry thudded to the floor, and Snape moved no more.

(Deathly Hallows, Chapter 32, page 658)

It's no accident that Snape's memories in "The Prince's Tale" come to us in Chapter 33 of *Deathly Hallows*. The three parts of *The Divine Comedy* are 33 Cantos or 'Chapters' long (with an introductory piece to make one hundred cantos in all). When we see "33," we're meant to think "Dante and *The Divine Comedy*," especially if we recall the importance of Beatrice's eyes in that epic poem.

We first learn Beatrice's eyes are green from the Four Virtues, nymphs that pull Dante from the ablutionary dip and drink he takes in Lethe after confessing infidelity of sorts to Beatrice. We are in the last cantos of the poet's trip through Purgatory as they tell him:

100 The lovely lady spread her arms,
101 then clasped my head, and plunged me under,
102 where I was forced to swallow water.

103 Then she drew me out and led me, bathed,
104 into the dance of the four lovely ladies
105 as each one raised an arm above my head.

106 'Here we are nymphs and in heaven we are stars.
107 Before Beatrice descended to the world
108 we were ordained to serve her as her handmaids.

109 'We will bring you to her eyes. But to receive
110 the joyous light they hold, the other three,
111 who look much deeper into things, shall sharpen yours.'

112 Thus they began their song and then
113 they took me to the griffin's breast,
114 where Beatrice stood and faced us.

115 They said: 'Do not withhold your gaze.
116 We have placed you here before the emeralds [the green eyes]
117 from which, some time ago, Love shot his darts.'

118 A thousand desires hotter than any flame
119 bound my eyes to those shining eyes,
120 which still remained fixed on the griffin.

121 Even as the sun in a mirror, not otherwise
122 the twofold beast shone forth in them,
123 now with the one, now with its other nature.

124 Consider, reader, whether I was struck by wonder
125 when I saw the thing itself remain as one
126 but in its image ever changing.

127 While my soul, filled with wonder and with joy,
128 tasted the food that, satisfying in itself,
129 yet for itself creates a greater craving,

130 the other three, who by their bearing
131 showed themselves of a higher order, moved forward,
132 dancing to their angelic roundelay.

133 'Turn, Beatrice, turn your holy eyes
134 upon your faithful one'–thus ran their song–
135 'who, to see you, now has come so far.

136 'Of your grace do us a grace: unveil
137 your mouth to him so that he may observe
138 the second beauty that you still conceal.'

139 O splendor of eternal living light–
140 even he who has grown pale in the shadow of Parnassus
141 or has drunk deeply from its well,

142 would not even he appear to have his mind confounded,
143 attempting to describe you as you looked,
144 Heaven with its harmonies reflected in you,

145 when in the wide air you unveiled yourself?

(*Purgatorio*, Canto XXXI, 100-145, translation courtesy *Princeton Dante Project*,[5]
emphases mine)

Dorothy Sayers here, as an aside, in her note on Beatrice's "emerald eyes" writes "the phrase [orbs of emeralds] probably means no more than "shining like jewels"; though, if we like to suppose that the eyes were of a greenish hazel, there is no reason why we should not" (Penguin, *The Divine Comedy 2: Purgatory*, p. 321). There may be no reason why we *should not*, but there is reason why we *should*. Beatrice is dressed in three colors, green, white, and red, we learned in the previous canto at her appearance:

31 olive-crowned above a veil of white
32 appeared to me a lady, beneath a green mantle,
33 dressed in the color of living flame.

Purgatorio, Canto XXX, 31-33, translation courtesy *Princeton Dante Project*

These colors are the traditional hues of the theological virtues: faith, hope, and charity. As the University of Texas online notes[6] for *Purgatorio* explain at Beatrice's entrance in Canto XXX:

*Beatrice will perform her role as Dante's guide for the rest of the journey in various ways, but she initially takes a harsh approach (she is compared to an admiral in 30.58-66) as the judge of Dante's past transgressions. Her appearance in this biblical location, the site of humankind's fall from innocence, contains multiple layers of symbolism. Donning the colors of the three holy virtues (**white veil for faith, green cape for hope, and red dress for love: 30.31-3**), Beatrice is greeted by her angelic companions with words echoing those used to announce Jesus' arrival in Jerusalem (30.19). After extracting a painful confession from Dante (31.31-90), she presides over an allegorical display of providential history and finally offers an enigmatic prophecy of future salvation (33.40-5).*

Beatrice's eyes are emerald green, then, rather than just "shining like jewels" of any color, because her face of pale skin, red lips, and green eyes reveal and reflect virtues essential to Dante's journey to God as clearly as do her clothes. And her eyes are critically important. Not only are looking deeply into these green eyes Dante's means of transport through the planetary spheres of Paradise, but at the entrance of Paradise in the passage above, Dante beholds the Christ in his beloved's eyes, both in his two natures and their resolution.

> 115 They said: 'Do not withhold your gaze.
> 116 We have placed you here before the emeralds
> 117 from which, some time ago, Love shot his darts.'
>
> 118 A thousand desires hotter than any flame
> 119 bound my eyes to those shining eyes,
> 120 which still remained fixed on the griffin.
>
> 121 Even as the sun in a mirror, not otherwise
> 122 the twofold beast shone forth in them,
> 123 now with the one, now with its other nature.
>
> 124 Consider, reader, whether I was struck by wonder
> 125 when I saw the thing itself remain as one
> 126 but in its image ever changing.

This griffin has "wings (stretching high out of sight) and other aquiline features are gold in color, while his hind quarters are a mixture of white and deep red."[7] Gryffindor, you'll recall, is French for "golden griffin" and, having met Dante's Griffin, you now know why the Gryffindor colors are red and gold. If you've read the traditional symbolism chapter of *Unlocking Harry Potter: Five Keys for the Serious Reader* (and you should if you haven't), you also know that the griffin – half-eagle, half-lion – is a cipher for Christ, King of Heaven and of Earth.

Dante, looking into Beatrice's eyes, sees what he cannot see looking at the griffin himself. Purified again and again on the mountain of Purgatory and standing on the threshold of Paradise, he sees in symbol– *in his beloved's green eyes* – the Transcendent/Immanent God/Man both in His two natures, and in the unity of these natures, a shadow of the Beatific Vision awaiting him at the end of his journey through Paradise.

People who complain about *Deathly Hallows* in my company at conferences have usually told me they didn't like the way Snape dies and they don't like the Epilogue. If anything, as Snape fans they should be thrilled. Severus Snape's death after his last wish has been granted and he stares into Lily/Harry's eyes, if it is the deliberate echo of Dante's vision through Beatrice's "orbs of emerald" as it seems to be, is both his redemption and salvation.

Dante's love for Beatrice was a beginning love that grew into a spiritual vision of Love Himself (cf., Socrates' speech about Diotima in *The Symposium* of which Dante's *Convivio* is an echo [both words mean "banquet" or "drinking party"]). Severus' childhood love for Lily, a marker of which lives in the eyes of her son, has grown, through courageous self-sacrifice and love of his enemy, to become his encounter with Christ in the figure of Harry and in Lily's eyes, at his death. Seemingly destroyed by the serpent of his Slytherin nature, he embraces and sees at his death his Golden Griffin reward for his heroic life.

A disappointing finish? Hardly. Snape's death is horrible, I'll grant you that, but his victory seems complete. Without the Dante echo, however, the death-with-memory-dump strikes the reader, I'm guessing, as just a plot-point necessity and neglects a large part of the epic ("this is the way to get Harry, at the last minute, in on Severus' and Albus' plan to defeat Voldemort..."). With the Dante echo, however, the huge Severus Snape sub-plot has a tie-up that congeals with much of Ms. Rowling's postmodern meaning and traditional symbolism. I cannot think of a way to change or improve it, especially as it seems to be the ending foreshadowed by Harry's fight with the Basilisk in *Chamber* and salvation through Fawkes' tears.

[For a note on Beatrice's green eyes in another bestselling novel, pick up a copy of *The Dante Club* by Matthew Pearl and read page 239. It's not just green-eyed ladies that think this is an important piece of *The Divine Comedy*.]

Candida Rosa:
The Meeting of Albus Potter and Rose Weasley in the Epilogue

The second Dante screamer that knocked me down was in the Epilogue. On the Hogwarts Express platform we're introduced to the children of Harry and Ginny and of Ron and Hermione. I've discussed the meaning of their names at some length in the next chapter but here's a preview:

- *James Potter:* namesake of James Potter, probable link to St. James, brother of the Lord and Patron Saint of Alchemists

- *Albus Severus Potter* (ASP): the longed-for resolution of Gryffindor/Slytherin antagonism, both a Potter/Gryffindor legacy and serpentine/Slytherin destiny

- *Lily Potter*: namesake of Lily Evans Potter, a token of the Severus/Lily love, and as "lily" a symbol of purity in general and of the white stage of alchemy specifically

- *Rose Weasley*: the Red Rose is a cipher for the Philosopher's Stone, the resolution of all contraries; inevitable, I guess, for the child of mercury and sulphur, which are the principal reagents of alchemy (her red hair makes her a "red Rose")

- *Hugo Weasley*: a stand-in for Victor Hugo, French poet, novelist and hermeticist, or another alchemical reference,[8] because the consonants of the first name, like Hermione's maiden name initials, are Hg, the periodic table abbreviation for mercury

- *"Potter"* is a Biblical cipher for God, Who "shapes the Human Vessel;"

- *"Weasley,"* as in "like a Weasel" is a pointer to Christ because of the traditional symbolism of the weasel as an animal that destroys the Basilisk by sacrificing itself for its loved ones.

The Dante screamer here is the conjunction, at the end of the story, of one character named "white" (Albus) and one named "rose" (um, Rose). In alchemy, the white rose has the same meaning as a lily, which wouldn't make much sense here, because this isn't the end of the white work by any means, and we already have a Lily on hand. The *white rose*,[9] though, or *candida rosa*[10] is one of Dante's most important mind pictures at the end of *Paradiso*. As the UTexas online notes for the Paradiso describe it:

> *The true home of all the blessed is with God in the Empyrean, a heaven of pure light beyond time and space. Dante sees the blessed systematically arranged in an immense white rose: like a holograph, a three-dimensional structure of light, the rose is formed from a ray of light reflected off the outer surface of the Primum Mobile (30.106-17).[11]*

Dorothy Sayers explains:

> *The White Rose: The circle of light, which is the light of God's glory, forms the yellow of the vast white rose which Dante next*

beholds. Its petals rising in more than a thousand tiers are the
thrones of the blessed, whom Dante can perceive despite the
distance, for he is now beyond the limitations of time and space.
The rose in medieval literature was the symbol of earthly love;
Dante's white rose is the symbol of divine love (Penguin, *The*
Divine Comedy 3: Paradise, p. 324).

Ms. Rowling, at the farewell to Hogwarts students at Platform 9 3/4, 19 years after Harry's victory, leaves us with the White Rose. It isn't the Beatific Vision, but as explained in the next chapter, it's the beginning of the resolution of remaining Gryffindor/Slytherin enmity. The peace consequent to young Albus' assumed victory-to-come in the wizarding world, if based, as we should expect, on sacrifice and love, will be the peace that passeth understanding, the peace of the Absolute/Infinite Father. About as close to the White Rose finish of the *Commedia* as we could get on a train station platform!

Three 'Dante' Places; Three Harry Potter Generations

My last Dante screamers in *Harry Potter* are variants on the hero's journey – one in space and one in time. Again, if you've read *Unlocking Harry Potter: Five Keys for the Serious Reader*, or just Chapter 1 of this book, you know the importance and the details of Harry's formulaic journey every year, and the specific variants Ms. Rowling has added to the Classical track of the *Odyssey* and *Aeneid*. These variants, especially as evident in *Deathly Hallows*, are specifically Christian ones, namely Harry's going underground before his resurrection from a figurative death in the presence of a symbol of Christ. In *Hallows*, Harry and friends, depending on how you count it, "harrow hell" or go underground to rescue someone or something between five and ten times.

The screamer in *Deathly Hallows* about Harry's journey echoing Dante's in *The Divine Comedy*, was the title to Chapter 34, "Into the Forest Again." Harry has been in a few forests in the last book, most notably the Forest of Dean in which "The Silver Doe" appears and Ron returns. But there hasn't been a forest entry in a chapter title in any of the books, or mention of "The Forbidden Forest" in a title since Chapter 15 of *Philosopher's Stone*. That might be the meaning of "Again" in the Chapter 34 title in *Hallows*. There is, however, a more obvious and more meaningful reference.

Chapter 33, "The Prince's Tale", you'll recall, linked Dante and Severus, because each book or cantica of the *Commedia* is 33 cantos. Chapter 34, the story of Harry's walk into the woods to sacrifice himself to defeat the Horcrux within him and the enemy outside him, is his fantasy-story "Holy Friday" walk to Calvary. Dante's journey through Inferno, Purgatorio, and Paradiso begins with his waking in the woods on Holy Friday in the year 1300:

> 1 Midway in the journey of our life
> 2 I came to myself in a dark wood,
> 3 for the straight way was lost.
>
> 4 Ah, how hard it is to tell
> 5 the nature of that wood, savage, dense and harsh –
> 6 the very thought of it renews my fear!
>
> 7 It is so bitter death is hardly more so.
> 8 But to set forth the good I found
> 9 I will recount the other things I saw.
>
> *Inferno*, Canto I, 1-9, translation courtesy *Princeton Dante Project*

Dante's walk in the woods to God ends at Easter, much as Harry's agony ends at the rising of the sun in the Great Hall ceiling at his conquest of Voldemort. The title "Into the Forest Again" is Ms. Rowling's hat-tip to the agony of Dante, the first and greatest Christian everyman and spiritual pilgrim, and a pointer to the meaning of Harry's trip into the Forbidden Forest. Ms. Rowling has said that when she finished this chapter, she wept both because of its events and her relief in finishing the chapter to which the series pointed. That this chapter begins with a Dante screamer title is no small thing.

But there's more...

Harry's adventure is not only a series of seven hero journeys in the present; his alchemical education is also a wave in the tide of generational cycles. At Hogwarts, his father had two close friends, a hanger-on, and a foe in Slytherin House he and his friends despised. Harry, too, has two close friends, a hanger-on, and a foe in Slytherin House he and his friends despise.

The differences? (1) The scar Horcrux and painful Muggle childhood which makes Harry less a wizard prince and more a Hogwarts

Hermaphrodite, (2) Harry's two friends include a Muggle-born witch of great intelligence who could and did confront him, and (3) Draco Malfoy isn't embittered by Harry winning his one true love. The result of these differences is Harry's transcendence of Gryffindor prejudices, victory over Voldemort, the redemption of sidekick Neville Longbottom and Draco's life-debt to Harry after the Battle of Hogwarts.

But there is a third wave of generations that we meet on the Epilogue platform. I think we can expect, just as Hermione was the infolding into the Inner Triumvirate of the Lily figure of Harry's father generation, that Draco's son Scorpius will be the inclusion of the Slytherin foe into Albus Severus' trio.

Albus, Rose, and Scorpius won't battle Voldemort, but they will, as the third generation and "white rose," enter the Paradise of Love and the end of the Four House metanarrative, which divides and causes the prejudices of all wizards and witches at Hogwarts. Dante journeys through the three "places" of hell, purgatory, and paradise in Holy Week to achieve the Beatific Vision of God's glory; Ms. Rowling has told us the central tale of three generations of heroic trinities that come to the same end and bring the magical world with them.

To begin the conversation about the Dante in Ms. Rowling's compost pile of books out of which Harry sprang, then, I offer these four assertions:

(1) The depth of Dante's influence on Ms. Rowling is surpassed only by Austen and, perhaps, Shakespeare, though she has never, to my knowledge, mentioned the Florentine poet in her answers to questions about "favorite authors;"

(2) The green-eyed girls connection, especially with reference to Severus' death and Dante's *Purgatorio* vision of the Griffin while staring into these eyes, is a key link in understanding the redemption of Snape;

(3) The "white rose" event of the Epilogue is a pointer to Dante's beatific vision and the ultimate resolution of the Gryffindor/Slytherin polarity in the Wizarding world; and

(4) The repeated character trinities across three generations in the Harry Potter epic point to the three canticas and three-laden structure of *The Divine Comedy*.

If it's been a few years since you pulled Dante off the shelf or, if you haven't read *The Divine Comedy,* I urge you to get started. "Firenze 2000+," my hoped-for *Harry Potter* conference in Florence, Italy, will be here sooner than you think! I look forward to hearing your thoughts there about the connection between the bestselling books of our times and what many feel is the best poem/epic/tale ever written.

Endnotes

1   http://www.dantesociety.org/mission.html

2   http://search.atomz.com/search/?sp_a=sp100168f8&sp_q=Dante&submit=Search&sp_p=any&sp_f=iso-8859-1

3   http://dante.ilt.columbia.edu/books/convivi/convivio2.html#01

4   http://iws.ccccd.edu/Andrade/WorldLitI2332/Dante/inf_dore_01.002.jpeg

5   http://etcweb.princeton.edu/dante/pdp/

6   http://danteworlds.laits.utexas.edu/purgatory/10terrestrialparadise.html#beatrice

7   http://danteworlds.laits.utexas.edu/purgatory/10terrestrialparadise.html#griffin

8   http://hogwartsprofessor.com/?p=211#comment-18702

9   see http://www.artsycraftsy.com/dore/dore34.html and click for Dore illustration

10   http://books.google.com/books?id=_ZkMAAAAYAAJ&pg=PA374&lpg=PA374&dq=dante+candida+rosa&source=web&ots=WPDmV47uVr&sig=zCVSx9fGG_unfAOMYYpmATIurOc

11   http://danteworlds.laits.utexas.edu/paradiso/10empyrean.html#rose

Chapter 5

The Seeing Eye

Deathly Hallows' Eye and Mirror Symbolism

If you have just finished Chapter 4's explanation of why Lily and Harry's eyes are green, and what this means in terms of Snape's death and redemption, I am obliged to forewarn you. That was only the opening salvo in our discussion of eyes, literature, transcendence, and symbolism.

Deathly Hallows has four other eye events, besides the Potion Master's plaintive "Look ... at ... me...", that Ms. Rowling brings to our attention and that, taken together, make eyes the central symbol of the series finale. The four other eyes in the *Deathly Hallows* story line are: Dumbledore's eye in the remnant shard of the mirror Harry received from his Godfather; Mad-Eye Moody's magical eye; Riddle's eyes in the Locket Horcrux; and the Hallows symbol, which Ms. Rowling describes twice as a "triangular eye."

Looking at these eyes and their meaning, *Deathly Hallows* appears to be a story-symbol about the importance of story and symbols. It's central symbol is the eye, whose traditional meaning and Ms. Rowling's argument is largely that we are *how* we see; our 'eye-dentity' in our self awareness is divine; and that the most real understanding of the world comes from seeing symbolically. This story-vision reveals God-in-everything and most especially in us. Ms. Rowling explains through story that reading symbolist literature – fables and fantasy – plays an important part in correcting our occluded vision so we can see and know things as they are, and with this vision, become human – three-dimensional symbols of God.

I assume you find this hard to believe, especially the last. I can't blame you. Like Hermione, we're all skeptical about stories having important, even life-changing meaning or real-world relevance and referents (and think "Elvendorks" who take fantasy that seriously are a lot like Xenophilius Lovegood, professional nut-job).

Getting to Ms. Rowling's traditional use of eye symbolism, consequently, will take three chapters, believe it or not. The first part of the trip requires a fresh look at *Deathly Hallows'* eye passages, and includeds side-trips to outer-space with C. S. Lewis, and to Xanadu with Samuel Taylor Coleridge, in order to arrive at an understanding of the "seeing eye," seeing symbolically, and what readers experience in stories as they suspend disbelief. Along the way, we'll learn about Harry's relationship with the Mirror of Erised and the "eye in the mirror," the Locket Horcrux eyes, and his corrected vision at King's Cross. In Chapters 6 and 7, we'll get to the three-dimensional meaning of the Hallows symbol and its story echo in the burial of Moody's "Mad-Eye."

Our first stop is the winter of 1961, and entertainment magazine article on why cosmonauts couldn't see God when they looked for him in outer space.

Looking for God – in Outer Space
and the Reflection of the Mind's Eye

Those of us Americans who grew up during the heat of the Soviet-American Cold War remember the "space race," especially the first lunar landing and walk-about, which was a defining national moment. C. S. Lewis, at home in the UK, thought this superpower race a waste of both money and effort.

> The more money, time, skill and zeal [the U.S. and U.S.S.R.] both spend on that rivalry, the less, we may hope, they will have to spend on armaments. Great powers might be more usefully, but are seldom less dangerously, employed than in fabricating costly objects and flinging them, as you might say, overboard. Good luck to it! It is an excellent way of letting off steam.[1]

The Soviets, though, used their space adventures to advance their atheist propaganda. They claimed that cosmonauts "have not found God in outer space." Lewis contributed an article on that subject to *Show: The Magazine of the Performing Arts* for their February 1961 issue. Originally titled 'Onward, Christian Spacemen' by the American editor, a title Lewis disliked, it has been republished in various essay collections since as 'The Seeing Eye.'

It is a short piece, but it has two responses to the Soviet implication "from their data" that God does not exist. The first is an argument from analogy. If God exists, he exists with respect to his creation the way Shakespeare exists to his plays.

> Looking for God – or Heaven – by exploring space is like reading or seeing all Shakespeare's plays in the hope that you will find Shakespeare as one of the characters or Stratford as one of the places. But he is never present in the same way as Falstaff or Lady Macbeth. Nor is he diffused through the play as a gas.[2]

Lewis allows that "if there were an idiot who thought plays existed on their own, without an author," and who did see all the plays, he probably would have "in reality been in some way affected by Shakespeare, but without knowing it." Which brings us to Lewis' second point and the reason his piece was titled "The Seeing Eye." The idiot "lacked the necessary apparatus for detecting Shakespeare."

The "necessary apparatus" for finding God, Lewis believed, is essentially conscience, or a mind-aware-of-itself. Listening to his "guide within" as a young man, he was surprised that his picture of himself came "down to something nearer life-size." He explains, while describing that experience to others, how obedience to conscience reveals the false-front of ego:

> And presently you begin to ponder whether you are yet, in any full sense, a person at all; whether you are entitled to call yourself 'I' (it is a sacred name).... You find what you called yourself is only a thin film on the surface of an unsounded and dangerous sea'. One's ordinary self, then, is a mere façade. There's a huge area out of sight behind it. And, then, if one listens to the physicists, one discovers that the same is true of all the things around us....

> Presently, if you are a person of a certain sort, if you are one who has to believe that all things which exist must have unity, it will seem to you irresistibly probable that what lies ultimately behind the one façade also lies ultimately behind the other. And then again, if you are that sort of person, you may come to be convinced that your contact with that mystery in the area you call yourself is a good deal closer than your contact through what you call matter. For in the one case I, the ordinary, conscious I, am continuous with the unknown depth.

And after that, you may come (some do) to believe that that voice – like all the rest, I must speak symbolically – that voice which speaks in your conscience and in some of your intensest joys, which is sometimes so obstinately silent, sometimes so easily silenced, and then at other times so loud and emphatic, is in fact the closest contact you have with the mystery and therefore finally to be trusted, obeyed, feared and desired more than all other things. But still, if you are a different sort of person, you will not come to this conclusion....

To some, God is discoverable everywhere; to others, nowhere. Those who do not find Him on earth are unlikely to find Him in space. (Hang it all, we're in space already; every year we go a huge circular tour in space.) But send a saint up in a spaceship and he'll find God in space as he found God on earth. Much depends on the seeing eye.[3]

Note two things here. First, the equation of "seeing" and "knowing," as in common speech. If a teacher asks us "Do you see now?", she isn't inquiring about our vision or ocular abilities but about our mental grasp of a given subject, that is, our knowledge or understanding. Seeing is knowing. "See?" Lewis writes here about "finding," "looking," discerning behind the "seeming," and "the seeing eye" as the work and name of conscience – the faculty by which we "see" what is more real, beneath what the physical eyes can see in objects or self.

Second, note the playful use of the assonant "I" and "eye." Lewis isn't the first to do this; Swift shoots Descartes – Mr. "I think, therefore I am" – in the eye in *Battle of the Books*. But Lewis is after much bigger game than Swift. He is saying "symbolically" that the ego-self "I" is a façade and hardly a person at all. The real self (over which the ego exists as a "thin film") is an "I" which is "sacred" and "continuous with" the unity of existence behind each person and everything. That part of us capable of thinking about thinking, what Lewis here calls the conscience, is the "seeing eye" or *"seeing."*

Lewis goes on to say that knowing God or seeing him is a function of a "certain faculty of recognition":

Indeed the expectation of finding God by astronautics would be very like trying to verify or falsify the divinity of Christ by taking specimens of His blood or dissecting Him. And in their own way they did both. But they were no wiser than before. What is required is a certain faculty of recognition. If you do not at all know God, of course, you will not recognize Him, either in Jesus or in outer space.[4]

"Methods of science" – analysis and measure of mass and energy quantities, the work of the eyeballs rather than the "seeing eye" – "do not discover facts of that order." Perceiving divinity and the sacred, even the Christ in the man Jesus, is a matter of "recognizing" him.

"Recognition" has two meanings or aspects linked to sight; the first is a function of memory and recall, the second one of reflection or, literally, "knowing-back." The first is common usage. We see someone or thing and we recognize it as an item or person we have seen before, even if it is changed or obscured in some way. "I would have recognized her anywhere." "Bob recognized the symptoms of his friend's paranoia peeking out from his questions."

This is not, except perhaps in a Platonic sense of memory, the case with "the faculty of recognition" that Lewis says allows perception of the sacred. Having said that awareness or "knowing" God is a function of "recognizing" him, Lewis ties a knot with the two strings of seeing/ knowing and eye/I mentioned earlier. If we look within ourselves, we will understand our "conscious I" is "sacred," and "continuous with" the greater reality and unity beneath and behind existence. This self-reflective act of seeing is our means of knowing God (or of his hunting us down) – and of being able, thereafter, to recognize him in things on earth, in outer space, or in Jesus of Nazareth. (Readers of Lewis will recognize this idea of the mind's self-awareness as his "argument from reason," contra scientism and naturalism, in *Miracles*.)

In his conclusion, Lewis characterizes this "reflective" meaning of recognition as the ability to see the sacred everywhere. In an abrupt closing paragraph he invites the reader to disregard what he has said as stuff "from the realm of fantastic speculation." The empiricist mind reads "fantastic speculation" and thinks "fairy tale thinking that is totally subjective." This reader turns the page of *Show* for a different article more worthy of his attention. Lewis the classicist, however, knows that "speculation" is from the Latin word *speculum* meaning "mirror;" hence, "fantastic speculation" is about the wonders revealed by looking at and through the transparency of oneself, into the depth of the unknown mystery. Much indeed "depends upon the seeing eye" and seeing the sacred "I" behind the façade of ego.

This can be called "epistemological theology," a very academic way of saying "knowing God by means of knowing how we know." Lewis holds that a specific faculty of soul – the mind or, more properly, the noetic and spiritual aspect of mind – is continuous with reality, and the Creator who is the Supreme Reality. The *logos* of the human mind, to risk simplification, is an extension of (if not identical with) the *Logos* or Divine Word that creates all things. Our knowledge of ourselves, ideas, and physical things, as well, is the divine in us, *recognizing* himself in the *logoi* of the things he has created.

Samuel Taylor Coleridge and the Transformed Vision

I imagine quite a few of you are rolling your eyeballs at this point, or just wondering if I am *really* trying to link a 1961 Lewis essay in a long defunct American magazine and the *Deathly Hallows* eyeball-in-the-mirror Harry sees several times. That would be a stretch, I admit. Fortunately for my argument and self-respect, "The Seeing Eye" and Lewis' epistemological theology aren't obscure intellectual items we can bet Ms. Rowling has never heard of. Assuming she hasn't read that 1961 essay is a good bet, I think; it's very unlikely that she's unfamiliar with the philosophical underpinnings of the literary tradition in which she writes. Because Lewis' ideas about the "eye/I" that sees and knows God everywhere is a big part of that tradition.

It's not insulting Lewis to point out that these ideas are not peculiar to him, and they certainly don't have their beginnings with him. Besides the German Romantics of the 19th century, the usual sources cited for these ideas are Plato, the neo-Platonists like Plotinus, and the gang of Florentine hermeticists we discussed in Chapter four that Ms. Rowling seems to be well aware of. If there is a specific single , specific person, though, in whom all these ancient, Renaissance, and Romantic sources intersect into a single starting point for English "high fantasy" or "symbolist literature," it is Samuel Taylor Coleridge, the Bard of Ottery St. Mary.

Lewis, of course, knew Coleridge at greater depth than passing familiarity with *Rime of the Ancient Mariner* and *Kublai Khan*. His personal library included, along with the *Complete Poetry*, Coleridge's important and challenging literary, philosophical, and theological texts, most notably, the *Aids to Reflection* and his *Biographia Literaria*. George MacDonald, too, the man Lewis referred to simply as his "master," was influenced by Coleridge, as well as the eminent theologian

F. D. Maurice, a disciple of Coleridge. Owen Barfield, the man Lewis called "the best and wisest of my unofficial teachers," was eyeball-deep in Coleridge's philosophy and theology; his *What Coleridge Thought* (1971) is considered a seminal work in Coleridge studies, as well as Inkling thought. And epistemological theology is a big part of both.[5]

In brief, Coleridge held that, to free ourselves from the cave-prison of empiricism (which holds that knowledge is restricted to information from sense experience of physical objects) and that to know God, that a "transformed vision" was necessary – a seeing of the world symbolically through the "communicative intellect," the *logos* within that is continuous with the *Logos* without.[6] The Inkling stream of iconological or symbolist literature – of which strong current Ms. Rowling is only the most recent wave – flowing from Coleridge's synthesis of Schiller and Bruno, Plotinus and Dante, echoes this understanding. Coleridge went so far as to assert that this transformed vision, and consequent experience and knowledge of God, is the heart and substance of Christian redemption.[7] More to the point, fostering this transformation and penetrating vision is the purpose of story. And story must be rich in symbols, because understanding the world and oneself *symbolically* reveals the mystery of the depth behind all facades.

The most telling Harry Potter illustrations for this point are Moody's Disillusionment Charm in *Phoenix* and the answers Luna and MacGonagall give to the Ravenclaw Common Room door in *Deathly Hallows*. The Charm Moody uses to conceal Harry for the flight from Privet Drive to Grimmauld Place makes him transparent, which Ms. Rowling calls "Disillusionment." The visible surface is the veil or illusion, and seeing clearly or to be freed from illusion is to see pass the surface to the greater reality within. The "inside greater than the outside,"of course, is a point made repeatedly in the books.[8]

Luna answers the magical equivalent of the chicken and egg riddle, "Which came first, the phoenix or the flame?" with the Gnostic truism "A circle has no beginning." (*Hallows*, Chapter 29, page 587). This is true but is important in highlighting the greater reality that a circle *does* have a defining center which is its *non-spatial*, invisible beginning or logical origin. MacGonagall puts her finger on this divine "intelligible sphere with a center which is everywhere and circumference nowhere"[9] when she answers the question, "Where do Vanished objects go?" by saying "Into non-being, which is to say everything" (*Hallows*, Chapter 30, page 591). On the analogy of the circle, vanished objects return to the unicity of existence in the interior origin (non-being, the Absolute) which center is common to all things.

This sort of interior or transcendent revealing symbol is not the sign, cipher, analogy, simile, metaphor, or allegory you may have studied in English classes or read about in semiotics textbooks. Coleridgean symbols, seen with a transformed vision, are a means to experience of and relationship with the unity beneath the façade:

> In Coleridge's vocabulary, symbols like polarities are therefore among the fundamental means of evoking true unity. As the fusion of general and concrete, idea and image, individual and representative, a symbol points to the relationship between a particular thing and the whole, between a particular object or event and the totality of all other things and events. Notice we do not say all *similar* things. That would be a simile, or even a metaphor.

> But a symbol is much more. It is the name for the relationship of a particularity to totality. In answer to the question, How can, in fact, each be in all? The Coleridgean response is: symbolically. How can a man have a vision of total introsusception, if everything he sees gets in the way? By seeing those things as symbols. Or rather, since this locution suggests a certain pretense or fabrication, by realizing that things *are* symbols. The transformation of vision means learning to see symbolically. And the visible phenomenon with which Coleridge most closely identifies the power of symbols, is translucence or transparency, the passage of light through a transmitting medium.[10]

Lewis' "seeing eye" looks through objects and self as transparent facades for the greater unity – even the divinity – in the "depth" and "mystery" beneath.[11] This is seeing the symbol or object as what it is more truly than as an object displacing space:

> For when it is a symbol, a thing becomes much more than itself. There is a melting away of the solidity of idem, an evaporating of the surface of its identity, as it assumes the value and meaning, even substance, normally enclosed in the identity of others. In the words of chemical Logic, a symbol "always partakes of the Reality which it renders intelligible; and while it enunciates the whole, abides itself as a living part in that Unity, of which it is the representative (*Aids to Reflection*, p. 156)."[12]

Imaginative literature, for Coleridge and his many disciples, most notably, I think, in MacDonald and the Inkling symbolist writers, is a powerful help in acquiring a knowledge of God, because symbols, in things and in stories, assume the value and meaning of their more real referents; and, as Lewis insisted, "imagination is the organ of meaning."[13] A neglected and atrophied imagination, in any child or adult, ensures mental and spiritual retardation and distortion, because it precludes a spiritually-minded (Romans 6:8) or sacramental world view. Story, myth, fairy tale, and legends, rich in imaginative substance and symbolic meaning, are delightful fare to exercise and nourish this faculty of soul. "Reading the right stories," as Lewis wrote in *Voyage of the Dawn Treader*, is the difference between a scientific, facade-focused Eustace Scrubb and the noble, heroic Prince Caspian.

The Symbolism of the Mirror: The Mirror of Erised

Though everything can be understood as a symbol, all symbols are not created equal. As a transparency to view one or more corresponding supernatural referents, or as a "'key' to supra-rational realities,"[14] some objects serve as symbols better than others. Martin Lings, tutorial student and friend of C. S. Lewis, explains:

> Since nothing can exist except in virtue of its Divine root, does that mean everything is a symbol? The answer is yes and no – yes for the reason just given, and no because 'symbol' means 'sign' or 'token', which implies an inoperative power to call something to mind, namely its Archetype. In the light of the initially quoted verse *Nor is there anything but glorifieth Him with praise*, we could say that whether this or that can rightly be called symbolic depends on whether its 'praise' is powerful or faint. The word symbol is normally reserved for that which is particularly impressive in its 'glorification.'[15]

An especially praise-powerful symbol is the mirror. Ms. Rowling, as suggested in Chapter 2, is probably familiar with the work of Swiss art historian and alchemy authority, Titus Burckhardt. In his essay "The Symbolism of the Mirror" Burckhardt explains:

> The mirror is the most immediate symbol of spiritual contemplation, and indeed of knowledge (*gnosis*) in general, for it portrays the union of subject and object.[16]

Remember "epistemological theology"? An objective, distinct human observer can't acquire *spiritual* knowledge (*gnosis* or *Sophia*) by gathering information from sense organs relaying data about physical objects in time and space. That is mechanical knowledge (*scientia*), derived from sense perception and extrapolation from same. Spiritual knowledge, in contrast (as understood by the traditional camp of Platonists, Romantics, and Orthodox Christians), is the *recognition* or *reflection* of object *logoi* in created things or ideas, by the *Logos* within the *nous* or communicative intellect of the subject. A mirror is the only thing in which subject and object are joined, and, as such, it is perhaps the best physical transparency or symbol through which we can "see" or experience what knowledge *per se* really is. Because this knowledge requires understanding every created thing as a symbol, the mirror, as a symbol of knowledge, is a "symbol of symbolism," as Burckhardt explains:

> [T]he symbolism of the mirror is as illuminating as it is because, in a sense, the mirror is the symbol of the symbol. Symbolism indeed can best be described as the visible reflection of ideas or prototypes that cannot be fully expressed in purely conceptual terms. In this sense, St. Paul says: 'For now we see through a glass [*di esoptrou, per speculum,* through a *mirror*], darkly, but then face to face: now I know in part; but then shall I know even as also I am known.' (1 Cor. 13;12.)
>
> What is the mirror in which the symbol appears as the image of an eternal prototype? Firstly, the imagination, if one is thinking of the visual or 'plastic' nature of the symbol in contradistinction from abstract concepts. But in a wider sense, it is the mind which, as the faculty of discrimination and knowledge, reflects the pure Intellect. In an even wider sense, the Intellect itself is the mirror of the divine Being. Plotinus says of the Intellect (*Nous*) that it contemplates the infinite One, and from this contemplation, which can never completely exhaust its object, the world proceeds as an ever imperfect image which may be compared to a continually broken reflection....
>
> The heart, centre of the human being, is therefore like a mirror, which must be pure, so that it may receive the light of the divine Spirit.... When the heart has become a pure mirror, the world is reflected in it as it really is, namely, without the distortions due to passional thought; in addition, the heart reflects the Divine Truth more or less directly, firstly in the form of symbols (*isharat*), then in the form of spiritual qualities (*sifat*) or essences (*ayan*), which lie behind the symbols, and finally as Divine Realities (*haqaiq*).[17]

Perhaps your head is hurting by now. Believe me, I understand. Let's take a break from Burckhardt and think about "pure hearts" and mirrors in *Harry Potter*. How about a look into the "Mirror of Erised"?

Dumbledore explained to Harry what the Mirror of Erised was in *Philosopher's Stone*:

"Let me explain. The happiest man on earth would be able to use the Mirror of Erised like a normal mirror, that is, he would look into it and see himself exactly as he is. Does that help?"

Harry thought. Then he said slowly "It shows us what we want ... whatever we want ..."

"Yes and no," said Dumbledore quietly. "It shows us nothing more or less than the deepest, most desperate desire of our hearts. You, who have never known your family, see them standing around you. Ronald Weasley, who has always been overshadowed by his brothers, sees himself standing alone, the best of all of them. However, this mirror will give us neither knowledge or truth. Men have wasted away before it, entranced by what they have seen, or been driven mad, not knowing if what it shows is real or even possible." (*Stone*, p. 213)

In *Half-Blood Prince's* critical "Horcrux" chapter, the Headmaster reviews Harry's achievement in *Stone's* battle between Harry and Quirrelldemort before the Mirror:

"In spite of all the temptation you have endured, all the suffering, you remain pure of heart, just as pure as you were at the age of eleven, when you stared into a mirror that reflected your heart's desire, and it showed you only the way to thwart Lord Voldemort, and not immortality or riches. Harry, have you any idea how few wizards could have seen what you saw in that mirror? Voldemort should have known then what he was dealing with, but he did not!

"But he knows it now. You have flitted into Lord Voldemort's mind without damage to yourself, but he cannot possess you without enduring mortal agony, as he discovered in the Ministry. I do not think he understands why, Harry, but then, he was in such a hurry to mutilate his own soul, he never paused to understand the incomparable power of a soul that is untarnished and whole." (*Prince*, p. 511)

Why should Voldemort have been impressed, even cowed, by the eleven-year-old Harry standing before the Mirror and seeing himself receiving the Philosopher's Stone? Review what happened way back then.

Harry only enters the final chamber after the feminine Hermes (Hermione) solves the puzzle of what Coleridge would certainly have recognized as "chemical Logic." The boy wizard passes through the fire, much as Dante passes through the purifying flames just before entering

Paradise, and finds himself in "the last chamber." After Quirrell explains the problem he's having getting the Stone out of the Mirror – as Quirrell himself says, he has a "special gift with Trolls" (p. 289), the dumbest of magical creatures, with whom he has a like capacity for liberating-knowledge (which is to say "none") – Harry realizes:

> Harry's mind was racing.
>
> *What I want more than anything else in the world at the moment,* he thought, *is to find the Stone before Quirrell does. So if I look in the mirror, I should see myself finding it – which means I'll see where it's hidden! But how can I look without Quirrell realizing what I'm up to?* (*Stone*, p. 291; italics in original)

The piggybacking Voldemort tells Quirrell to "use the boy" to get the Stone from the Mirror, so Harry gets his chance to act on his plan:

> He saw his reflection, pale and scared-looking at first. But a moment later, the reflection smiled at him. It put its hand into its pocket and pulled out a blood-red stone. It winked and put the Stone back in its pocket – and as it did so, Harry felt something heavy drop into his real pocket. Somehow – incredibly – *he'd gotten the Stone.* (*Stone*, p. 292; italics in original)

Recall Dumbledore's explanation to Harry of what he had done, once Harry arose from the dead in the infirmary, three days after his battle with the Dark Lord:

> "How did I get the Stone out of the mirror?"
>
> "Ah, now, I'm glad you asked me that. It was one of my more brilliant ideas, and between you and me, that's saying something. You see, only one who wanted to *find* the Stone – find it, but not use it – would be able to get it, otherwise they'd just see themselves making gold or drinking Elixir of Life. My brain surprises even me sometimes..." (*Stone*, p. 300; italics in original)

As I explain in *How Harry Cast His Spell*'s chapter on the traditional symbols Ms. Rowling uses in *Harry Potter*, the Philosopher's Stone, because the Elixir of Life that flows from it is a guarantor of eternal life (immortality) and spiritual riches (gold), it is a story-transparency or symbol for Christ. Christ is the Word or *Logos* of God. Unlike the troll-brained, evil-empiricist, Dark-Lord headset-wearing wizard standing before the Mirror of Erised in the last chamber, Harry has a pure heart. Consequently, Subject and Object, noetic logos and Christ-*Logos*, unite and the "pure of heart sees God" as Jesus Christ promised (Matthew

5:8). How? Harry's noetic faculty, or communicative intellect in the heart, sees the Stone as the *Logos* it is. The God who is Love (1 John 4:8) lives within Harry's pure heart and recognizes himself in the mirror.

Dumbledore thought Voldemort should have recognized that "the incomparable power of a soul that is untarnished and whole" made Harry a more-than-worthy opponent. As Burckhardt explains in his explanation of the mirror symbol, Harry's pure heart is his participation in or "continuity with" the divine unity:

> The process of reflection is perhaps the most perfect image of the 'process' of knowing, which is not exhausted at the rational level. The mirror *is* what it reflects, to the extent that it reflects. As long as the heart – i.e., the cognitive Intellect – reflects the multiplicity of the world, it *is* the world, according to the way of the world, namely with the scission of object and subject, of outward and inward. To the extent, however, that the mirror of the heart reflects divine Being, it *is* precisely this, according to the undivided mode of pure Being. In this sense, the Apostle Paul said: 'But we all, with open face beholding as in a glass [*avakekalummeno prosopto, speculantes*, seeing in a mirror] the glory of the Lord are changed into the same image....' (2 Cor. 3:18.)...
>
> If the universe as a whole is the mirror of God, so also is man in his original nature, since this qualitatively contains the whole universe, the mirror of the One.[18]

As for the circle symbolism explained earlier (Chapter 1, p. 20), Harry's purity of heart, and the reflection or dissolution of his "otherness" with the Divine Being, is his identity with the Absolute, represented by the circle's center—the unity, cause, and totality of the whole. Even the Dark Lord, if he could understand or "see" such things and still *be* the Dark Lord (cf. *Hallows*, p. 710), would not want to face such an opponent in mortal combat.[19]

The Eye in the Godfather's Mirror

It's time we fast forward to *Deathly Hallows*.

Harry's Phoenix-core wand (another Christ/logos symbol – see Chapter 1, page 27-28, for wand sentience and their Christ/*Logos* cores) "recognized," in Dumbledore's words, Harry's shadow-self in Lord Voldemort, during the flight from Little Whinging. As Dumbledore explained at King's Cross:

"I believe that your wand imbibed some of the power and qualities of Voldemort's wand that night [the graveyard battle at the end of *Goblet*], which is to say that it contained a little of Voldemort himself. So your wand *recognized* him when he pursued you, *recognized* a man who was both kin and mortal enemy, and it regurgitated some of his own magic against him, magic much more powerful than anything Lucius's wand had ever performed. Your wand now contained the power of your enormous courage and of Voldemort's own deadly skill: What chance did that poor stick of Lucius Malfoy's stand?" (*Hallows*, p. 711; emphasis added)

This "recognition" explanation is reminiscent of Harry, the Mirror of Erised, and the Philosopher's Stone in the first book, as well as with epistemological theology. But it's a faint echo compared to the eye Harry sees in the shard of the mirror given him by his godfather. Let's review Harry's experiences with the mirror shard from beginning to end of *Deathly Hallows*.

When we first meet Harry, he has hurt his hand cleaning his school trunk. The mirror shard is to blame:

Minutes previously, Harry had plunged his hand into this mulch, experienced a stabbing pain in the fourth finger of his right hand, and withdrawn it to see a lot of blood.

He now proceeded a little more cautiously. Kneeling down beside the trunk again, he groped around in the bottom and, after retrieving an old badge that flickered feebly between *SUPPORT CEDRIC DIGGORY* and *POTTER STINKS*, a cracked and worn-out Sneakoscope, and a gold locket inside which a note signed R.A.B. had been hidden, he finally discovered the sharp edge that had done the damage. He recognized it at once. It was a two-inch-long fragment of the enchanted mirror that his dead godfather, Sirius, had given him. Harry laid it aside and felt cautiously around the trunk for the rest, but nothing more remained of his godfather's last gift except powdered glass, which clung to the deepest layer of debris like glittering grit.

Harry sat up and examined the jagged piece on which he had cut himself, seeing nothing but his own bright green eye reflected back at him. Then he placed the fragment on top of that morning's *Daily Prophet*, which lay unread on the bed, and attempted to stem the sudden upsurge of bitter memories, the stabs of regret and of longing the discovery of the broken mirror had occasioned, by attacking the rest of the rubbish in the trunk. (*Hallows*, pp. 14-15)

Harry reads the *Daily Prophet* interview with Rita Skeeter, which features nasty bits of misinformation about Dumbledore and himself, and is outraged:

> "Lies!" Harry bellowed, and through the window he saw the next-door neighbor, who had paused to restart his lawn mower, look up nervously.
>
> Harry sat down hard on the bed. The broken bit of mirror danced away from him; he picked it up and turned it over in his fingers, thinking, thinking of Dumbledore and the lies with which Rita Skeeter was defaming him....
>
> A flash of brightest blue. Harry froze, his cut finger slipping on the jagged edge of the mirror again. He had imagined it, he must have done. He glanced over his shoulder, but the wall was a sickly peach color of Aunt Petunia's choosing: There was nothing blue there for the mirror to reflect. He peered into the mirror fragment again, and saw nothing but his own bright green eye looking back at him.
>
> He had imagined it, there was no other explanation; imagined it, because he had been thinking of his dead headmaster. If anything was certain, it was that the bright blue eyes of Albus Dumbledore would never pierce him again. (*Hallows*, pp. 28-29)

When Harry first looks in the mirror, he sees what he expects to see – his own eye. Or, as with all mirrors, even magical ones, his façade-self or "I" that is not sacred. The second time, he is more than half-convinced, however skeptical, that he has seen an otherworldly eye, rather than his own. He denies such a possibility.

Still, as the only keepsake of his godfather, he treasures the mirror shard. Hagrid gives him a mokeskin bag in which he can secure his most valuable items. Harry puts in it the Marauder's Map, R.A.B.'s locket, and the mirror shard (*Hallows*, Chapter 7, p. 132). We don't see the shard again until after Harry and Hermione's disastrous trip to Godric's Hollow on Christmas Eve, during which Harry's wand was broken in the battle with Nagini. Given the sentient Christ/*Logos* symbolism of his wand's core, its breaking is an apt story-transparency for Harry's crisis of faith:

> He pulled the pieces of the broken wand out of his pocket and, without looking at them, tucked them away in Hagrid's pouch around his neck. The pouch was now too full of broken and useless objects to take any more. Harry's hand brushed the old Snitch through the mokeskin and for a moment he had to fight

the temptation to pull it out and throw it away. Impenetrable, unhelpful, useless, like everything else Dumbledore had left behind –

And his fury at Dumbledore broke over him now like lava, scorching him inside, wiping out every other feeling. Out of sheer desperation they had talked themselves into believing that Godric's Hollow held answers, convinced themselves that they were supposed to go back, that it was all part of some secret path laid out for them by Dumbledore; but there was no map, no plan. Dumbledore had left them to grope in the darkness, to wrestle with unknown and undreamed-of terrors, alone and unaided: nothing was explained, nothing was given freely, they had no sword, and now, Harry had no wand. And he had dropped the photograph of the thief, and it would surely be easy now for Voldemort to find out who he was....Voldemort had all the information now.... (*Hallows*, p. 351)

As you know from reading Chapter 3 of this book, "The Life and Lies of Albus Dumbledore" is the nadir chapter of Harry's alchemical *nigredo*. He considers the magical mirror shard from his godfather as just another "broken and useless" object. When he next looks into it, his life and faith will be changed forever.

No Atheists in Fighting Holes: The "Hail Mary" in the Malfoy Manor Basement

Things get better for Harry and then a lot worse. Ron comes back in time to save his best friend's life and destroy the Locket Horcrux (about which, more in a minute). The trio learns from Xenophilius Lovegood the meaning of the Hallows symbol, and that the Deathly Hallows actually exist. They debate pursuing the Hallows to keep Voldemort from the Elder Wand, when Harry breaks the Name Taboo by saying Voldemort's name.

A troop of Snatchers led by Fenrir Greyback are upon them in an instant. Despite Hermione's best effort to disguise Harry, the Snatchers recognize him and take the three heroes (with Dean and Griphook) to Malfoy Manor, to claim the reward for capturing The Chosen One. Lucius almost contacts the Dark Lord by Dark Mark messaging, but Bellatrix recognizes the Sword of Gryffindor and panics. The prisoners are thrown in the basement with Luna and Ollivander, except for Hermione, whom Bellatrix tortures to learn where the trio got the Sword, a treasure supposedly safe with Voldemort's Horcrux in her Gringotts vault.

Luna cuts the bonds holding Harry, Ron, Dean, and Griphook. Agonized in their helplessness as they hear Hermione's tortured screams, Harry and Ron run about the stone room, seeking a way out. Desperation drives Harry to empty Hagrid's gift pouch that hangs around his neck:

> Hermione was screaming again: The sound went through Harry like physical pain. Barely conscious of the fierce prickling of his scar, he too started to run around the cellar, feeling the walls for he hardly knew what, knowing in his heart that it was useless.
>
> "What else did you take, what else? ANSWER ME! *CRUCIO!*"
>
> Hermione's screams echoed off the walls upstairs, Ron was half sobbing as he pounded the walls with his fists, and Harry in utter desperation seized Hagrid's pouch from around his neck and groped inside it: He pulled out Dumbledore's snitch and shook it, hoping for he did not know what – nothing happened – he waved the broken halves of the phoenix wand, but they were lifeless – the mirror fragment fell sparkling to the floor, and he saw a gleam of brightest blue –
>
> Dumbledore's eye was gazing at him out of the mirror.
>
> "Help us!" he yelled at it in mad desperation. "We're in the cellar of Malfoy Manor, help us!"
>
> The eye blinked and was gone.
>
> Harry was not even sure that it had really been there. He tilted the shard of mirror this way and that, and saw nothing reflected there but the walls and ceiling of their prison, and upstairs Hermione was screaming worse than ever, and next to him Ron was bellowing, "HERMIONE! HERMIONE!" (*Hallows*, p. 466)

And the eye delivers. Dobby suddenly appears, but is wounded by a knife thrown by Bellatrix. (Presumably the house-elf catches the silver blade she meant for Harry).

In Chapter 3 of this book (pp. 93-97), I explained how Dobby's sacrificial death crystalizes Harry's decision to believe in Dumbledore and pursue Horcruxes, as instructed. We know he makes this choice, that sets the course for the remainder of the novel, in Dobby's grave (Harry tells us this in his talk with Aberforth, much later in the story; *Hallows*, p. 563). But the decision is not arbitrary, nor the first time Harry has made the choice to believe.

The first time Harry chooses to believe is in desperation, while in the Malfoy Manor lock-up.

> He walked into the little kitchen, to the basin beneath a window overlooking the sea. Dawn was breaking over the horizon, shell pink and faintly gold, as he washed, again following the train of thought that had come to him in the dark garden....
>
> Dobby would never be able to tell them who had sent him to the cellar, but Harry knew what he had seen. A piercing blue eye had looked out of the mirror fragment, and then help had come. *Help will always be given at Hogwarts to those who ask for it.* (*Hallows*, p. 483; italics in original)

The eye first appears in Harry's bedroom, remember, when he is enraged by a Skeeter article about Dumbledore. It appears again, when Harry cries out. It seems to respond to loyalty and need, in Dumbledore fashion. In the bedroom, Harry is the skeptical empiricist with limited vision. "If anything was certain" to Harry at story's beginning "it was that the bright blue eyes of the Headmaster would never pierce him again" (*Hallows*, p. 29).

In the basement, Harry speaks to the "seeing eye" in the mirror (which should show only his reflection). In desperation, he acts as if he *knows* it is Dumbledore and throws the equivalent of a "Hail Mary" pass in the mirror's direction. However, he is still somewhat skeptical about what he has seen, after the eye "blinked and was gone." His later decisions and choices, in the grave and at Shell Cottage, were only deliberate continuation of his desperate faith at the Malfoys. In Dobby's grave, please note that Harry is thinking of Dumbledore at least as much as the house-elf (*Hallows*, Chapter 24, page 480).

As the choice to believe is the heart of the book's meaning (namely "love's victory over death") and the turning point of the story, we should take a moment to unpack the translucent story point that is both trigger and pivot for this shift – namely, the eye in the mirror.

Harry's victory (seeing only himself) before the Mirror of Erised in *Philosopher's Stone*, is possible only because he has acted selflessly. The mirror from his godfather has a different magic, it seems, but operates on a similar principle. It doesn't show the heart's desire. The mirror shard becomes unconventional when Harry thinks of Dumbledore in loyalty, love, or need; it then reflects the "seeing eye" or "knowing I" "continuous with" the depth of the mystery behind the façade "I" of ego and selfishness. Dumbledore tells Harry he is a "remarkably selfless person" (*Hallows*, p. 716).

Seeing this eye/I is one thing, but deciding to trust it is another. I said in chapter 3 that Dumbledore was more of a super-ego stand-in than God symbol (because of his confession to Harry at King's Cross). The eye of Dumbledore in the mirror, however (despite it "actually" being the eye of *Aberforth*, not *Albus*, Dumbledore) is a symbol of the sacred unity behind everything existent; Harry's seeing this eye as his reflection points to his eye-dentification with the divine beneath the façade and his participation or communion with it. His "choice to believe" is not so much a conversion or change of mind as it is his acknowledgement and acceptance of the *logos*/Christ within – his "inner Dumbledore" – as his master. It is a "*god*father mirror," after all.

The Eyes in the Horcrux Locket

Too much? Ms. Rowling points to this "inner Dumbledore" meaning in her description of Voldemort's disembodied eyes in the Locket Horcrux, a study in contrasts with the single eye of the mirror shard. Let's leave Shell Cottage and go back to the Forest of Dean, where Harry has asked Ron to destroy the Horcrux with the Sword of Gryffindor.

Speaking in Parseltongue, Harry tells the Horcrux to open. Inside are two eyeballs behind glass, which are the inversion of the single blue Dumbledore eye in Harry's mirror shard; they are two red Tom Riddle eyes behind "windows." Not surprisingly, making contact with these eyes is something like dancing with demons:

> The last word came as a hiss and a snarl and the golden doors of the locket swung wide with a little click.

> Behind both of the glass windows within blinked a living eye, dark and handsome as Tom Riddle's eyes had been before he turned them scarlet and slit-pupiled.

> "Stab," said Harry, holding the locket steady on the rock.

> Ron raised the sword in his shaking hands: The point dangled over the frantically swiveling eyes, and Harry gripped the locket tightly, bracing himself, already imagining blood pouring from the empty windows.

> Then a voice hissed from out of the Horcrux.

> "*I have seen your heart, and it is mine.*"

> "Don't listen to it!" Harry said harshly. "Stab it!"

> "*I have seen your dreams, Ronald Weasley, and I have seen your fears. All you desire is possible, but all that you dread is also possible....*"

> "Stab!" shouted Harry; his voice echoed off the surrounding trees, the sword point trembled, and Ron gazed down into Riddle's eyes.
>
> *"Least loved, always, by the mother who craved a daughter ... Least loved, now, by the girl who prefers your friend ... Second best, always, eternally overshadowed ..."*
>
> "Ron, stab it now!" Harry bellowed: He could feel the locket quivering in his grip and was scared of what was coming. Ron raised the sword still higher, and as he did so, Riddle's eyes gleamed scarlet.
>
> Out of the locket's two windows, out of the eyes, there bloomed, like two grotesque bubbles, the heads of Harry and Hermione, weirdly distorted. (*Hallows*, pp. 375-376; italics in original)

These bubble-heads become full-figure Riddle-Harry and Riddle-Hermione nightmare-caricatures and they torment Ron with his worst fears, self doubts, and feelings, until his eyes, too, show a "trace of scarlet" (p. 377). Ron finally destroys the Locket, using the Sword of Gryffindor, and, with the locket's container shattered, the eyes and nightmare figures are destroyed as well.

The Mirror of Erised is about the heart's greatest desire; these eyes, too, seem to be a gauge of the heart, albeit the heart's basest fears and darkest doubts. When the Riddle eyes tell Ron, *"I have seen your heart, and it is mine,"* they aren't talking about the light of the Deluminator in Ron's heart that brought him back to his friends, *or* the love in his heart that prompted him to dive into the pool to save his friend, *or* the nobility there, rewarded with the Sword of Gryffindor. The heart the Riddle eyes see is the heart of darkness.

The differences between these eyes and Dumbledore's eye are in their number, their color, their frame, and their "point of view." Each difference deserves comment and highlights the symbolism of the mirror-eye as the sacred "I" or inner-Dumbledore.

- **Number:** There are two Riddle eyes and only one of Dumbledore's. One is the number of unity and totality; two is the number of polarity, partisanship, division, and discord. One eye is assonant with "I"; two eyes are the appearance of the façade ego-self. Just as the Dark Lord is the Prince of Discord and Division, the number of his eyes in the Horcrux, contrasted with the one blue eye in the mirror fragment, represents multiplicity rather than unity.

• **Color:** Riddle's eyes first appear "dark and handsome," then "gleamed scarlet" (pp. 375-376). Dumbledore's eye is the "brightest blue" (p. 29). Ron's eyes, like Dumbledore's, are blue, but, as he is possessed by the taunts made by the figures of his heart's basest fears and suspicions, a "trace of scarlet" appears in his eyes, too. After destroying the Locket Horcrux, "his eyes were no longer red at all, but their normal blue; they were also wet" (p. 377). The reflex referents I think most readers supply here given Ron's psychological purification, are of the flames of the afterlife and the blue sky of heaven. Certainly Ron's experience—what amounts to an exorcism—seems a small taste of purgatory's fires, if not hell.

Red eyes, though, can just be cloudy, bloodshot eyes, usually caused by lack of sleep, a bit too much to drink the night before, or both. Red eyes are a marker of dissipation and mental confusion, even illness. Dumbledore's eyes, in the mirror or in person, are always described as "piercing," "brilliant," "bright," etc. Their blue is a sign of mental clarity, transparency, and penetration or, in the language of Coleridgean symbolism, translucency.

• **Frame:** Dumbledore's eye is framed in a mirror shard. The shape is probably a triangle, at least one edge coming to a point, but the important thing here is only that it is a mirror. Riddle's eyes are each behind a glass window, out of which "bloomed" the "distorted" Harry and Hermione figures. As we have seen, a mirror, like the singular eye, is a symbol of unity; in the mirror the subject and object distinction evaporates, and knower and known are the same. Glass windows, in contrast, though transparencies, are not symbols or means to greater realities; like the number two, a window is an artificial division creating an "inside" and "outside," an idem and alter, a meaningless "here" and "out there." A mirror is a point of passage to the unity beneath multiplicity; a glass window is a vehicle of *Maya* or the delusion of multiplicity. The opaque and occluding quality of Aberforth's glasses is instructive on this point; he and his brother share the same quality blue eyes, but Aberforth, in his self-focused and bitter grief, is effectively blind to reality.[20]

• **Vision:** Dumbledore was noted for "only being able to see the good in others." Harry believes it is the Headmaster's eye which first appears when he is enraged by Skeeter slander about Albus and then, again, when Harry is desperate in the Malfoy Manor dungeon. It *seems* to be proof of Albus' promise made in *Chamber* that he would only truly depart "when none here are loyal to him" (cf., *Prince*, p. 649, *Hallows*, p. 483). Riddle's eyes, in contrast, see that darkness within the heart trying vainly to comprehend the light; their aim is to create a vision from fear and wounded self-importance, one that destroys loyalty, friendship and trust.

As you'd expect, Harry's decision to trust in this single "seeing eye" – his almost-divine inner-Dumbledore – leads to the destruction of his inner-Voldemort of division and doubt, the way light destroys darkness, harmony destroys chaos, and unity destroys division. The Dumbledore at Harry's King's Cross makes this clear in his comments to Harry about knowing, knowledge, and reality.

The Meeting at King's Cross

Harry learns, in the Pensieve, that Dumbledore's plan was for him to sacrifice himself to Voldemort when the time was right (ideally after all the other Horcruxes had been destroyed), so that the Dark Lord soul-fragment beneath his scar would die with him. The Chosen One, in a state of something like shock, walks out of the Hogwarts Castle and into "The Forest Again." He opens the Snitch left him by Dumbledore for just this moment – "I open at the close" (*Hallows*, page 134). Using the Resurrection Stone within, he is accompanied by the shades of his mother, father, godfather, and favorite teacher to the clearing occupied by Death Eaters and Voldemort. Harry is killed without raising his wand in self-defense. (*Hallows*, Chapter 34).

What follows is certainly the most mysterious and surreal, or better, the *most real* chapter in the 4100-page adventure. Harry finds himself in a place that is not a proper place, a non-location with no proper "when;" it is a "place to be" and know things as they truly are. At King's Cross, Harry sees for the first time with "transformed vision," rather than through corrective lenses, and what he learns there, in the end, is what Ms. Rowling had been aiming at through the whole series.

But I'm way ahead of myself. Let's take a look around Harry's King Cross.

When Harry comes to, after being blasted by Lord Voldemort, he struggles to understand where he is. The place he finds himself seems to have no *where* there. "He was not perfectly sure that he was there himself" (page 705). He understands from clear sensory impressions (first touch, then sight, when he "discovered that he had eyes"), that he is "more than disembodied thoughts" (p. 705). Contact with the surface he is on convinces Harry "that he must exist," although it only "seemed to be white, neither warm nor cold, but simply there, a flat, blank something on which to be" (pp. 705-706).

If that isn't odd enough, he finds himself in a "bright mist," but it isn't a sunny fog, or what he had experienced before. "His surroundings were not hidden by cloudy vapor; rather the cloudy vapor had not yet formed into substance" (705). In fact, "his surroundings seemed to invent themselves before his eyes" (706). Harry thinks of clothing and "barely had the wish formed in his head than robes appeared" (706). This ain't Kansas, Harry, and Oz had a lot more color, not to mention recognizable substance.

His first indication of where he is comes from the "great domed glass roof" he sees that "glittered high above him in sunlight" (706) and the" sparkling" (707) "high, vaulted ceiling" (713). "Perhaps it was a "palace" (706), "if an odd [palace]" (709). After Dumbledore tells him how it was possible to have survived the Dark Lord's curse, Harry asks the Headmaster where they are. Dumbledore says he had the same question.

> Until Dumbledore asked, Harry had not known. Now, however, he found that he had an answer ready to give. "It looks," he said slowly, "like King's Cross Station. Except a lot cleaner and empty, and there are no trains as far as I can see" (712).

They are in a place where the features of space – most notably objects displacing emptiness and other objects – are congealing and "inventing" themselves from ideas "before his eyes." From an unconditioned substance just "on which to be," Harry's surroundings take shape as what he considers a "palace," and then as a railway station sans trains. Even taking Ms. Rowling's word for why she placed Platform 9 ¾ at King's Cross – that she was thinking of Euston Station[21] – and assuming she meant the Euston Station with Arch demolished in 1961, none of these places have "domed" or "vaulted" ceilings. Harry, having grown up with the Dursleys, has no experience of churches, so he associates the architecture with royalty and a palace. He finally comes up with an answer: it's *King*'s Cross. I'll say more on the idea of King and Cross as divine intersection in a moment, and in the next chapter.

As odd as the space is, in this place still becoming a recognizable place, time is not any better. He's confused about the place-ness, but time just doesn't exist, in a durative way, in the not-quite-there. He notes between thoughts "a long time later, or maybe no time at all, [an idea] came to him" (705). Later (or so it seemed to me, a reader), "Harry sat in thought for a long time, or perhaps seconds. It was very hard to be sure of things like time, here" (712).

Harry's condition is much changed and improved from the battered, exhausted young man who had entered the Forbidden Forest.

This not-quite-there person is naked, is "unscathed" (706), has "clean, unblemished hands," feels "great at the moment" (712), and, perhaps most remarkably, has no glasses (706), but sees clearly. Until his transition to, well, wherever he is, Harry been essentially blind without his glasses. Hermione, as one of the seven Potters escaping Privet Drive, made only this comment when becoming her good friend: "Harry, your eyesight really is awful" (52).

The King's Cross Dumbledore is, if anything, in even better shape, especially for a man who admits "matter-of-factly" (707) to being dead. His Horcrux-cursed arm is healed; in fact, "his hands were both whole and white and undamaged." "Everything," Harry thinks after looking him in the face, "was as he remembered it" (707). "Happiness seemed to radiate from Dumbledore like light, like fire: Harry had never seen a man so utterly, so palpably content" (708). The Headmaster *is* wearing spectacles, though! (707)

Both of their bodies seem in excellent condition, then – and they do both have solid, sensing bodies as Harry was "glad to find" when he grabbed the Headmaster's arm to support and console him in his grief (717). If all physical systems are looking great and working well, how are the mental works? Knowing seems a lot easier and surer in the not-quite-there.

As we saw in Harry's epiphany about his King's Cross almost-location above, understanding seems to come with the asking, or just waiting for it. When Harry asks Albus how he could have survived the Killing Curse, the Headmaster throws the question back at him with an "I think you know" (708). Sure enough, after letting "his gaze drift over his surroundings," "the answer rose to his lips easily, without effort." And it was the right answer (709). For Harry, never a candidate for classroom "Best in Show" awards, this effortless and exact insight is as bizarre as ideas turning into robes. The only thing he doesn't figure out, before deciding to return to the Forest, is "whether Dumbledore had ever found out who struck Ariana dead," and this failure is because "he did not want to know" (719). The will and intelligence are joined here.

It could be said that Harry, as he suspects, is just knocked out in the Forbidden Forest, and his experience at King's Cross and conversation with Dumbledore were just a nice dream. One of the better arguments for this is that Harry doesn't learn anything from Dumbledore in their conversation that he couldn't have figured out on his own from what he learned in the Pensieve.

If a "better argument," it's still quite the stretch, even for a plot device to quickly lay out the facts of the matter, before the final confrontation in the Great Hall. It means that Harry figured out everything from the wand connections and his surviving the Killing Curse again, to the deep story of Ariana's death *on his own*. Assuming he did it without the Dumbledore explanations means the King's Cross Headmaster is a fancy figment Harry has only dreamed up, either as a stand-in for his own intelligence or as an exercise in wish fulfillment. (It is perfectly understandable that Harry would want to talk with an honest and open Headmaster, who both begs Harry's forgiveness and insists "I have known, for some time now, that you [Harry] are the better man"! 713). This Harry, smart as he is, has become *in his unconscious mind* (!) Hermione's better, even Dumbledore's and Snape's real-world master in deduction, logic, and magic theory.[22]

If this argument is understandable, even plausible, it is because of the number of times Dumbledore tells Harry that he knows the answer already and doesn't need an explanation from the Headmaster, or prefaces his explanations with an anything but throw-away "you know" and "you already know." Count them up. We've already seen Dumbledore ask Harry to answer his own questions about how he survived and where they are. In ten pages (708-717) Dumbledore says variations of "you know" to Harry *fourteen times*. If this isn't wish fulfillment on Harry's part, it seems at least a pointer to Harry's already knowing what is supposedly being revealed. Which opens the door to the possibility that the meeting never really happened except in Harry's fancy or dream state.

So, where is he really? In an otherworldly place like Heaven, or in his own unconscious mind? Or someplace else not a place? The scene, imagined or real, is certainly otherworldly in being unlike any familiar place or even a place; the absence of a durative time that Harry can sense, too, has a note of Eternity in it. As mentioned in Chapter 3 (p. 121), the soul fragment that cannot be consoled has an obvious element of Christian afterlife: there is a non-local, non-temporal, place of judgment in which nothing can be done to help the lost. In Harry's and Dumbledore's physical and mental near-perfection, too, there is the not-so-subtle suggestion of the age-to-come expectations of the saints or elect.

It being a very realistic dream, as noted, is only plausible because the Dumbledore here doesn't bring into the conversation anything that Harry has never even heard *about*. It is bizarre, certainly, but Harry believes he has died. Why wouldn't Harry imagine himself into a paradise of sorts, in which he gets to spend time with the mentor he has wanted to quiz all year, and get to make a choice about coming back? The poor guy's spent his whole life fighting battles he felt obliged to fight, and fighting his way out of corners that circumstances and a Prophecy forced him into.

Either position is possible, even probable. And, as you might have guessed, it's easy for secularists to argue that Harry's King's Cross fantasy is an *Alice in Wonderland* dream, and for Christians to say it is his taste of paradise in the life to come. How each side dismisses the other and neglects Harry's very real-world sensorial experience there – an experience I don't expect souls stripped of bodies or minds in dreams to have – is interesting, because the sum of the two arguments seems to be a dilemma of "either" or "neither" possibility being true. Both are logically possible, if you imagine heaven will be an embodied state immediately after death, and if you think imaginative experience can include brain experiences identical to sense impressions; both are not possible if you don't.

Is there a third possibility? Are we even supposed to be asking this question?

That Ms. Rowling wants us to be asking this question about the reality of Harry's King Cross is clear in Harry bringing it up himself, in the last moments of his conversation with Dumbledore, at the end of his something-like-time at what-might-be-King's-Cross:

> "Tell me one last thing," said Harry. "Is this real? Or has this been happening inside my head?"
>
> Dumbledore beamed at him, and his voice sounded loud and strong in Harry's ears even though the bright mist was descending again, obscuring his figure.
>
> "Of course it is happening inside your head, Harry, but why on earth should that mean that it is not real? (723)

The author has confided that this exchange is perhaps *the* critical part of the book:

> *Q: There's this dialogue between Harry and Professor Dumbledore: "Is this real? Or has this been happening inside my head?"*
>
> *A: And Dumbledore says: "Of course it is happening inside your head, but why on earth would that mean that is not real?" That dialogue is the key; I've waited seventeen years to use those lines. Yes, that's right. All this time I've worked to be able to write those* **two phrases***; writing Harry entering the forest and Harry having that dialog (sic).*[23] *(emphasis added)*

That's a pretty remarkable statement, so let me run that answer by you again.

Ms. Rowling says that Harry's question and Dumbledore's response are "the key" (emphasis on the restrictive definite article: "*the* key"), and that for seventeen years she has worked on this series "to be able to write those two phrases."

This chapter, believe it or not, has really just been about making sense of those two lines. Harry's question reflects the everyday postmodern understanding of reality and what we can know of it. The late Albus' answer is the response of Samuel Taylor Coleridge and friends, to include Ms. Rowling. If Ms. Rowling wasn't misquoted or mistranslated (and the comment was translated from English into Spanish, and then back into English again), then understanding these lines mean you have understood what she has been hoping you will take away from the experience of reading her novels.

Let's start with Harry's question.

He offers Dumbledore two possibilities for everything that he has experienced since taking the Green Shower of Power fire hose in the Forbidden Forest. "Is this real? Or has this been happening in my head?" By "real," Harry means what David Hume and the dead 18th and 19th century empiricists who rule our thinking from the grave, meant by real. Harry's "real" is the world of quantities of energy and matter occupying space, having measurable qualities, from temperature and weight to dimension and charge. (Time is considered real because duration can be tracked, if not measured, *per se.*) "Real" means, in short, something we have understood, from information we have acquired via our physical senses, or pictured and abstracted out of that information we recall. Studying the "real world" is the realm of the physical sciences, in which scientific method produces objective knowledge.

Harry asks the question, though, only because his experience at his King's Cross has been in several important ways *unreal.* From the cloudy vapor becoming both his surroundings and items he wants, to his having a lively chat with a radiant, certifiably solid, and brilliant dead man, the interlude "underground" isn't the stuff of energy and matter quantities, or even the magical curriculum at Hogwarts. The trick is, if it's not "real" the way both Muggles and Magical folk think things can be real, what else can be it be?

Harry's alternative to "real" is: "or has this been happening inside my head?" To Harry, events "happening inside my head" are "what isn't real" or "what is less real," something rising involuntarily in human gray matter while sleeping or day dreaming, or from mistaken ideas and abstractions. Given Harry's track record at Hogwarts in being stunned at the end of every year by how little he understood of what was really going on, it's little wonder he asks the equivalent of "Did this really happen, or have I mistaken what *I* think is happening for reality again?"

Dumbledore's response reveals that he thinks Harry has created a false dichotomy. There is *another* option to account for his experience than just either/or: either scientific knowledge or delusional opinion, either objective or subjective thinking. Harry, like the rest of us, is a *de facto* materialist. If he cannot touch, see, smell, taste, or hear it, he thinks it is less real than something he can know by sense perception. All abstraction, thinking, feeling, fancy, imaginings, and dreams, the things that "happen in our heads," because they are not-material by definition, are not dependable ways of knowing the hard, and therefore real, facts. Prejudices, limited views, unfounded speculation and private animosity can distort our thinking, so, like Harry, we don't count "inside our head" experience as *real*. Harry asks Dumbledore the skeptic's question, with the empiricist's only two options: "real" or "head games."

"Dumbledore beamed at him" means, I think, that he is delighted and amused with the Boy Who Lived's question, as we should be. "Materialist wizard" is a funny idea, after all, and Harry is also asking something of a ridiculous question. First, in suggesting the possibility he's in a fantasy of his own delusional production, he's necessarily denying the very substantial and detailed *sense* experiences he has just had. The place-not-quite-a-place is very real, in a material way, as have been Harry's experiences with Dumbledore. He has seen, touched, heard, spoken with the Headmaster rationally and discursively, and had only believable experience in talking with the dead Dumbledore as a physical reality and human being. If sense is the standard of reality, this place must be real, whatever its differences from prior experience.

Second, if this palatial King's Cross, the screaming baby object that cannot be consoled, and Dumbledore are *not* real, what is the value of any answer Harry's delusion might give to Harry's question? Not much.

Dumbledore, however, delivers a literally high-sounding answer: "Of course it is happening inside your head, Harry, but why on earth should that mean that it is not real?" This can be read in at least three ways: as the statement of a relativist, of a psychologist, or of a symbolist.

The relativist's answer of "head happenings are real" means that not even sense perception is a direct understanding of reality. Because everything is filtered through our head-box of passions, pride, and prejudices, the only thing we can know for sure is what we think. Because we cannot be truly sure about the dependability or correspondence of our thinking with anything else, a dream is as real as a logical demonstration.

The psychiatric understanding of Dumbledore's answer (i.e., "head happening are real") is that thinking is just brain and nerve cell chemistry, period. This is the materialist's position and it winds up in the same unsurety as the relativist's. If our thinking is the consequence of more or less arbitrary chemical reactions, then belief that we are able to know anything real, or discern the true from what is false, is delusional. Some folks may put on a better show rhetorically but, qua chemistry sets, we can never know better or discern more truly than can another person's arbitrary chemical reactions. The molecules causing our psychological profiles, which bring about our equally valuable (because none are valuable) opinions and sureties, have no relationship with an independent or objective truth, so neither can our ideas or conceptions.

Frankly, I have a hard time believing that Dumbledore of Hogwarts or Harry's King Cross is a relativist or gray matter materialist. He says things that contradict these positions head on. He calls Harry a "better man," and admits to "shame." He's obviously consumed with knowing (even guessing), in hope of gaining greater proximity to the true, good, and beautiful – meaning, what is real *within* the measurable world, but which is not matter or energy itself. That Dumbledore "beamed at" Harry (remember that his happiness and contentment are like radiant light!) means, I think, that he is amused, yes, but also delighted by the opportunity to explain to him, however opaquely and obliquely, where he has been.

Dumbledore's position asserts there is a nonmaterial (albeit, anything but immaterial) unity between what is real and what is happening in our heads. Unlike Harry's idea of "real" – the man-in-the-street empiricism and materialism we all share in this historical period to one degree or another – Dumbledore's reality doesn't reduce to a wave-particle polarity of matter and energy quantities. The Headmaster's unity of "real" and "thinking" is the unity we met in Lewis' "seeing eye" and Coleridge's "transformed vision."

To review, the "seeing eye/I" of our self-awareness or conscience, is that part of ourselves that can never see itself any more than we can touch touching or hear hearing. It is the reality beneath the ego façade of self, that is also the reality beneath all things, ideas, and other thinking persons. This transpersonal mental reality is the *logos* continuous with, and, in at least one sense then, identical with the divine *Logos* or Word that is the Creator and unity of all things. Seeing with this eye/I means seeing God everywhere – both in our space and outer space – because this *logos* faculty or eye recognizes itself, the *logos* or *Logos*-shadow, in every existent thing or person, insofar as each of us is a transparent symbol of the Absolute.

When Ron Weasley pulls Harry out of the pool in the Forest of Dean (371), and again, when he is disappointed that Harry decides to forsake the Elder Wand (748), he asks Harry, incredulously, "Are – you -- *mental*?" (371; italics and spacing in original). Harry doesn't respond on either occasion. But the "key" to the *Potter* stories – which Ms. Rowling says is in Dumbledore's "the real is happening in your head" reply to Harry's question – is that, yes, Harry is *mental*. The unity of existence as *logos* means we – Muggles, wizards, with all created things – are *mental*. We are also, insomuch as we identify with the reality beneath the façade – the eternal behind the ephemeral – are images of God, three dimensional symbols or transparencies of the divine. Coleridge's hermetic epistemological theology, the heart of fantasy and symbolist tradition in English letters, is the message of the *Harry Potter* novels.[24]

Where, then, is Harry's King's Cross station? Just beyond the veil of time, space, matter, and ego obscuring the *logos* reality that is the unity of everything existent. Harry isn't blasted to his subconscious or unconscious mind; he "comes to" his *super*conscious mind. Call it "*Logos*-Land," "*Nous*-ville." or even "The Kingdom of Heaven."[1] It isn't a place of "disembodied thoughts," but of matter done right, which is to say thoughts-becoming-bodies, ideas congealing into substance. It is *more* real than the world consumed and distracted by multiplicity, that denies the creative unity of the Word; it seems unreal only because of our mistaken and relatively restricted, even pathetic, space-time ideas of reality.

Harry knows everything he wants to know here – and Dumbledore knows he knows – because will and intelligence are joined there, and, more incredible, intelligence and matter and time seem to be one as well. Harry's understanding this place as "King's Cross," as I'll explain in the next chapter on three different levels, has something to do with Calvary; symbolically, of course. Harry's sacrificial and salutary death to his ego self brings him to the unity or intersection of all worlds, the

---

1   Harry's meeting with Dumbledore in a place-that-is-not-a-place is described as a "palace" three times, as "King's Cross" once, and as a basilica cathedral in terms of its structures (dome, arched ceiling, etc.); as it is also the place where Harry knows all, I think we are meant to recognise the several regal references and otherworldly signatures as the kingdom of heaven or of God within us (Luke 17:20-21), the uncreated or noetic faculty of soul, the "sacred I," and *logos*.

Logos, the hypostasis of God that became humanity in Jesus of Nazareth. Only love, the resolution of contraries and lifting of veils, could bring Harry to this place beneath all places that is spiritual knowledge. The dead are alive there but only if and because they died to themselves and became incarnations of love and *logos* while living.

Harry's King Cross, then, is Coleridge's *Via Media* between godless empiricism and abstract fideism[25]; Harry is in Lewis' "mystery of the depth," the *logos* mind "in his head" which is the non-local place where time and space are resolved in eternity and have their origin, as do all things in ideas, more real than space-time reality, more physically human and knowing in being "within" the creative Word.

The goal of Harry's hero journey in *Deathly Hallows* was to bring him out of his relative blindness up to this "corrected vision," Coleridge's "transformed vision," in which the world and man are theophanies. Purified by his choices, beliefs, and sacrifices, his "remarkable selflessness" and death to ego, he sees behind the veil; his knowledge is spiritual knowledge and the "mind (nous) of Christ:" (1 Cor. 2:16). At the noetic King's Cross, he experiences this as a "palace." Harry's head has the divine center, the unicity of existence within it, an "inside greater than the outside" that puts even Hermione's beaded bag to shame, and this creative center is "where" Harry goes when he is finally cleansed of his Scar Horcrux soul fragment. He sees through the Disillusionment Charm of all things.

Ms. Rowling's goal for reader, Harry's fellow traveler, is a little less ambitious. She just doesn't want us to wind up like the soul fragment beneath the chair at King's Cross. Her stories aim to transform our vision so that we might avoid the fate of Voldemort, who has none of Harry's spiritual knowledge or *logos* awareness. Dumbledore is explicit that the Dark Lord's genius and power were nothing as compared to his profound ignorance of children's tales:

> And his knowledge remained woefully incomplete, Harry! That which Voldemort does not value, he takes no trouble to comprehend. Of house-elves and children's tales, of love, loyalty, and innocence, Voldemort knows and understands nothing. *Nothing.* That they all have a power beyond his own, a power beyond the reach of any magic, is a truth he has never grasped. (*Hallows*, pp. 709-710; emphasis in original)

The world is mental, and, consequently, a person *is* as much as they *know* or commune with the mental principle joining all things. Voldemort "knows and understands nothing" of this symbolist or fairy tale cosmology, epistemology, and anthropology, so he cannot know the "power beyond any magic." Ms. Rowling tells us her story so we *can* know this power and love's victory over death. Our experience in Harry's adventures of the transpersonal self and *logos*, which is continuous with the *Logos*/Christ, transforms our vision to the degree our mind allows the heart this cathartic and purifying initiation. In this, she is a disciple and descendant of Coleridge and the symbolist writers of English literature, whose hermetic instruction is only found in the experience resulting from willing suspension of empirical disbelief.

Conclusion

Snape was redeemed, as we saw in the last chapter, by transcending the world through the eyes of his Beatrice, Lily Potter. Harry's victory, too, is in the eyes he chooses to look into and trust. The perfect understanding (discussed in Chapter 1) that allows him to defeat Voldemort, is really his "corrected vision" and eye-dentification with the eye-in-the-mirror, his "faculty of recognition" or Dumbledore-within. His desperate choice in the Malfoy Manor basement, and deliberate decision to believe that he makes in Dobby's grave – to trust the eye-in-the-mirror," the sacred "I" continuous with the Mystery behind the façade – is what brings him from the narrow skepticism of his Privet Drive bedroom to the perfect vision he enjoys at King's Cross. The Boy Who Lived, by becoming the spiritual knowledge made possible by sacrificial love and selflessness, destroys both the Voldemort piece within him and the as-real Dark Lord without. Ms. Rowling invites us to this transformation and gives us an experience of seeing the world symbolically. Like Harry and Snape, our transcendence is in how we identify with the seeing eye of conscience.

Deathly Hallows, in brief, is the story of Harry becoming the rightful heir of Ignotus Peverell, the brother who created the Invisibility Cloak and "escaped death," because the wearer of the Invisibility Cloak is a symbol of the transpersonal and sacred I/eye. Dumbledore says its "true magic" is that it is shared with others (p. 716), it is the invisible, seeing person, who "gladly" goes with Death "as an old friend," even as "equals" from this life (p. 409). Harry and friends under the Cloak are "the Seeing Eye," hence his decision to keep it, alone among the three Hallows. It is a story-symbol of his means to victory over Voldemort, even his apotheosis as hero.

Remarkably, though, *Deathly Hallows* is not just about thinking symbolically per se; it actually has a symbol in it and the interpretation of this "triangular eye" is a large part of the surface story. The next chapter is about understanding this eye – the Hallows symbol – and the eye of Alastor "Mad-Eye" Moody. To pull back the veil from these transparencies, I'll explain why we know there is a greater depth to these stories, a second and third layer beneath the storyline, in fact, and how reading them correctly is best understood as a Quidditch match. For the next step in the iconological or esemplastic[26] understanding of Harry Potter and symbolist literature, turn the page.

Endnotes

1   C. S. Lewis, *Essay Collection*, HarperCollins (2002), chapter 8, 'The Seeing Eye,' p. 63

2   Op. cit., p. 59

3   Op. cit., p. 59-61

4   Op. cit., p. 62

5   This is not the place to argue for a definitive link between Lewis and Coleridge which will have to wait for another day. Lewis' knowledge of Coleridge is not restricted to catalogued information, however, as a check of the indices to three volumes of his collected letters reveal, the argument in *The Abolition of Man* against the authors of *The Green Book*, and his comments about imagination in *Surprised by Joy* and *On Three Ways of Writing for Children* mention and reflect Coleridge's "primary imagination" as defined in the *Biographia Literaria* (cf., *C. S. Lewis: Companion and Guide*, p. 565).

6   I urge any reader interested in Coleridge's epistemology to read James Cutsinger's *The Form of the Transformed Vision: Coleridge and the Knowledge of God*, Mercer University Press, 1988.

7   "[Coleridge] would agree that divinity, or theology, and the knowledge of God that is its object depend for their meaning upon certain points of contact with the world of nature. The knowledge of God depends, he would say, upon the introsusception of mental power that is required in the presence of living symbols – (sic) upon the conscious and willing release of thinking from its habitual assumptions concerning out-ness and solidity. This according to Coleridge was the whole point of the Christian dispensation, the explanation and unraveling of which is the central work of theologians.

It was one of the great purposes of Christianity, and included in the process of our redemption, to arouse and emancipate the soul from [its] debasing slavery to the outward senses. For this end, our Lord, who came down from heaven to take captivity captive, chose the words and names, that designate the familiar yet most important objects of sense, the nearest and most concerning things and incidents of corporeal nature: -- water, flesh, blood, birth, bread! But he used them in senses, that could not without absurdity be supposed to respect the mere phaenomena, water, flesh, and the like (Aids to Reflection, p. 349)."

James Cutsinger, *The Form of the Transformed Vision: Coleridge and the Knowledge of God*, Mercer University Press, 1988, p. 85

8   A key motif in the Potter stories suggestive of layered meaning – and that the greater meaning is beneath the surface reading -- is that "the inside is greater than the outside."

Magic cars, for example, appear to be mid-sized or compacts, but open up miraculously on entering to be remarkably spacious and much more than what their visible exterior suggested. The Knight Bus, with its "wood-panelled walls" and "brass bedsteads," resembles a country inn more than public transportation (*Prisoner*, Chapter 3, p. 35). How about the Sorting Hat that is really a "sword-in-Hat," and a very large sword at that? The outsides of Wizard Tents, too, promise cramped quarters and the insides deliver palatial or at least ranch house comforts. Much of *Deathly Hallows* takes place in the "tent" that is really a cabin which Hermione borrows from Mr. Weasley and keeps in her "small beaded handbag."

This magical bag, too, created by her Undetectable Extension Charm (*Hallows*, Chapter 9, p. 162), holds a "cargo hold" worth of necessities and grows at need (e.g., to fit in the portrait of Phineas Nigellus: *Hallows*, Chapter 12, p. 228). The archway and veil in the Department of Mysteries, too, though Harry walks around it, front and back, conceals an "in there" that is invisible and as indefinite, possibly infinite, as the afterlife (*Phoenix*, Chapter 34, pp. 773-775).

The critical adventure in *Deathly Hallows* "inside Harry's head" at what he thinks looks like King's Cross nut which strikes him also as a "palace" and "giant Room of Requirement" because it was "a wide-open space, bright and clean, a hall larger by far than the Great Hall" (*Hallows*, Chapter 35, p. 706). Besides responding to the wishes of wizards, this place that is not a place resembles the ever expanding Room of Requirement in being immeasurable and yet within something as spatially restricted as Harry's head. The Room of Hidden Things, one aspect of the Room of Requirement, in which the Trio battle Draco, Crabbe, and Goyle in the Battle of Hogwarts to retrieve the Diadem Horcrux is described as "a place the size of a cathedral with the appearance of a city" (*Hallows*, Chapter 31, p. 627). No wonder Dumbledore mentioned it on the sly to Harry at the Yule Ball in his Fourth Year as a "Hogwarts Secret" (*Goblet*, Chapter 23, p. 417).

The entire Wizarding World, in fact, should probably be understood as the "greater thing" hiding within the lesser exterior. Think of Platform 9 ¾ as King's Cross. Behind a wall in plain sight on the busiest underground station in metropolitan London is the point of transition to the world of magical education. But like The Leaky Cauldron and The House of Black, the outside surface is invisible to most and impenetrable to the rest. As Stan Shunpike tells Harry, "Them [Muggles]!" said Stan contemptuously. "Don' listen properly, do they? Don' look properly either. Never notice nuffink, they don'" (*Prisoner*, Chapter 3, p. 36)

9   James Cutsinger explains the necessity of symbols for attempts to

express the Absolute Reality being simultaneously transcendent and immanent:

How to capture at least something of the truth? Many different strategies and approaches have been used. One of the most famous is found in a classic definition of God that can be traced back at least as far as the medieval Catholic theologian St Bonaventure (1217- 74), whose biography of St Francis of Assisi you'll be reading later this term. According to Bonaventure, God is *an intelligible sphere the center of which is everywhere, but the circumference nowhere.* This image is chosen because the sphere is traditionally understood to be the most perfect of geometrical shapes in that all of its points are equidistant from a common center. The center of this particular sphere—this Divine "globe", we might say—turns out to be "everywhere" because of God's immanence. God is wherever there is any "where", and He is present "there" fully and completely. On the other hand, the circumference of the sphere is "nowhere", and this is because of God's transcendence. You can never get to God's edge, as it were, for it's He who is always beyond.

James Cutsinger, *Lectures on Christian Theology*, p. 48; http://www.cutsinger.net/pdf/that_man_might_become_god.pdf

10 Cutsinger, *Vision.*, p. 76

11 "Whether God be the mirror of man or man be the mirror of God, the mirror in both cases signifies the knowing subject, which as such cannot also be the object of knowledge. In an absolute manner this is true of the Divine Subject alone...; this is the infinite mirror whose 'substance' can in no wise be grasped, but which nevertheless is knowable in a certain sense, because one can know that only in it can all be creatures be known."

Titus Burckhardt, 'The Symbolism of the Mirror,' *Mirror of the Intellect: Essays on Traditional Science and Sacred Art*, Quinta Essentia (1987), p. 122

12 Cutsinger, Op. cit., p. 77

13 'Bluspels and Flalansferes' (1939), cited in 'Meaning, meanings, and epistemology in C. S. Lewis,' Mythlore, Spring-Summer 2007, Charlie W. Starr, http://findarticles.com/p/articles/mi_m0OON/is_3-4_25/ai_n27253241/pg_2

14 Burckhardt, Op. cit., p. 117

15 Martin Lings, 'What is Symbolism?,' *Symbol and Archetype: A Study in the Meaning of Existence*, Quinta Essentia (1991), p. 6

16 Burckhardt, Op. cit., p. 117

17 Op. cit., p. 11

18 Op. cit., p. 120

19 This is also why Dumbledore is able to defeat Grindlewald and the unbeatable Elder Wand in their legendary 1945 duel. "The owner of the wand must capture it from its previous owner" (*Hallows*, p. 412). But unlike Grindelwald, who stole the wand from Gregorovitch, and Draco, who surprised Albus on the Tower, Dumbledore didn't capture the Elder Wand by either stealth or surprise (*Stone*, page 102-3). As Dumbledore explained at King's Cross to Harry, "I was fit to own the Elder Wand, and not to boast of it, and not to kill with it. I was permitted to tame and to use it, because I took it, not for gain, but to save others from it" (*Hallows*, p. 720). Dumbledore's selflessness and humility are the equivalent of "purity of heart" and identity with the Absolute, the sure way to victory, even against a wizard with an unbeatable wand.

20 It is worth noting here that Aberforth's eyes are strikingly like his brother Albus,' so much so that throughout the story Harry assumes the eye in the mirror is the Headmaster's, though Harry knows he is dead (hence it's supernatural quality to him and its value as a marker of his faith). In "The Missing Mirror" (*Hallows*, chapter 28), Aberforth's eyes and "gaze" are described as "strikingly like his brother's. The bright blue eyes gave the same impression that they were X-raying the object of their scrutiny..." (*Hallows*, p. 563). Several times in the chapter, however, Aberforth's glasses are described, "dirty lenses" (*Hallows*, p. 559), "grimy lenses" (*Hallows*, page 563), as refracting light and becoming "opaque," effectively blinding Aberforth.

The firelight made the grimy lenses of Aberforth's glasses momentarily opaque, a bright of flat white, and Harry remembered the blind eyes of the giant spider, Aragog.... (p. 563)

[Aberforths'] eyes were briefly occluded by the firelight on the lenses of his glasses. They shone white and blind again. (p. 566)

Aberforth's eyes in person are not the red eyes of the Locket Horcrux, but they are not the eye-in-the-mirror shard, either. Light reflects from a mirror to show the unity of subject and object; light through glass or glasses is bent and distorted, preferably to improve vision, but always to make a difference in the way things would otherwise appear. Ms. Rowling makes her point about eyes, mirrors, and glasses with the blindness of Aberforth Dumbledore reflecting his consumption with his personal grief as clearly as she does with Harry's mirror and Voldemort's Horcrux. He cannot see what is greater than himself in others, *or* in himself, until Harry's pure-of-heart example shames him into heroic action in the Battle of Hogwarts.

21 Wikipedia.com, 'King's Cross Station in Fiction: Harry Potter,'

http://en.wikipedia.org/wiki/London_King%27s_Cross_railway_station#Harry_Potter

22 Not to mention Dumbledore's expansion of the Grindelwald story (pp. 716-719) that Harry heard from Aberforth in "The Missing Mirror" (566-568), which Albus says rightly Harry "cannot imagine." This is the only time, in fact, he doesn't note Harry's existent understanding with a "you know."

23 http://www.the-leaky-cauldron.org/2008/2/9/jkr-discusses-dursley-family-religion-us-presidential-election-and-more-in-new-interview

24 On the world being "mental" or *logos* driven, we need return to Lewis and Barfield. James Cutsinger explains Lewis' learning about the identity of mind and creator from Barfield, whom Cutsinger met and interviewed this way:

Barfield once told me, "Lewis taught me how to think, and I taught him what to think." The wry smile which he had on his face at the time made it clear that this maxim was by no means his last word on the subject, and yet, as you may remember from Surprised by Joy, Lewis was the first to admit to how great an extent the content of his mature philosophy had been shaped by his friend. "Barfield never made me an Anthroposophist," writes Lewis, "but his counterattacks destroyed forever two elements in my own thought."[Lewis, Surprised by Joy: The Shape of My Early Life (New York: Harcourt, Brace, Jovanovich, 1955),207] The first was "chronological snobbery", that is, "the uncritical acceptance of the intellectual climate common to our own age and the assumption that whatever has gone out of date is on that account discredited."(Surprised by Joy, 207) We readers of Lewis can easily see the lasting importance of this lesson throughout his many books. Indeed in my experience, no author has been more successful in driving home the fact that "our own age is also 'a period'".(Surprised by Joy, 208) But it is Barfield's other contribution that I would have us focus on here. "In the second place," Lewis continues, Barfield

convinced me that the positions we had hitherto held left no room for any satisfactory theory of knowledge. We had been, in the technical sense of the term, "realists"; that is, we accepted as rock-bottom reality the universe revealed by the senses. But at the same time we continued to make, for certain phenomena of consciousness, all the claims that really went with a theistic or idealistic view. We

maintained that abstract thought (if obedient to logical rules) gave indisputable truth, that our moral judgment was "valid", and our aesthetic experience not merely pleasing but "valuable". . . . Barfield convinced me that it was inconsistent. If thought were a purely subjective event, these claims for it would have to be abandoned. . . . I was therefore compelled to give up realism. . . . I must admit that mind was no late-come epiphenomenon; that the whole universe was, in the last resort, mental; that our logic was participation in a cosmic Logos (Surprised by Joy, 208-209).

Take particular note of the fact in this passage that man's aesthetic experience, and not only his thinking and moral willing, had become for Lewis a proof of our participation in the Logos or Word.

James Cutsinger, 'C. S. Lewis as Apologist and Mystic,' Lectures delivered for the Narnia Clubs of New York, December 1998; http://www.cutsinger.net/scholarship/articles.shtml

25 Cutsinger, *Transformed Vision,* chapter 2, "Coleridge's Via Media"

26 "Esemplastic" is a word of Coleridge's invention "from the Greek words, *eis en plattein,* i.e., to shape into one" (*Biographia Literaria,* 1:168; cited in Cutsinger, Op. cit., p. 15, note 1) to describe the power of the imagination to lead one to a unified, spiritual knowledge. See also Lewis' use of the word to describe Charles Williams' effect on the Inklings as a group:

[T]he importance of [Williams's] presence was, indeed, chiefly made clear by the gap which was left on the rare occasions when he did not turn up. It then became clear that some principle of liveliness and cohesion had been withdrawn from the whole party: lacking him, we did not completely possess one another. He was (in the Coleridgian language) an 'esemplastic' force.

(C. S. Lewis, Preface, *Essays Presented to Charles Williams,* 1947. Grand Rapids, MI: Eerdmans, (1966), page xi; cited in "The centre of the Inklings: Lewis? Williams? Barfield? Tolkien?," *Mythlore,* Fall-Winter, 2007 by Diana Pavlac Glyer, http://findarticles.com/p/articles/mi_m0OON/is_1-2_26/ai_n21118779/pg_1?tag=artBody;col1)

Chapter 6

Taking Harry Seriously

Learning to Read With Triangular Vision

The last chapter was, in large part, an argument for reading symbolically. We discussed the transforming vision, seeing God everywhere, and understanding ourselves and everything created as symbols. We also looked at the eyes in the mirror shard and Locket Horcrux. It would be strange if we didn't explore the meaning of the actual *Deathly Hallows* symbol and how the characters understand it. But a discussion of the two *other* eyes in *Deathly Hallows* – Moody's Mad-Eye and "the triangular eye" – will have to wait until Chapter 7. First we must learn to read with "triangular vision," the heart of traditional iconology,[1] which interprets images and symbols on many levels.

Before we jump headlong off the pier into the depths of this tradition, let's check the depth of the pond. Does *Harry Potter* warrant or require a search for "deep, hidden meaning," or is that a risible overreaching? Is it possible this "unlocking analysis" is just the frenetic thinking of an overheated *Da Vinci Code* fan, and you're being "taken in" by a nutter?[2]

I guess that's possible, but the evidence in hand is heavily against it. Ms. Rowling's interview comments on this subject, the book's storyline and details, and the symbolist tradition in which she writes, not only stand up to a serious reading, they require it. For the books and their popularity to be understood beyond superficial classification as "a wonderful coming of age" story, we need to get beneath the surface of things, under the veil. The meaning inside is much greater than their storyline outside.[3]

The smart guy in *Harry Potter*, the wizard to whom everyone defers even when he is "just guessing," is Albus Dumbledore, "the greatest wizard of the age." At three different times in the books, and about three different things, the Headmaster refers to a power "greater than magic." In *Philosopher's Stone*, it is music that is "a magic beyond all we do here!"[4] In *Phoenix*, it is love, "a force that is at once more wonderful and terrible than death, than human intelligence, than forces of nature."[5] In *Deathly Hallows*, "the power beyond the reach of any magic" is the knowledge "of house-elves and children's tales, of love, loyalty, and innocence."[6] Dumbledore sees beneath the surface of people and things and has the knowledge of "children's tales."

If we are to share Dumbledore's knowledge, and understand the power of Ms. Rowling's artistry (given her comments, writings, and story requirements), we must learn to see with triangular vision, which will enable us to discover the Hallows symbol's layered meanings.

Ms. Rowling's Comments

Near the end of Chapter 5, I quoted Ms. Rowling's answer to a Spanish reporter's question regarding the last lines of Harry's experience at his noetic King's Cross with Albus Dumbledore. She told him *"That dialogue is the key; I've waited seventeen years to use those lines. Yes, that's right. All this time I've worked to be able to write those two phrases."*[7] We wouldn't need a key to open unlocked, transparent texts whose meaning is on the surface, right? You need a key to understand what map symbols represent. Without the key, a map is only so many colored, squiggly lines; with a key, the text opens up into another world of meaning.

But that key comment she made in 2008 is the icing on the interview cake. Ms. Rowling has been standing on or pointing to the elephant of meaning beneath her storyline for years.

Ms. Rowling's signatures as a writer, for example, are the surprise ending and meticulous planning. She has told reporters that she took *five years* planning the seven book series, filling boxes with notebooks of backstory, before she finished the first book. She also spent six months *planning* how each of her *Potter* novels would work, before beginning the process of writing them. She tells writers aspiring to her kind of success that *planning* their books – knowing where their book is headed and why – is the great secret to writing a good book. **Planning, though, means an author has a purpose in writing, toward which goal, every chapter, action, and writing device points.** If planning is

Ms. Rowling's hallmark, her books deserve a close reading to discern the purpose or meaning she is aiming at.[8]

Her responses about how readers have misunderstood her books suggest, too, that there are wrong ways to read her books and at least one right way. She was asked, for example, in her 2000 *Today* show interview, what she thought about Christians who believed her books promoted witchcraft. She paraphrased George Chistoph Lichtenberg and said, "A book is like a mirror. If a fool looks in, you can't expect a genius to look out."[9] The Lichtenberg original quotation? "A book is a mirror: if an ape looks into it an apostle is hardly likely to look out."

Sidestepping the mirror symbolism, and its equation with reading (see Chapter 5), this exchange reveals Ms. Rowling's belief that the mental capacity and receptivity one brings to the text determines how much its meaning can be understood. Her assertion that readers seeing nothing (or something not in the text, like occultism) is reflective of their idiocy, not the text, suggests in turn that the book can be *profitably* explored by those who read closely and who are not idiots.

She reinforced that idea in a 2008 interview with Adeel Amini :

> *Moving on to a more contentious issue, Rowling has categorically said that she does believe in a higher power, a statement reinforced by her childhood church-going ("Till I was 17," she clarifies). It must be difficult to reconcile her religious beliefs with those that denounce Harry Potter as anti-Christian, I wonder aloud. Rowling's expression does not change a fraction.* **"There was a Christian commentator who said that Harry Potter had been the Christian church's biggest missed opportunity. And I thought, there's someone who actually has their eyes open."**[10]
> (emphasis added)

Ms. Rowling reiterates the idea of her "books are mirrors" view, in saying that they can be read "with eyes open," i.e., with discernment and understanding, or "with eyes closed." That books require interpretation to be understood properly – and that this "eyes open" understanding is not common – is the heart of these remarks.

I think her comments about "fundamentalists" echo this idea, too. She said in the 2007 *Time* magazine "Person of the Year" article: "I'm opposed to fundamentalism in any form," she says. "And that includes in my own religion."[11] Her understanding of "fundamentalism" isn't historical or theological, of course; she uses it in the vernacular sense of "ideological dogmatist" and "literalist fanatic." As much as the epithet "fundamentalist" means, in street usage, "someone whose understanding has been shaped by a literal and narrow interpretation of scripture," Rowling, in speaking against "fundamentalism in any form," is arguing in favor of a more subtle and nuanced reading, or at least one that includes more than just the surface text or literal meaning.

Anyone who has read many of the interviews Ms. Rowling gave between 1997 and the publication of *Deathly Hallows* will tell you the one answer she gave inevitably gave to every reporter, at least once, was "I cannot answer that." To her credit, her two priorities in life, for the greater part of a decade, seem to have been protecting her family from the media and protecting her storyline from anyone and everyone. Not giving clues outside the existing books was certainly, in large part, to prevent "spoiling" the experience of the ending. But there was more to it than that.

Ms. Rowling would not, and still will not, answer questions about her story's meaning. When asked what Harry's name means, for example, she says she always liked that first name, and that a family named Potter lived in the neighborhood where she grew up. This response, I think we can say without unkindness, tells us nothing about the meaning of the name and not much more about why she chose them. Similarly, in answer to a question about why Harry and Dumbledore met at King's Cross station, she said that she thought the name worked "rather well" (!).[12] She confirms here, at least, that there is a connection between the location name and the events of the chapter, but again, she only gives the equivalent of "I liked it" in answer to a request for meaning.

If I asked you what time it was and you responded "6 foot, 7 inches," I would have to think you misunderstood my question. If you repeatedly answered my request for the time with an answer about height, I would be obliged to conclude you were either a moron or you don't want to tell me the time. Ms. Rowling is no moron. That she refuses to answer questions about meaning, then, means (1) she doesn't want to answer the question and (2) we are left to find that out for ourselves.

I suppose that could mean she is saying "there is no meaning," but then we're left with the years of planning and her noting that there are blind and observant readings of her books. Because she's not talking about meaning beyond statements of preference, I believe this is her way of telling us there *is* such meaning to find. And she won't be spoon-

feeding readers not serious enough to see – or look further beyond
– what the texts say.

I think my favorite pointer in Ms. Rowling's references to possible
layered meanings (some deeper than others) comes from her 2000
interview with Larry King:

> KING: Did you think it would do as well with adults?
>
> ROWLING: No. In all honesty, I didn't think it would do this well
> with anyone. I thought I was writing quite an obscure book that
> if it ever got published would maybe have a handful of devotees
> because I thought -- **it is kind of a book for obsessives**. I thought,
> well, maybe a few people will like it a lot. I never expected it to
> have broad appeal.
>
> KING: You might have thought it would be a cult following, a
> small intense group.
>
> ROWLING: Yes, I think if you'd sort of given me a multiple choice
> one and one of them had been mass acclaim and one had been
> cult I'd have picked cult, yes.[13] (emphasis added)

When planning the series, then, she thought of it as "obscure," a "kind
of book for obsessives" that "a few people will like... a lot." Describing
her books as somehow opaque, and making the distinction between "the
few" and "the many," are red flags for texts with sub-surface meanings,
reserved for those serious enough to discern them. Call those readers
"obsessives" if you must; clearly she thought, while planning the books,
that there would be meat beyond the milk (1 Corinthians 3:2) in these
stories to reward those with eyes to see the more substantial meaning.

Books and Lessons About How To Read
Books Inside the *Harry Potter* Books

More importantly, given the limits of auctorial interpretation, the
Harry Potter novels themselves are about reading texts diagonally and
with a transformed vision, by which the reader sees the greater meaning
below the surface and behind the veil. Think on these points:

- Magical terms used by witches and wizards to perform spells
  are not in a language they understand or use. Instead, the Latin
  or East African dialect, or whatever, is all "speech with power."
  However, all the spells, rightly translated, do meaningfully
  correspond with magical effect; they therefore need interpretation

to be understood as more than nonsense. The meanings are in the words, but the surface meanings don't yield these meanings to English-only readers, who must learn another language to interpret and understand the correspondence between spell and magic.

• The principal characters of the books have names that are best described as "Dickensian cryptonyms," which is to say, "name puzzles reflecting the meaning and character of the person so tagged." You don't have to decipher "Remus Lupin" to understand that he is a werewolf, but it was a clear indication of that condition. The name-game Ms. Rowling plays consistently points to a text beneath the surface, a reward for thoughtful readers willing to hold their breath, duck their heads into the deep, and open their eyes.

• The books are mystery stories, driven almost entirely by Nancy Drew and the two Hardy Boys trying to solve a puzzle every year they are at Hogwarts. Readers are invited to play literary detective alongside Harry, Ron, and Hermione; joining them, we scour the text for clues and pointers, even while we are still readers with suspended disbelief. Anyone familiar with the legions of Fandom who spent the greater part of 2001-2007 trying to figure out who Hermione loved, and Snape's true allegiance, knows the books invite second and third readings for greater penetration of the mystery.

• The Ministry of Magic has a Department dedicated to solving or reflecting on the mysteries of time, space, memory, mind/brain, love, and even death. The fittingly-named Department of Mysteries is in the deepest dungeon of the Ministry, a placement suggesting that the big questions are being asked and answered in the depths well beneath the surface.

• Most of the story's various plot twists and surprise endings turn on mistaken identities and misreadings of events, not to mention prejudice crippling understanding. The moral again of each is that, in the language of *Martin Chuzzlewit* and *Pride and Prejudice*, we need to be more "penetrating" in our understanding of others rather than judging by outward appearances. The Wise Man of the books, Albus Dumbledore, is noted especially for his ability to see what others miss; readers are called by his example to "penetrate" the story-line for the "surprise inside."

• In *Chamber of Secrets*, the critical plot point is a book hidden inside another book—Riddle's diary placed in Ginny's textbook. I explain in the chapter on *Chamber,* in *How Harry Cast His Spell,* that the second book is largely about how to read a book and get inside it; even how to confront the author's meaning and intention, with Harry's adventure, in the book the reader is holding, being the counter-spell to the poison hidden in textbooks.Ms. Rowling seems to have been answering her "fundamentalist" critics with an illustration of how to read books -- and why hers are especially rewarding to those who "get inside" them.

• *Deathly Hallows,* too, largely turns on the interpretation of a text. Dumbledore didn't tell Harry flat-out about the three Hallows during his *Half-Blood Prince* tutorials; he leaves Hermione Granger a copy of *The Tales of Beedle the Bard,* in the expectation that she will turn her remarkable intelligence to figure out the meaning of the seemingly innocuous and trivial fairy tales and marginalia. Though a skeptical reader with limited imagination, Hermione does spot the symbol, though she cannot translate or understand it, which proves to be the key that unlocks the mystery. [The fairy tale book's title is significant, too, as I'll explain in a second.]

• Rufus Scrimgeour, the Minister of Magic himself, couldn't figure this out, though he locked himself in a room to study the book at length. He tried to understand the text because he knew Dumbledore wouldn't have given this book to Hermione without reason. Dumbledore tells Harry in King's Cross that Lord Voldemort's great weakness and failing was his certainty that "children's tales" were beneath him; he was consequently ignorance in understanding them as valuable knowledge, even the pearl of great price. As we read in the last chapter's conclusion:

> *"And his knowledge remained woefully incomplete, Harry! That which Voldemort does not value, he takes no trouble to comprehend. Of house-elves and children's tales, of love, loyalty, and innocence, Voldemort knows and understands nothing.* **Nothing.** *That they all have a power beyond his own, a power beyond the reach of any magic, is a truth he has never grasped."* (Chapter 35, pages 709-710; emphasis in text)

The ability to read and understand "children's tales," then, is the way to "a power beyond the reach of any magic." Unlike her public comments, I think Ms. Rowling in her novels is being anything but opaque, or even subtle, with the message that reading her "children's tales" with discernment and penetration will be rewarding exercise, even a transforming experience.

I freely admit that I may be wrong in what I see "between the lines" of *Deathly Hallows*. It isn't likely at all, though, that there is *no meaning* between those lines; both the author and her books have told us there is.

Symbolism: The Path to Meaning

As we discussed in the previous chapter, a symbol (especially in the literary tradition post-Coleridge) is not a stand-in simile ("tit-for-tat") or metaphor ("x" is another way of saying "y"). Symbols are transparencies, even windows, through which veiled greater realities can be seen by the discerning eye. As Coleridge put it:

> A Symbol . . . is characterized by a translucence of the Special in the Individual or of the General in the Especial or of the Universal in the General. Above all by the translucence of the Eternal through and in the Temporal.

As Cutsinger explains, "a thing becomes a symbol by allowing the precedence of something more, something higher and other, to shine through it."[14] Seeing this greater reality is perceiving the unity of existence behind the façade of things.

This sight results from an act of Self-recognition. The *logos* within us (called the *nous* or "mind" in Plato, the Bible, and Church Fathers; "intellect" to the scholastics and philosophers, and, specifically, the "communicative intellect" and "primary imagination" by Coleridge) "recognizes" itself in the *logoi* of created things. Both *logos*-within and *logoi*-outside the person are "continuous with" the *Logos*/Christ – the Word of God and immanence of the transcendent Absolute. Lewis, after Coleridge, identifies this faculty with self-consciousness or simply conscience.

Therefore, the key to symbolism is self-reflection, and the symbol of symbolism is the mirror, the only natural object in which subject-object and self are joined (*nous/logos* to *Logos*). Coleridge put the importance of reflection to our humanness succinctly, even harshly:

READER! – You have been bred in a land abounding with men, able in arts, learning, and knowledges manifold, this man in one, this in another, few in many, none in all. But there is one art, of which every man should be master, the art of REFLECTION. If you are not a *thinking* man, to what purpose are you a *man* at all? In like manner, there is one knowledge, which it is every man's interest and duty to acquire, namely, SELF-KNOWLEDGE: or to what end was man alone, of all animals, endued by the Creator with the faculty of *self-consciousness?* Truly said the Pagan moralist, *e caelo descendit, Gnothi seauton.* ['Know Thyself' is a revelation from heaven](The Author's Preface, page xix)

A reflecting mind, says an ancient writer, is the spring and source of every good thing. (*'Omnis boni principium intellectus cogitabundus.'*) It is at once the disgrace and the misery of men, that they live without fore-thought. As a man without Fore-thought scarcely deserves the name of a man, so Fore-thought without Reflection is but a metaphorical phrase for the *instinct* of a beast. (Aphorism IV, page 2)

In order to learn we must *attend*: in order to profit by what we have learnt, we must *think* – *i.e.* reflect. He only thinks who *reflects*. (Aphorism VII, page 3)

As Lewis wrote, "much depends on the seeing eye" inasmuch as it is the "sacred I" becoming more aware of itself, through reflection in conscience and creation.[15]

Catholic theologian Jean Borella explains what human beings are in terms of our recognizing ourselves:

Man is essentially and first of all an intellectual being, a knowing being, even though this knowing may be of the most humble sensory kind; as loudly and as keenly as desire might speak within him, it speaks to someone who hears and recognizes it, someone for whom it makes sense or is repudiated. But neither is he a believing machine, a "religious automaton" invested with some wholly external revelation or salvation completely incongruous to his nature. He also needs to recognize the Divine Word [*Logos*] – it needs to make sense to him and, in return, he needs to recognize himself in it.[16]

Borella's distinction between "knowing" or intellectual persons (human by their *logos* recognition) with "religious automatons" or "believing machines" (for whom the Divine Word exists and works something "wholly external") is relevant to a discussion of Ms. Rowling's faith. As noted above, she is overtly hostile to "fundamentalism of any kind" and deeply suspicious of a mechanical, evangelical Christianity. She holds the didactic and proselytizing Christian, C. S. Lewis (a man she calls a "genius" and a tremendous influence on her work[17]), at arm's length[18] and says she is not teaching Christianity, per se.[19]

Ms. Rowling's artistry is "subversive," and meant to challenge the conceptual range of a reader living within a corrupt, materialist society. In contrast, literary critic Colin Manlove considers C. S. Lewis' stories to be more "conservative" in trying to encourage resistance to takeover by materialist ideas.[20] Harry Potter's story is meant to inspire us to pursue, as well as give us some experience of, the greater human life consequent to reflection and recognition. So countercultural is this pursuit that Ms. Rowling puts it in a story about resistance to those in power that ends in regime change.

Harry, then, is a revolutionary? Yes, but as an intellectual or, better, as a symbol of the intellect.

Harry Potter as Intellect

Yes, I know Harry is not an "intellectual" in the normal sense that word is used. He only does well in Defense Against the Dark Arts and struggles along with Ron in Hermione's wake in all other Hogwarts classes. Harry is a symbol of the "intellect," however, in the proper use of that word; not as a synonym for "reason" and the discursive part of the soul, but as the noetic or spiritual faculty (the so-called "eye of the heart") – the power of reflection and recognition as discussed by Borella, Coleridge, and Lewis. As I explain at some length in *How Harry Cast His Spell* (pages 95-99), Harry, Hermione, and Ron (like Alyosha, Ivan, and Dmitri in *The Brothers Karamazov;* Kirk, Spock, and Bones in *Star Trek,* and Luke, Leia, and Han in *Star Wars*) are a soul triptych, or story transparencies through which we can see the spirit/mind/body aspects of the human person shining through.

Harry, as the Intellect or Spirit part of this "troop," is in charge when everything is in its right place. (When Spirit becomes obedient to mind or body, or is removed from either, the agonizing "nothing is going right" parts in the books begin). Harry leads because the noetic aspect of the person is the "home," of the "sacred I," or *logos,* that is the conscience and the self-recognizing Word making perception possible – "all-forms" perceiving itself in the forms in all other things.

"Wait a minute," I can hear you thinking, "if Harry is Mr. Intellect, how come he's almost never right? The end of the first six books is about how wrong Harry was." Good point. The reason Harry doesn't get it right until the end of the seventh book is because, in addition to being a symbol of the intellect in the spirit-mind-body trio with Ron and Hermione, as such, he is also something of a "Christian Everyman" on a hero's journey towards spiritual purification and perfection. In the first six books, as good and as heroic as Harry is, he is still straddled with an inner-Voldemort, the soul fragment of the Dark Lord quite literally on his mind. We know this is his "heart of darkness" because of "where" Harry goes the moment his scar-Horcrux is destroyed.

As discussed in the last chapter, Harry finds himself naked, feeling great, and with perfect vision in a place that doesn't have the usual aspects of place about it. His first attempts at understanding it result in vague ideas of a palace, the home of a king, with a vaulted, domed ceiling through which light shines. He then realizes "where" he is can be described as "King's Cross," though it isn't the London underground train station he is used to.

Before we discuss the iconological meaning of the Cross, I'd note here that the London King's Cross, especially Platform 9 ¾, is the place of intersection and transition between Harry's mundane, Muggle existence with his Aunt and Uncle's family (who must be related to the magical Thicknesse clan) and his life at Hogwarts and the Wizarding World. Every young witch and wizard, as Steve Vander Ark has pointed out in his "Wizard Geography" talk at Harry Potter conventions, has to come to London to get on the Hogwarts Express, no matter how silly this is in terms of efficient point A to point B travel. Mr. Vander Ark calls this a classic example of "wizard logic." If he meant by that, it isn't practical or rational, I'd have to agree.

The logic of King's Cross as a point of transition and intersection – and the reason Harry describes the place-that-isn't-a-place "where" he meets Dumbledore as "King's Cross" – is that it is the world within both worlds, the equivalent of Lewis' "Wood between the Worlds" (cf., Chapter 3, *The Magician's Nephew*). Paul Ford describes that non-local and timeless place:

> [The Wood between the Worlds is] the wood where Polly and Digory arrive after leaving Uncle Andrew's study via the magic rings. Polly first calls it the Wood between the Worlds after

Digory reasons that they are indeed between worlds. It is so dense and leafy that the light is green, the air is warm, and no sky can be seen. There is no sound of life or wind, and the wood is characterized by a feeling of timelessness. There are pools everywhere, and although they look deep they are really shallow. It is hard for the children to feel frightened in the wood, and at first it is difficult for them to remember who they are and where they've come from. They feel as if they have always been in the Wood.

Curiously, the Wood seems to affect people in varying ways, according to their innate goodness. When Digory and Polly return there from Charn, the Wood seems "rich and warmer and more peaceful" by contrast. But Queen Jadis looks paler and far less beautiful in its atmosphere; in fact, the air seems to stifle her. The children lose their fear when they realize that they are stronger than she. Upon her return to the wood, Jadis becomes "deadly sick." Uncle Andrew is shivering there (probably with fear), but Strawberry seems to look and feel better. (*Companion to Narnia*, HarperCollins (1984), page 446)

Both Rowling and Lewis describe characters experiencing these "between worlds" places in a sensory way; these places are something like the worlds of time and space from which they came. The timelessness, and non-spatial aspects and qualities, however, especially the sense of reward and vitality for the pure in heart and discomfort or punishment for the wicked, give them an "otherworldly" feel. The good *feel* good and the bad *feel* bad, and it is the *same* place. This is reminiscent of Quirrelldemort's burning at contact with Lily's sacrificial love in Harry's skin (*Stone*, Chapter 17, page 295). It also echoes the Christian doctrine of Heaven and Hell being the same "place,"—God's glory—experienced by the righteous and selfish as light and fire respectively (cf., *How Harry Cast His Spell*, pages 132-134, and Lewis' *The Last Battle*, Chapter 13, "How the Dwarves Refused to be Taken In").

I think, though, it is a mistake to understand these places of transition and intersection as an "afterlife" or "otherworld." The fantasy places "between worlds" are better pictured as non-local reality "behind" or "within" time=space duality and experience. They are, in brief, story transparencies of the eternal point of creation and unity of existence, with which the conscience or *logos*-mind and intellect are "continuous." Harry Potter, Christian Everyman and symbol of Intellect, "goes there," i.e., "returns to himself" as soon as he is rid of his inner Voldemort, the scar-Horcrux, by an act of loving self-sacrifice.

Ms. Rowling's has described Dumbledore's revelation at the end of the King's Cross dialog (that what is real is what is happening "in your head," especially Harry's head, qua intellect) as the "key" to the books she waited seventeen years to write.[21] It is "key" because bringing Harry and us to this realization and understanding has been the point of Harry's seven year hero's journey. Harry Potter's name is instructive on this point. The hero of the piece, in contrast with Voldemort's puppet at the Ministry, has a name meaning 'Heir of the Father,' or, at least in keeping with Biblical usage of 'Potter' as "shaper of the human vessel," 'Heir of God.'[22] At his death to ego-self and the destruction of his inner-Voldemort, Harry becomes the "sacred I" and travels non-locally to the point of intersection uniting all existence, just beneath the veil of every person and thing—God the Word.

That is very hard for postmodern readers to consciously grasp. Because "reality," to us, is the surface multiplicity of our time and space-material world, a world Lewis, Rowling, and symbolist authors, from Shakespeare to our times, see both as unreal and as real a story as the fantasies they write. The meaning is beneath the surface, where the greater reality "fillest all things" or gives the surface its substance.

Martin Lings, student and friend of C. S. Lewis and disciple of Frithjof Schuon, defined a symbol as "the reflection or shadow of a higher reality" (*Symbol and Archetype*, Quinta Essentia, 1991, page 2); this definition clues us into our problem in "getting this." We don't believe in an immanent "greater reality" above or behind us. Or that there is a hierarchy of being in which *anything* is more real than any other thing, or by which these things are joined. In an ontologically flat world, in which everything is perceived as a distinct and separate object of energy and matter, quantities devoid of qualities, realities like truth, virtue, and beauty, symbolism can't be taken very seriously. Contrast this attitude with what Lings says of Shakespeare's audiences:

> The first spectators of Shakespeare were probably more receptive than we are. We tend to take art less seriously than they did. For modern man the supreme distinction is between 'fiction' and 'truth', as we say, between art on the one hand and 'reality' on the other. Now naturally our medieval ancestors made the same distinction, but for them it was not so sharp. They were not in the habit of speaking and thinking of life as 'truth'. **By truth, by reality, they meant something different; for them the supreme distinction was not between life and art, but between the next**

world, that is, Truth, and this world, which is the shadow of Truth. The sharpness of that distinction took the edge off all other distinctions.

Moreover, art for them was not merely a copy of life, that is, it was not merely the shadow of a shadow; it was also by inspiration, partly – and is some supreme cases even almost wholly – a direct copy or shadow of the 'substance' itself. **The distinction between art and life is therefore not so much between a shadow and a reality as between two shadows.** This sounds exaggerated, and no doubt the divergence in outlook between then and now was far slighter for the vast majority than might appear from what has just been said. But it went certainly further than a mere verbal quibble over the meaning of the word 'reality', and it would have been enough to make an appreciable difference in the attitude of an audience to a play. **By attributing a less absolute reality to life they attributed more reality to art. They no doubt entered into it more whole-heartedly.** (*Secret of Shakespeare*, Inner Traditions, 1984; page 136; emphasis added)

Shakespeare took his Globe audiences, people more apt to suspend their disbelief in the exclusive reality of the visible world, as imaginative participants into his alchemical dramas. Their cathartic experience there, in identifying with the character symbols on stage, brought them only to themselves, which is to say, to King's Cross, the Wood Between the Worlds, the intellective unity of existence behind the veil.

Three Dimensional Texts:
The Surface, the Edifying, and the Alchemical

Northrop Frye, whose *The Anatomy of Criticism* is the foundational study of symbolic, mythic, and archetypal literary criticism, refers to an "iconological tradition"[23] of criticism that stretches from Dante through Spenser[24] to Ruskin.[25] Frye, in his pursuit of a "science of literary criticism," arrives at a theory of symbols, with the levels of meaning corresponding to this tradition's understanding of art symbolism, nature, and literature.[26]

We need to understand the "iconological tradition" because of Ms. Rowling's evident ties to Dante and the importance of getting literary symbols right, to understand what the Wade Center (a C. S. Lewis and Inklings study/research center in Illinois) calls "symbolist literature." Understanding story transparencies means seeing them as three-dimensional texts, with surface, moral, and alchemical meanings.

In Chapter 4 I discussed the Dante influence on Ms. Rowling and the layered writing of the *Divine Comedy*. Thomas Aquinas detailed in the *Summa Theologia* that there are four levels of meaning in an inspired text. Dante writes at all four levels, but is rarely read at the most important one. As I wrote then to introduce the iconological approach to profound texts:

> Rene Guenon, in his *The Esoterism of Dante* (Sophia Perennis, 1996), reminds us that Dante urges his readers, first, "to search beneath the veil of my strange allegory" (*Inferno*, IX, 61-63) and that in *Convivio* (The Banquet), II:1, he says his poetry has diverse meanings and "they may be understood, and they must be explained in four senses." In this, Dante follows the Angelic Doctor and traditional understanding of the four layers of text – literal , allegorical, moral, and anagogical—of text, especially scripture.

About this last, the poet explains, "The fourth sense is called anagogical, that is to say, beyond the [physical] senses; and this occurs when a scripture is expounded in a spiritual sense which, although it is true also in the literal sense, signifies by means of the things signified a part of the supernal things of eternal glory." Guenon writes that Dante today, however, is interpreted on three levels exclusively — the literal or poetic, the allegorical or "philosophical-theological" "hidden meaning," and the moral, political or social. However profound the exegesis of the exoteric religious meaning at the level of allegory, the neglect of the anagogical or metaphysical means the kernel of the nut has not been revealed (*Esoterism*, p.2).

I'm not going to quarrel or naysay either Dante or Aquinas, but I do want to simplify their four levels of meaning down to three. Taking out the "literal," because not even Harry's most devoted reader believes these stories actually took place, we're left with:

1. The Surface Meaning

2. The Edifying Meaning

3. The Alchemical Meaning

The surface meaning is the story itself, the vehicle in and behind which the other meanings are carried. In *Romeo and Juliet*, it is the tale of star-crossed lovers in a city divided by feuding families. In Lewis' *The Lion, the Witch, and the Wardrobe*, the story line is the fantasy adventure of four children in service to Aslan and their attempts to free

Narnia from a wicked witch. Some of the themes play across the surface of these stories; most readers and audiences, however, experience them *consciously* "just" as tales well told.

As engaging as these adventures are, and as interested as we are in the characters, the edifying or moral meaning of the story is where we first experience the depth of the playwright's and novelist's meaning. We identify with the heroes and suffer alongside them, assimilating something of their cathartic agonies, and the virtues and morality consequent to them. Lewis like to call this "training in the stock responses." Beyond recognition of – and right understanding – of right and wrong, virtue and vice, this training included an appreciation of beauty and the transcendent. Traditional images and symbols cue the reader to grasp what is true and good and beautiful in character, in choices, and in nature.

In the tragedy in Verona, we experience a play of light and dark, of love's brilliance and hatred's blindness and violence. Like the Capulet and Montague parents reconciled at story's end, we are obliged to acknowledge how all contraries had been resolved in the light and love of their children's sacrificial union. Aslan's sacrifice on the Stone Table in *The Lion, the Witch, and the Wardrobe* gives us an almost allegorical transparency of Christ's victory over death on the Cross, and, with Edmund, we accept this sacrifice as being for us. Both stories have didactic philosophical and theological points to make, delivered just below the story's surface, for our edification and moral or religious education.

Beneath this level, though, Dante, Shakespeare, and Lewis are artists reaching for our transformation. Shakespeare is writing an implicitly alchemical work,[27] resolving the contraries of the city in the vessel of the joined lovers; the play is heavy with contrary images and even has alchemical items in the apothecary shop. *Romeo and Juliet* is a dramatization of the Great Work, in which the king and queen die, and all contraries are resolved into one (hence, too, the golden statue the families erect at play's end).

Lewis, too, is a hermetic writer, and his first Narnia novel, as Michael Ward has demonstrated in *Planet Narnia* (Oxford, 2007), is written with astrological artistry to initiate the reader into the Jovian qualities of Christ. This metaphysical or anagogical layer is in the story as symbol; its esoteric images and structures are just out of plain sight, *unless* one is looking diagonally at what seem to be arbitrary stage settings and directions. All of this meaning is centered on the divinization or apotheosis of the players, by their contact and communion with a greater reality. You might want to think of these three layers as a Quidditch game you can play in an armchair, while reading your favorite book. Unlike Muggle sports, as you know, Quidditch is a *three*-dimensional challenge that adds height to the breadth and width of a surface-only playing field.

- The *surface* meaning of Quidditch – the larger part of the visible game – is the battle between the Chasers and Keepers to score or prevent goals, with the Beaters and Bludgers present to keep things interesting in the largely horizontal match.

- In every one of Ms. Rowling's Quidditch matches, there is a moral issue, mystery, or question of character that comes into play. Layered on top of the game, this makes the match more important than "who wins the game," and an *edifying* experience for the reader.

- And, above and beyond the game and the moral, flies the Seeker, searching for the difficult-to-grasp and harder-to-see Golden Snitch. Until the Seeker sees and catches the Snitch (an alchemical symbol, by the way, for prime matter), the game is not over.

The sport is in this way a metaphor for reading. What you see in Quidditch is the surface meaning of, say, Gryffindor battling Ravenclaw. If you look a little harder, you will see the drama of characters making right and wrong choices to win the contest. But what really matters is the Reader/Seeker seeing and grasping the greatest meaning, the alchemical prize that resolves the contraries and ends the game, win or lose. The Seeker is *in* the game but his important role and is *above,* and independent of, the surface story and evident moral instruction.

The Harry Potter novels operate on these three levels as well. On the surface, we have the great "beach-read": a mystery-driven narrative of good versus evil *bildungsroman* in fantasy sub-creation, with postmodern themes celebrating tolerance and diversity while condemning prejudice and discrimination. The Death Eater Nazis are bad, opposing them is good, and the stories are exciting, funny, and totally engaging. The movies, with the inevitable chase scenes and strictly visual story-telling ("no thinking, please!"), excel at delivering the surface story and at least some part of its postmodern meanings.

Harry's legion of fans among librarians, literacy advocates, and youth ministers, love him because of the celebration of the "stock responses" in the stories. Yes, the students misbehave and are disrespectful. *And*, peccadilloes like these aside, they deliver the most powerful magic of "love, loyalty, and innocence" in these children's stories with a truckload of traditional Christian symbolism and theology.

Because I was the first to write at length about the Christian content of the stories' imagery, themes, and meaning (and received my share of nasty grams from those who wouldn't or couldn't see any of it), I can say in all modesty that Ms. Rowling is right to describe this symbolism as "obvious." If you have to squint or strain to see that the Good Guys are lions in a House named "Golden Griffin," and the Bad Guys are underground and like snakes and serpents a lot, the problem is with your eye-wear prescription, not the difficulty of the story-signage, which is largely transparent.

And then there is the third layer, consisting largely of symbols and story structures without clear referents. Here is the alchemical structure of the books, the hero's journey story-scaffolding, and the multitude of seemingly arbitrary stage settings and images. Like the astrological backdrop and meaning in the *Narniad*, Ms. Rowling's anagogical work here is very subtle, even if naming the first book *Philosopher's Stone* was not an obscure reference. Would it have taken fifty years for Lewis scholars to break code (as did Michael Ward) if, instead of *The Lion, the Witch, and the Wardrobe*, Lewis had titled his first Narnia book *The Pevensie Children By Jove?*. Subtle or not, though, the alchemical, transformative layer of meaning is there. It's the meat behind the milk of the surface and moral layers.

Conclusion

Having picked up the tools of seeing with triangular vision, we can turn to the symbol in *Deathly Hallows* that Albus Dumbledore leaves to Hermione and friends to decipher. The meaning of the symbol is fascinating in itself; what is startling is how Ms. Rowling has written a textbook for us to understand and practice symbol interpretation, wearing traditional tri-focals, if you will, in the story of various characters interpreting the triangular eye. She even throws in a short scene as a vignette, or story-picture, of the symbol's anagogical meaning. If you're ready to see just how much bigger the symbol's inside can be than a symbol's outside would suggest, read on.

Endnotes

1   Webster says iconology is "the study of artistic symbolism." As we'll see, there is a tradition of iconological criticism of multi-valent texts especially appropriate for symbolist literature.

2   For this kind of skepticism about "taking Harry seriously," see 'The Code Breakers' by Alan Jacobs (*First Things*, August/September 2006; http://www.firstthings.com/article.php3?id_article=5332).   Dr.   Jacobs, an English professor at Wheaton College and biographer of C. S. Lewis, dismisses the alchemical structure of the narrative Ms. Rowling has said sets "the magical parameters" of the series (see chapter 2) as so much frenetic nonsense.

3   See chapter 5, note viii, for the many times Ms. Rowling shows "an inside greater than its outside" in the *Harry Potter* novels.

4   *Stone*, Chapter 7, p. 128

5   *Phoenix*, Chapter 37, pp. 843-844

6   *Hallows*, Chapter 35, pp. 709-710

7   http://www.the-leaky-cauldron.org/2008/2/9/jkr-discusses-dursley-family-religion-us-presidential-election-and-more-in-new-interview

8   See Introduction, *Unlocking Harry Potter*, John Granger, Zossima Press, 2007

9   www.accio-quote.org/articles/2000/1000-nbc-couric.htm

10   http://www.adeelamini.com/JKR/ESTE012C_adeelaminicom_JKR.pdf

Ms. Rowling read "the Christian commentator's" comments almost certainly in the *Time* magazine piece about her from December 2007:

It turns out that Rowling, like her hero, is a Seeker. She talks about having a great religious curiosity, going back to childhood. "No one in my family was a believer. But I was very drawn to faith, even while doubting," she says. "I certainly had this need for something that I wasn't getting at home, so I was the one who went out looking for religion." As a girl, she would go to church by herself. She still attends regularly, and her children were all christened. Her Christian defenders always thought her faith shined through her stories. One called the books the "greatest evangelistic opportunity the church has ever missed." (emphasis added)

http://www.time.com/time/specials/2007/personoftheyear/article/0,28804,1690753_1695388_1695436,00.html I was interviewed for this article and I am probably the unnamed "Christian defender" quoted in the piece.

11 http://www.time.com/time/specials/2007/personoftheyear/article/0,28804,1690753_1695388_1695436,00.html

12   www.accio-quote.org/articles/2007/0730-bloomsbury-chat.html

13   www.accio-quote.org/articles/2000/1000-cnn-larryking.htm

14   *The Statesmens Manual, 30,* quoted in *The Form of the Transformed Vision,* James Cutsinger, Mercer University Press, pages 79-80:

> Thus, symbols serve true unity because they reveal an open existence in which the being of all is made possible by the fluidity and transparency of each. Symbolization is akin to "Gravitation, all in all/nothing in any one part, as fluid, either, or such like"; like gravity, and like the soul, which is also "all in every part," and to which it is analogous, a symbol is "that nothing-something, something-nothing." It is with this in mind that Coleridge offered his most commonly quoted definition: "A Symbol . . . is characterized by a translucence of the Special in the Individual or of the General in the Especial or of the Universal in the General. Above all by the translucence of the Eternal through and in the Temporal." In each case, a thing becomes a symbol by allowing the precedence of something more, something higher and other, to shine through it.

15   Cf., the discussion in Chapter 5 of this book, C. S. Lewis, *Essay Collection,* HarperCollins (2002), chapter 8, 'The Seeing Eye,' and Coleridge, *Aids to Reflection,* Chelsea House (1983)

16   *The Secret of the Christian Way,* Jean Borella, edited and translated by G. John Champoux, SUNY Press (2001), page 20

17   *The names of Dahl and C S Lewis are frequently mentioned alongside Ms Rowling's, a comparison at which she has balks. "C S Lewis is quite simply a genius and I'm not a genius," she said. "And while I think Dahl is a master at what he did, I do think my books are more moral than his. He also wrote very overblown comic characters, whereas I think mine are more three-dimensional."*

Williams, Rhys. "The spotty schoolboy and single mother taking the mantle from Roald Dahl," *The Independent* (London), 29 January 1999; http://www.accio-quote.org/articles/1999/0199-independent-williams.html

"Although I love C. S. Lewis, I have a problem with his imitators." At 33, Rowling still re-reads The Chronicles of Narnia, famous for The Lion, the Witch and the Wardrobe (she likes The Voyage of the Dawn Treader best), along with other childhood favourites, E. Nesbit, Paul Gallico and Noel Streatfield.

Blakeney, Sally. "The Golden Fairytale," *The Australian*, 7 November 1998; http://www.accio-quote.org/articles/1998/1198-australian-blakeney.html

18 Grossman, Lev. "J.K. Rowling Hogwarts And All," *Time Magazine*, 17 July, 2005; http://www.accio-quote.org/articles/2005/0705-time-grossman.htm

19 http://www.mtv.com/news/articles/1572107/20071017/index.jhtml

20 Perhaps the easiest way of understanding Ms. Rowling's simultaneous discomfort with and admiration for C. S. Lewis is in Colin Manlove's essay 'Parent or Associate? George MacDonald and the Inklings' (*George MacDonald: Literary Heritage and Heirs*, Roderick McGillis, editor, Zossima Press, 2008, pp. 235-236). Manlove distinguishes two types of fantasy or symbolist writers: the subversive and conservative. The subversive writer "aims to undermine his reader's assumptions and ways of seeing the world" either "for the sake of broadening our perspective on life" or for the purpose of leading us towards God. His fantasies are full of paradoxes, riddles, and other reverses to point us to a new and transcendent level of discourse." Speaking about MacDonald as a subversive, Manlove says his fantasies "are founded on words, scenes, and events that continually reverse one another, pushing a deeper knowledge beneath a shallower one; and characters frequently change shape, according to their inner natures, or the spiritual nature of the person looking at them." *Conservative* fantasy writers, in contrast, "seek to preserve something, to keep things as they are;" Manlove says this is especially true of Lewis' Space Trilogy and *Narniad.* Rowling and Lewis are both Christian symbolist writers, but as "subversive" and "conservative" authors, their works differ in tone and posture. And one appeals to conservative Christians much more than the other!

21 http://www.the-leaky-cauldron.org/2008/2/9/jkr-discusses-dursley-family-religion-us-presidential-election-and-more-in-new-interview

22 *How Harry Cast His Spell*, John Granger, Tyndale (2008), pages 120-124

23 Northrop Frye, *The Anatomy of Criticism*, Princeton University Press, 1957, page 10

24 Spencer, famous as a writer of allegory, transcends the allegorical in his choice of images because their "depth or thickness" make them reach to Dantean symbolic, even alchemical meanings. C. S. Lewis writes that this "depth or thickness" is "why work on Spencer's philosophical and iconographical background seems to be so much more rewarding than work on his historical allegory."" What is clear in Spenser is the image" (C. S. Lewis, *Oxford History of the English Language, 16th Century Excluding Drama)*, Oxford University Press, 1954, pages 388, 387) The multi-layered

quality of these images and their association with the four levels of meaning beneath Dante's veils are evident in Frye's exegesis of Spencer's St. George:

> The battle with the dragon lasts of course, three days: at the end of each of the first two days St. George is beaten back and is strengthened, first by the water of life, then by the tree of life. These represent the two sacraments which the reformed church accepted; they are the two features of the garden of Eden to be restored to man in the apocalypse, and they have also a more general Eucharist connection. St. George's emblem is a red cross on a white ground, which is the flag borne by Christ in traditional iconography when he returns in triumph from the prostrate dragon of hell. The red and white symbolize the two aspects of the risen body, flesh and blood, bread and wine, and in Spenser they have a historical connection with the union of red and white roses in the reigning head of the church. The link between the sacramental and the sexual aspects of the red and white symbolism is indicated in alchemy, with which Spenser was clearly acquainted, in which a crucial phase of the production of the elixir of immortality is known as the union of the red king and the white queen. (Northrop Frye, *The Anatomy of Criticism,* Princeton University Press, 1957, pages 194-195)

You recognize the Alchemical Wedding from Chapter 2's discussion of *Deathly Hallows'* alchemical images, structures, and meaning, and we will get to the tree of life, but here we need only note the allegorical, moral-political, and anagogical-spiritual meanings in Spencer's image. Iconographical, indeed.

25   John Ruskin, most famous during his life as an art critic, extended his ideas about painting to literary criticism, even political philosophy. His influence, though not especially well known today, is hard to over-estimate; M. K. Gandhi, for example, frequently cited Ruskin and Tolstoy as the greatest Western influences on his idea of *satyagraha,* or peace-force in political action. Ruskin's "reach" and continuing influence in the worlds of art and literary criticism are more profound.

And he explained both how we are to understand the sort of books Ms. Rowling writes, both in the experience and work involved. In his *Queen of the Air* (1869), Ruskin described how a symbolist poem or story-as-myth affected a reader, and the effort that reader would have to make to understand it fully – not surprisingly, in terms of art appreciation. Note his insistence that there is a didactic or moral layer in all good art; that the sub-surface meanings are hidden and require a key to open; and that there is a spiritual level whose meaning probably escapes even the understanding of the inspired artist:

> [The Homeric poems] are not conceived didactically, but are *didactic in their essence, as all good art is.* There is an increasing insensibility to this character, and even an open denial of it, among us, now, which is one of the most curious errors of modernism, -- the peculiar and judicial blindness of an age which, having long practiced art and poetry for the sake of pleasure only, has become incapable of reading their language when they were both didactic....

And even the celebrated passage of Horace about Iliad is now misread or disbelieved, as if it was impossible to believe that the Iliad could be instructive because it is not like a sermon. Horace does not say that it is like a sermon, and would have been still less likely to say so, if he ever had had the advantage of hearing a sermon. "I have been reading that story of Troy again" (thus he writes to a noble youth of Rome whom he cared for), "quietly at Praeneste, while you have been busy at Rome, and truly I think that what is base, and what is noble, and what useful and useless, may be better learned from that, than from all Chrysippus' and Crantor's talk put together."

Which is profoundly true, not of the Iliad only, but of *all other great art whatsoever; for all pieces of such art are didactic in the purest way, indirectly and occultly,* so that, first, you shall only be bettered by them if you are already hard at work at bettering yourself; and when you **are** bettered by them, it shall be partly with a general acceptance of their influence, *so constant and subtle that you shall be no more conscious of it than of the healthy digestion of food; and partly by a gift of unexpected truth, which you shall only find by slow mining for it; -- which is withheld on purpose, and close-locked, that you may not get it till you have forged the key of it in a furnace of your own heating.*

And this withholding of their meaning, is continual and confessed, in the great poets. Thus Pindar says of himself: "There is many an arrow in my quiver, full of speech to the wise, but, for the many, they need interpreters." And *neither Pindar, not Aeschylus, nor Hesiod nor Homer, nor any of the greater poets or teachers of any nation or time, ever spoke but with intentional reservation: nay, beyond this, there is often a meaning which they themselves cannot interpret, --in what they said, so far as it recorded true imaginative vision.* (emphasis added in italics)

Ruskin ends this passage with the suggestion that modern critics who deny this layer of meaning do so because they are incapable of seeing, not to mention interpreting it:

> "For all the greatest myths have been seen, by the men who tell them, involuntarily and passively, -- seen by them with as great distinctness, (and in some respects, though not in all, under conditions as far beyond the control of their will) as a dream sent any of us by night when we dream clearest; and it is this veracity of this vision that could not be refused, and of moral that could not be foreseen, which in modern historical inquiry has been left wholly out of account: being indeed the thing which no merely historical investigator can understand, or even believe; for it belongs exclusively to the creative or artistic group of men, and can only be interpreted by those of their race, who themselves in some measure also see visions and dream dreams."
> John Ruskin, *The Queen of the Air*, John Wiley & Son, 1873 (1.17, pp. 15-18)

Ruskin, the giant of Victorian and Edwardian criticism, whose ideas of typological symbolism inspired the Pre-Raphaelite Brotherhood of painters and several generations of 19th century architects, thinks of the influence of literature as instructive, but "indirectly and occultly," working its influence first by an unconscious "constant and subtle" action, and then, after the labors of "slow mining" to extract meaning, by epiphany. This mining work is necessary because the treasured gems are not on the surface; none "of the greater poets and teachers of any nation or time, ever spoke but with intentional reservation" and the anagogical meaning, "of true imaginative vision," even they could not have understood sans explanation.

Appreciation of the best literature, ancient and modern, is the union of receptivity to the action of images, and the meditative effort to understand them in their "depth or thickness," as Lewis would have it. Dante, Spencer, Ruskin, Lewis, and Frye all speak to the necessity of getting well beneath the surface of images as multi-valent symbols, if we are to grasp the artistry, genius, and meaning of a work (or its lack of same).

26   Frye, op. cit., pages 71-130; cf., http://en.wikipedia.org/wiki/Anatomy_of_Criticism#Second_essay_-_Ethical_Criticism:_Theory_of_Symbols

27   See *The Secret of Shakespeare*, Martin Lings, Inner Traditions (1984), page 14

Chapter 7

The Triangular Eye

*The Symbol of the Three Hallows as an Exercise
in Reading Books and Their Images on Three Levels of Meaning*

This is a test.

The tool we've just learned about is a lens for reading symbolist stories on three levels: the surface, the moral, and the alchemical. Ms. Rowling has been generous enough to write the story of a symbol being interpreted at different levels into the story of *Deathly Hallows*. Reflecting on those three levels, and how symbols work as a rule, gives us leverage to do three things: open up the anagogical meaning of the Hallows symbol, recognize its three-part meaning in context of the book, and answer questions about why the books are loved by so many and despised by others.

It *is* a test, but less like an English exam than a driver's test. Pass this practical application of what you've learned about the trifocal lens, and you can enter into the "greater inside than outside" of the best books ever written. You'll have earned your license to read the Greats with greater pleasure than you could have imagined.

When the monitor gives the signal, you may begin the test. Please write me a note when you are finished to let me know how you did.

The Deathly Hallows Symbol: Three Levels of Interpretation Represented by Three Story Characters

We find the Deathly Hallows symbol, the "triangular eye," in four places: around Xenophilius Lovegood's neck, in the *Tales of Beedle the Bard* as marginalia, on the Peverell gravestone at Godric's Hollow, and finally, on the Resurrection Stone. It is a triangulated circle bisected by a perpendicular line running apex to base. The surface meaning we get from Viktor Krum, Hermione and Ron give us the moral interpretation, and Lovegood and Dumbledore separately give Harry the "real" meaning concealed beneath the other layers.

• **Surface Meaning:** We first see the Hallows symbol at Bill and Fleur's wedding. Xenophilius Lovegood wears it; "an odd symbol, rather like a triangular eye, glistened from a golden chain around his neck" (Chapter 8, page 139). One of Fleur's guests, the star Seeker Viktor Krum, recognizes it and becomes very angry. To him it is "the symbol" (Chapter 8, page 148) of Gellert Grindelwald and the "Greater Good" fascism that Grindelwald brought to his country. To the Bulgarian, Grindelwald represents a "wizard-twin" of Hitler, the leader of the National Socialists, with the Hallows symbol a stand-in for the Nazi swastika, and those who would wear it, Neo-Nazis.

This Nazi-like wizard responsible for the death of Krum's grandfather. As a point of honor, Victor confronts Lovegood, though we aren't told if he challenged him to a duel; the party is broken up by Death Eaters before we learn Viktor's plan.

Krum's response to what is described twice as a "triangular eye" and "symbol," is its surface meaning, in that he doesn't interpret anything about the symbol *per se*. What it means to Viktor is the knee-jerk association it brings to mind for him with the murderers of his family and young punks who act tough. The symbol's surface meaning tells us nothing about the bisected and triangulated circle.

• **Moral Meaning:** The symbol turns up again after Ron departs the trio. Hermione points to "that symbol" (Chapter 16, page 316) at the top of a *Beedle the Bard* page and Harry assumes it is a rune: "a picture of what looked like a triangular eye, its pupil crossed with a vertical line." He recounts his experience with Viktor and Xenophilius at the wedding. They see the sign next in the Godric's Hollow graveyard on Ignotus Peverell's headstone. "Hermione showed him the symbol beneath [Ignotus Peverell's name]" (Chapter 16, page 326). When Ron returns and they travel to the Lovegood ziggurat to learn more, Harry asks Xenophilius point blank: "It's about that symbol you were wearing around your neck at Bill and Fleur's wedding, Mr. Lovegood. We wondered what it meant" (Chapter 20, page 404).

Having been identified again and again as a "symbol," variously as "odd" (139, 148) and "weird" (316), the players have discovered through *Beedle* and the headstone that the triangular eye predates Grindelwald and must have a meaning beyond Krum's reaction to its associative, surface meaning. After Hermione reads "The Tale of the Three Brothers" in *The Tales of Beedle the Bard*, Lovegood, odd bird that he is, explains the "real" meaning of the symbol discovered on the edifying story's first page. The symbol is a cipher for three real, powerful magical objects, each of which is represented in the triangular eye glyph.

After debating with Lovegood, until he leaves the room to fetch dinner, "Hermione, *looking skeptical*" Chapter 21, page 415; emphasis added) tells Harry, "It's a pile of utter rubbish. This can't be what the sign really means. This must just be his weird take on it. What a waste of time" (page 414). She agrees with Ron that Xenophilius' Hallows interpretation can be dismissed as wizard "superstitition," and the 'Tale of the Three Brothers' is "just a morality tale" (page 414). As Ron put it, "that story is just one of those things you tell kids to teach them lessons, isn't it? 'Don't go looking for trouble, don't pick fights, don't go messing around with stuff that's been left alone! Just keep your head down, mind your own business, and you'll be okay'" (414).

Ron and Hermione, then, interpret the symbol within the tale as a teaching point or vehicle for "training in the stock responses." They're profoundly skeptical and dismissive of Lovegood's belief that the Hallows are real, which is remarkable on two counts. First, they are fascinated with the idea of the Death Stick, Resurrection Stone, and Invisibility Cloak, and debate which would be best to have.

Their skepticism about the real-world meaning of the symbol is a real head-slapper, though – it's in Dumbledore's specific gift to Hermione and on a Godric's Hollow gravestone, and they have used the Invisibility Cloak, which Xenophilius describes to them in detail, for more than six years. "[Hermione, Ron, and Harry] glanced at one another [during Lovegood's Cloak talk], and Harry knew that they were all thinking the same thing. It so happened that a cloak exactly like the one Xenophilius had just described was in the room with them at that very moment" (page 411). Harry comes to believe in the Hallows but Hermione insists; "That symbol doesn't mean anything" (Chapter 22, page 433).

> • **The Alchemical Meaning:** No character champions an anagogical or spiritual meaning for the Hallows in the book, at least not in the way Viktor expresses the surface meaning, and Ron and Hermione the "morality tale" interpretation. All Ms. Rowling does is have Xenophilius insist the Hallows symbol stands for

very real things, an interpretation Harry eventually accepts and Dumbledore confirms (Chapter 35, page 714).

As Xenophilius understands and explains it, the symbol is a three-part ideogram, each part representing one very real Hallow: the vertical line is the Elder Wand or Death Stick, the circle is the Resurrection Stone, and the triangle is Harry's Invisibility Cloak. Xenophilius dismisses Viktor's understanding (which is restricted to the symbol's *surface* meaning) as "ignorance" and "crude." He discounts, too, the *edifying* or moral meaning of the "children's tale" in *Beedle* as a story "told to amuse rather than to instruct." He accepts as demonstrated fact, though, that the items exist, and winning all three and uniting them "will make the possessor master of Death" (Chapter 21, page 407, 409-410).

To Lovegood, undeniably a nutter in the eyes of a skeptic, the only level of meaning worth taking seriously is the most fantastic and incredible – and the trio would probably have ignored his thoughts on this if they didn't possess the Invisibility Cloak Hallow he described. The level of meaning Xenophilius describes is not alchemical, metaphysical or even abstract, but *allegorical*: the symbol has three parts which have tit-for-tat "real world" counterparts. Ms. Rowling offers a third level of meaning but, because *Deathly Hallows* is not a textbook on symbolism and anagogical interpretation, she doesn't present that in the book as the third level of interpretation. The deepest level of interpretation she offers in the story – the allegorical one – is one that skeptics like Hermione will deny; even though this interpretation of the symbol is more real, or at least more solid, than the surface or edifying meanings of the Three Brothers story.

Real symbols, though, have a metaphysical meaning beneath the surface and moral layers – and so does the triangular eye. Before interpreting it and confirming that meaning in the text, let's look at three symbols and their layers of meaning for practice.

Interpreting the Cross, Swastika, and Fish: Surface, Moral and Alchemical Meanings

Symbols have a Surface, Edifying or Moral, and Alchemical or Metaphysical meaning. Keeping Viktor, Hermione, and Dumbledore in mind, we can see such meanings in three common symbols that are rarely explained or understood anagogically or metaphysically. The cross, the swastika, and the "Jesus fish" are good examples for practicing iconological interpretation. Starting with the Cross:

• **The Surface Meaning** of a symbol is the shell concealing the nut, that is, the popular understanding, which usually associates a symbol with the people who have used it, e.g. the Hallows with Grindelwald and the Cross with Christians. This is what most people in our flat culture "get" when they see a multivalent symbol: just a historical linkage with a group, and attendant feelings about that group's being good or bad, rather than an interpretation of the symbol per se. Often these surface associations affix a meaning, or create hostility to, the symbol, having nothing to do with the symbol's transcendent referent (see Lao Tsu: "if the fool did not laugh, it would not be the Way").

• **The Edifying Meaning** of a symbol could be called its Moral, "Religious," or Temporal meaning. We see this in The Hallows with the *Beedle* "morality tale," and the Cross with Christ's historic, sacrificial death at Calvary. This level of meaning, as is certainly true of the Cross, can have a supernatural aspect, but is restricted to the exoteric understanding of a particular faith group from a catechism manual or the academic, naturalist explanation you can find on Wikipedia.

• **The Alchemical Meaning** of a symbol is its esoteric meaning – the supernatural Reality which can be seen through the transparency of the symbol in space-time. The Seeker who sees the symbol, which only veils that Reality, may experience the greater Reality and grasp its meaning. The Cross is a snapshot representation of the Absolute or Supreme Reality in the Point of Intersection, which point, in its being non-spatial, symbolizes "non-Being" and this Reality's "knowability," that is, how God's reflection in creation exists only in consequence of the Absolute's infinitude (a non-spatial quality represented spatially as the extension from the point of the vertical and horizontal arms of the cross). In the Cross we can see a transparency of the polarity without duality in the Godhead, the simultaneous transcendence and immanence of God.

The surface meaning of the Cross is what people take it to mean by association, which can be positive or negative ("he's wearing a cross. Great! That means he's a Christian!" or "she's wearing a cross. Oh, no! She's a puritanical do-gooder who wants to deprive me of my right to an abortion..."). The historical, moral, or devotional meaning links the cross to Jesus of Nazareth's sacrifice on Calvary and makes the symbol positive or negative, again, depending on the observer's relationship with those events.

The anagogical or "leading upward"[1] meaning, what I have been calling "alchemical" or "metaphysical," has no direct relationship with the surface meaning of popular association but informs the historical and devotional layer of meaning. **As Rene Guenon explains:**

> In particular, if Christ died on the cross, it can be said that this was by reason of the symbolic value which the cross possesses in itself and which has always been recognized by all traditions; thus, without diminishing in any way its historical significance, the latter may be regarded as directly derived from the symbolical significance that goes with it. (*Symbolism of the Cross*, page xiii).[2]

Christ, the "begotten Son of the Father" becomes humanity as Jesus of Nazareth, dies on a cross because he is the Word of God, the resolution of contraries, and the means to the Father, the Absolute or Supreme Reality. The Crucifixion, literally "an action of the cross" or "being made a cross," in this respect is a second Theophany and Transfiguration in which the Christ's supernatural divine nature is seen through the symbolism of events in natural time and space.

We can see this same relationship of surface, moral, and alchemical meanings in the swastika, the "Jesus Fish," and the triangular eye symbol of the Hallows.

We first meet the triangular eye at Bill and Fleur's wedding – and the first person that reacts to it is Viktor Krum. As noted above, the associations he has with it are clearly meant to make us think of Grindlewald and the triangular eye as story-equivalents, or stand-ins, for Hitler and the Nazi swastika. The swastika, then, is relevant both as an example of the three levels of symbolic meaning, and as an illustration of how to understand the Hallows symbol.

To anyone living in the West after the Second World War, Viktor Krum's visceral anger at seeing the symbol at a wedding is more than understandable, if it is a stand-in for the swastika. When seeing the Nazi symbol, Holocaust images, Nazi atrocities, and neo-Nazi racism is the first thought that come to mind in countries that fought to overthrow National Socialism. In Germany, the swastika is illegal and, when the Germans took their turn as heads of the European Union in 2007, they proposed legislation that would have made this ban EU-wide.

This move failed, though, because the surface meaning, or popular and historical association with Hitler and National Socialism, has nothing to do with what the symbol means either historically to Hindus, or metaphysically in itself. Hindus in the UK, France, and the Netherlands protested the proposed EU ban, because to them the swastika is not a symbol of Hitler and of Nazi crimes against humanity, but of peace and their ancient faith. "Swastika" is the *Sanskrit* name for the symbol, after all; *hakenkreuz* is the rarely used German name.

> Ramesh Kallidai of the Hindu Forum of Britain said the swastika had been a symbol of peace for thousands of years before the Nazis adopted it. He said a ban on the symbol would discriminate against Hindus....
>
> "The swastika has been around for 5,000 years as a symbol of peace," he said. "This is exactly the opposite of how it was used by Hitler." He said that while the Nazi implications of the symbol should be condemned, people should respect the Hindu use of the swastika.
>
> "Just because Hitler misused the symbol, abused it and used it to propagate a reign of terror and racism and discrimination, it does not mean that its peaceful use should be banned." The group said banning the swastika was equivalent to banning the cross simply because the Ku Klux Klan had used burning crosses.[1]

The swastika does not "belong" to Hindus, though. According to Guenon, "it is found in the most diverse and widely separated countries and from the most remote periods" (*Cross*, page 54). It is essentially a symbol of "the Pole," sometimes called the "vertical axis," and more commonly, the "Tree of Life." Though it is sign of the "horizontal cross," whose circular motion are defined by the center Pole, the "swastika is not a symbol of the world" – the circle and its motion being described by the arms at right angles – "but rather of the Principle's action upon the world" (*Cross*, page 55; cf., *The Lord of the World*, Coombe Springs, 1983, Chapter 2, page 9). The Hindu explanation of the symbol as a sign of "peace," of course, may be in reaction to its associations with war and German fascism, but it also is, in concordance with the symbol's referent, namely, the unicity of Creation.

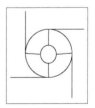

swastika

I know very few people my age who can see a swastika, though, and not have Viktor Krum's response; I know I can't. We can find a less charged illustration of the layers of interpreting symbols by looking at the "ichthus" or "Jesus Fish" seen on the back of cars everywhere in the U.S. It is a marker for "Christian" in its surface meaning, and to many non-believers, has unfortunately come to mean "religious-right voter, fundamentalist, anti-abortion radical, and six-day Creationist." That may not cause the visceral response a swastika does but it obviously upsets some people (hence the "Darwin fish" many secularists put on *their* car bumpers).

As with the swastika, the "Jesus Fish" identification with an American Christian "culture war" political movement is well removed from both its religious and its metaphysical meanings. The Fish becomes a Christian symbol because the Greek word *ichthus'* five letters are an acronym or anagram for the five Greek words meaning "Jesus Christ, Son of God, Savior." Many believe early Christians used it as a "secret sign" used by Christians to silently identify their faith or point the way to Christian gatherings during persecutions. No less an authority than St. Clement of Alexandria recommended its use as a seal.

One metaphysical meaning, apart from the initials spelling the Greek word for fish, is evident in the shape (which doesn't look that much like a fish, after all). The fish symbol as drawn is the intersection of two circles; as such, it is a symbol of manifestation per se, a lesser image of the Divine, and a symbol that especially highlights the Principle of Creation.

Don't see it? Draw two circles on a piece of paper one above the other so their intersection is a "Jesus Fish." (If necessary, see Chapter 1, page 28, on circle and center symbolism.) Of the intersected circles, the top circle is Divinity, with the invisible center the Absolute or "God the Father." The radiance from this point, to the visible circle and beyond, is the procession of the Holy Spirit. The visible Circle itself is the Word or "Son of God." The bottom circle is "existence." It is a distant, but obvious,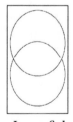

Jesus fish

echo of the Divine in its being another circle. It is an echo consequent to the Infinitude of the Absolute. The Intersection of the original and echo circles—the intrusion of the Divine into the human world of relativity, and "by whom all things were made"—is the Word of God, the relative Absolute, Which became Jesus of Nazareth. Hence the "Jesus Fish."

Grasping the *surface* meaning of the "Jesus Fish" will allow anyone to understand the various players in the American culture war, just by glancing at the back of their cars. Understanding the *moral*, religious or historical meaning of "Ichthus" as an acronym, reveals the connection with Jesus of Nazareth, historical person and object of Christian devotion. Reflection and meditation on the *alchemical*, which is to say, "transforming" meaning shows us a picture of Creator and Creation and the activity of the Word in Creation as Mediator and Means to the Father, which activity is the cause of said devotion.

The Triangular Eye

"All very interesting, I'm sure," you may be thinking. "So what is the deep, secret meaning of the "triangular eye" symbol then?" I hear you.

Oddly enough, this symbol *does* have a metaphysical meaning like the Cross, the swastika, and the *ichthus*. The Hallows symbol, like the allegorical fable elements, has three parts: a "triangular eye" called the "All-Seeing Eye," the perpendicular line as both "Tree of Life" and "World Axis," and the bisected circle and triangle, or "Mirrored Image." [There are other symbols that are in the Hallows glyph – the irradiating point, the triangle, and the circle most obviously – but I think you'll see why I chose the three I have in a minute.]

The Eye: You may think a circle inside a triangle is an exotic image, but I bet you have a picture of it in your wallet. It's on the Great Seal of the United States, believe it or not, albeit it on the reverse side, which radiating "triangular eye" has been on the back side of $1 bills since 1935. Called the "Eye of Providence," in popular Masonic usage, it symbolizes God's eye

triangular eye

and omniscience. It's on the seal because God was thought to have looked favorably on the beginnings of our country (*annuit coeptis*); it's on the currency and the seal, some say, because Benjamin Franklin and Franklin Roosevelt were both Lodge masons of advanced degree.

I'm pretty sure the edifying meaning of "Big Brother God watching over us" is not why Ms. Rowling calls the Hallows symbol a "triangular eye." Such an idea would be more F. Scott Fitzgerald, with his *Gatsby* scary road signs, than *Deathly Hallows*. For the meaning of the "Eye of Providence," we must review what we learned from Lewis and Coleridge about the "seeing eye" and "transforming vision" in Chapter 5. Think about how we equate sight, light, and knowledge, and what the word "eye" and "I" mean in English.

First, common usage makes "seeing" something synonymous with "understanding" or "knowing" it. For example: "You have to see that – you see that, don't you?" If we want an explanation, we ask the genius in the room to "throw some light on the subject, so we can see" what she's talking about. Sight and knowledge, because of sight's centrality in grasping things and events on the physical plane, are colloquial equivalents.

Second, the word "eye" and "I" in English are both consonant and assonant. With reference to the "Eye of Providence/Triangular Eye," this assonance is important because the word "I" in English (as the "eye" is a means to, and "sight" synonymous with, "knowledge") is a path to God, the all knowing.

> Ask yourself the questions, "Why is it that 'I' am 'I'? And "why is the 'other' an other?" Have you ever stopped to consider that the first person singular personal pronoun is the only word which we all apply to completely different things, but which always means the same thing? How is it that we can still communicate? If I used the word X to name a tree, and you used it to label an elephant, and someone else to signify the sun, and so on and on, with no one ever intending a univocal object, we would all be completely confused. But not in this case. Although few people make it a topic of deliberate reflection, each of us intuitively knows that I means more than me, that there is a fundamental difference between the one who says I and the individual thus named. This difference, deeply pondered – "the phenomenon of an 'I' that is unique, yet multiple" – can lead the person who is "sensitive to the essence of things" to "the dazzling intuition of the absolute Subject, whose unicity, at once transcendent and immanent, is unambiguous." It can lead, in other words, to God. (*Advice to the Serious Seeker,* James Cutsinger, SUNY Press, 1997, page 24)

Lewis explained in "The Seeing Eye" how our self-awareness, or conscience, was "continuous with" the unity of existence behind the façade of surfaces. This is an echo of Coleridge's epistemological theology and "transforming vision," by which we understand time-space reality as a transparency or symbol veiling God, whom our *logos*-within perceives in everything by recognizing itself in the principles therein. The "Eye of Providence" is the Absolute Subject and Transpersonal "I" who, as Creative Other and reality of creation, is both subject and object in our knowing. As Schuon explains:

[T]he symbolism of sight is universal and is therefore applicable also to the macrocosm and to all its degrees: the world is an indefinitely differentiated vision whose object in the final analysis is the divine Prototype of all that exists, and, conversely, God is the Eye that sees the world and which, being active where the creature is passive, creates the world by His vision, this vision being act and not passivity; thus the eye becomes the metaphysical center of the world of which it is at the same time the sun and the heart.

God sees not only the outward, but also – or rather with all the more reason – the inward, and it is this latter vision that is the more real one, or strictly speaking, the only real one, since it is the absolute or infinite Vision of which God is at once the Subject and the Object, the Knower and the Known. The universe is merely vision or knowledge, in whatever mode it may be realized, and its entire reality is God: the worlds are fabrics of vision, and the content of these indefinitely repeated visions is always the Divine, which is thus the foremost Knowledge and the ultimate Reality – Knowledge and Reality being two complementary aspects of the same divine Cause. (Schuon, *The Eye of the Heart*, World Wisdom, 1997, pages 3-5; see also Guenon, *Fundamental Symbols: The Universal Language of Sacred Science*, Quinta Essentia, 1995, 'The All-Seeing Eye,' pages 294-296)

In the first chapter of this book, I discussed how the five keys that unlock *Harry Potter* all reveal points about how we think, and how the way we see and understand things restricts or opens our experience of reality. Therefore, it shouldn't be a surprise that the symbol of the book's subject (according to the title!) is a glyph of sight and understanding, telling us true vision is the very fabric of reality.

No wonder Rufus Scrimgeour couldn't figure out the triangular eye.

The Tree of Life: The next part of the Hallows glyph is the perpendicular line bisecting the triangle from tip to base. The edifying meaning is that this vertical post symbolizes the Tree of Life growing in the center of the Garden. That Tree, in turn, is a natural image of the supernatural World Axis around which Creation turns, and by which it is "connected" to the transcendent Creator. (In the *Odyssey*, Homer used the ship's mast as a sign of the World Axis.) As Cirlot explains:

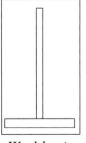

World axis

In its most general sense, the symbolism of the tree denotes the life of the cosmos: its consistence, growth, proliferation, generative and regenerative processes. It stands for inexhaustible life, and is therefore equivalent to a symbol of immortality. According to Eliade, the concept of 'life without death', stands, ontologically speaking, for 'absolute reality' and, consequently, the tree becomes a symbol of this absolute reality, that is, of the centre of the world....

The tree also corresponds to the Cross of Redemption and the Cross and is often depicted, in Christian iconography, as the Tree of Life. It is, of course, the vertical arm of the Cross which is identified with the tree, and hence with the 'world-axis'. The world-axis symbolism (which goes back to the pre-Neolithic times) has a further symbolic implication: that of the central point in the cosmos. Clearly, the tree (or the cross) can only be the axis linking the three worlds if it stands in the centre of the cosmos they constitute. (Cirlot, *Dictionary of Symbols*, Dorset, 1991, page 347; see also Eliade, *Images & Symbols*, Sheed & Ward, 1968, page 44, Guenon, *The Symbolism of the Cross*, Luzac, 1975, page 46-48, 100)

The vertical line, then, symbolizes the axis or still-point around which creation turns. It represents the Unmoved Mover, and in being eternal, immortality for the person who can cling to this cross (Odysseus had a great difficulty holding on). In a book featuring a sacrificial death and a trip to King's Cross as some kind of afterlife preluding resurrection, the vertical line—glyph for the Tree of Life, World Axis, and Cross at Calvary—is an excellent overlay on the Triangular Eye.

But the bisection of the triangle and eye creates another symbol, our friend the mirror.

The Mirrored Image: The vertical line, rising from the triangle base to the apex, bisects both the triangle and the circle. The "triangular eye" is simultaneously cut in half *and* joined by the World Axis. Cut the figure along the bisecting line and you have mirrored images. Putting them together shows how the glyph—like the cross, the yin/yang circle, or Tao, and the fish, as explained above—represents the union of complements

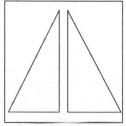

Mirrored image

and the resolution of contraries in existence within God (panentheism). The contraries and complements are shadows of God's simultaneous transcendence and immanence; their resolution and union in the symbol are the peace or "stillness" of the Unmoved Mover and the unicity of God (cf. Guenon, *The Symbolism of the Cross*, Luzac, 1975, pages 95-103). The mirrored image of triangles in the Deathly Hallows symbol—like the *yin-yang* symbol of the Taoists, the *swastika* of the Hindus, the Jewish Star of David, and the Christian Cross—are icons of Creator and Creation, revealing the polarity without duality in the Godhead (and, consequently, in everything created).

And recall that the mirror is the "symbol of symbolism" in which subject and object are resolved, because of the seeing subject's self-recognition in the seen object—the "seeing eye" beholding the "sacred I" as intellect. (See discussion of the Mirror of Erised and the eye-in-the-mirror shard in Chapter 5.) The bisected triangular eye becomes a picture of our double vision: seeing both empirically—"stuff as matter filling space"—*and* symbolically—"everything as a *logoi* veiling transparency." The Hallows symbol (understood as metaphysical glyph) is about our means to transcendence—seeing with triangular vision the three layered reality behind and within things, people, and stories.

I wrote above that *Deathly Hallows* wasn't a textbook on symbolism, as such, because its third level of symbol interpretation was tit-for-tat allegory from Xenophilius, rather than alchemical exegesis like the above. Curiously, though, Ms. Rowling points almost explicitly to this interpretation within her storyline, in the last of the disembodied eyes in the book left for us to discuss: Moody's Mad-Eye. In the burial of Moody's eye, *Deathly Hallows* is not only an example of symbolist literature, but a textbook in iconological interpretation.

The Eye, the Tree, and the Cross

Mad-Eye Moody is killed by Lord Voldemort himself during Harry's escape from Privet Drive (Chapter 5, page 78). Alastor's friends try to recover his body, but Bill and Lupin are unsuccessful in this attempt (page 81). Beyond a toast to his memory by his friends in the Order, the heroic, irascible auror's life and death are not commemorated. There is no funeral service.

This would not be the first time that has happened. There is, for example, no mention in the books of a service or burial for Sirius Black, who was blasted by Bellatrix through the Veil in the Department of Mysteries. For all we know, "No body, no funeral" might be the rule of the Wizarding World.

But Alastor Moody *was* loved and remembered by his friends, even without a big-deal service like Dumbledore's. Bill and Remus' dangerous attempt to recover the body the night of Harry's escape, when Death Eaters would almost certainly have assumed an attempt would be made and laid a trap, speaks to that. Harry, too, remembers Mad-Eye.

When the trio enter the Ministry of Magic clandestinely clandestinely, in search of the Horcrux Locket taken by Dolores Umbridge from Mundungus, Harry heads to the first floor to search her office. Seeing an office worker look nervously at Umbridge's door, he is shocked to find a memento, an actual fragment of Moody:

> For a split second Harry forgot where he was and what he was doing there. He even forgot that he was invisible: He strode straight up to the door to examine the eye. It was not moving: It gazed blindly upward, frozen.

Harry sets off a Decoy Detonator to distract the office workers and enters Dolores' office. It is just as her Hogwarts Office had been – with one exception:

> Behind Mad-Eye's eye, a telescopic attachment allowed Umbridge to spy on the workers on the other side of the door. Harry took a look through it and saw that they were all still gathered around the Decoy Detonator. He wrenched the telescope out of the door, leaving a hole behind, pulled the magical eyeball out of it, and placed it into his pocket. (Chapter 13, pages 249-251)

Harry has reason to regret this act. After recovering the Horcrux Locket from Umbridge, Harry, Ron, and Hermione are almost caught, and the "just-barely" quality of their escape leaves Ron splinched and the trio unable to return to Grimmauld Place. Harry accepts the blame for this. As he tells Hermione in the tent:

> "Don't be stupid, it wasn't your fault! If anything it was mine...."
>
> Harry put his hand into his pocket and drew out Mad-Eye's eye. Hermione recoiled, looking horrified.
>
> "Umbridge had stuck it to her office door, to spy on people. I couldn't leave it there... but that's how they knew there were intruders."(Chapter 14, page 271)

Now this eye is no token trinket belonging to an old friend. As we learn from faux-Moody in *Goblet,* and the genuine article in *Phoenix,* this "Mad-eye" is as close to "All-Seeing" as one eye sans elevation can hope to get. It has full 360 degrees of rotation, is able to see through almost everything—through walls, doors, and most impressively, even the back of his own head. It can even see through Invisibility Cloaks, much to Harry's surprise. If it had heat-vision and telescopic powers, it would be the eye of Superman or the "triangular eye" on the money in your pocket. Harry doesn't think to use it, of course, feeling that what Umbridge did was something of a desecration. Instead, *Harry buries it.*

> Early next morning, before the other two were awake, Harry left the tent to search the woods around them for the oldest, most gnarled, and resilient looking tree he could find. There in its shadow he buried Mad-Eye Moody's eye and marked the spot by gouging a small cross in the bark with his wand. It was not much, but Harry felt that Mad-Eye would have much preferred this to being stuck on Dolores Umbridge's door. Then he returned to the tent to wait for the others to wake, and discuss what they were going to do next. (Chapter 15, page 284)

The burial service's *surface* meaning is Harry's paying his respects to a "fallen warrior" (the title of the chapter in which we learn about Mad-Eye's death). It neatly closes off the plot point of how the trio was detected at the Ministry and then forced to live on the run, their circumstances during the greater part of *Deathly Hallows*.

The second layer of meaning, the *moral and religious*, are evident, too. Harry's love for the gruff Auror, and loyalty to this comrade who gave his life to save him in the war against the Dark Lord, show themselves in his rash, but gallant decision to take the magical eye and then bury it alone, in a private service. The religious symbolism of marking the burial place with a cross is duly observed, in keeping with Christian practice. It is the first time we have any indication that Harry is in any way familiar with Christian belief and practice, but this "gouging a cross in the bark" is hard to overlook.

The whole ceremony, however, is more than a little unusual. Harry is no Bible-literate Christian or funeral director; when he reads the inscription on his parents' grave marker later in the story, he thinks St. Paul's words are those of a Death Eater, and after burying Dobby, to whom he owed a similar life-debt, he doesn't make the sign of the cross on the house-elf's grave.

And why the *secret* burial, without Ron or Hermione? Why at dawn? Why "the oldest, most gnarled, most resilient looking tree"? Why bury it in the tree's shadow?

The third layer of meaning, the *alchemical or esoteric* level of interpretation about Harry's corrected vision and spiritual perfection, is in these details. The All-Knowing Eye, as described above, is a symbol of God's knowledge and the panentheistic nature of Creation. The Tree of Life, here—with marks of eternity and omnipotence in being long-lived, hardened, and strong—is the World Axis that binds us to God. The Cross is the union of complements and resolution of contraries – a symbol-snapshot of the Supreme Reality's Transcendence and Immanence – and the self-recognition of the transforming vision.

Harry performs this service alone because divinization is not Ron's or Hermione's burden or destiny. He observes this commemoration to note what he knows intuitively will be his end: to die willingly and sacrificially in love for his friends as Moody had. He buries the eye in the tree's shadow as a marker that this is a symbolic act ("a symbol is a representation or shadow of a higher reality"). He does it at dawn, "early next morning," in the hope of the resurrection that each new day represents.

This is perumbration, or fore-shadowing, of Harry's ultimate victory over the interior and exterior Voldemorts in the story, his death, resurrection, and conquest at dawn months later in the Great Hall. It is also a story echo of the three parts of the "triangular eye" Hallows symbol. I understand that the All-Knowing Eye, World Axis, and Mirrored Image interpretation I gave the Hallows symbol above may seem a bizarre "stretch," or over-reaching, to anyone uncomfortable with the esoteric interpretation of story or symbol. To the skeptical Hermiones, who see this as so much Lovegood nonsense, the Invisibility Cloak hints that skepticism is not logical on this point. It might be *as bizarre,* at least, to believe the author would include, either by accident or coincidentally, a story-point with three symbols that resonate with the exact three parts of the Hallows symbol and their meaning, as explained above.

Love's Victory Over Death

And, if this bizarre exegesis and echo of the Hallows symbol in story form weren't a part of *Deathly Hallows*, I think the consonance of the symbol's meaning with the meaning of the Harry Potter epic itself – especially as played out in *Deathly Hallows – would* be sufficient evidence to accept the three-part interpretation of the "triangular eye."

If I had to explain what *Harry Potter* means in five words or less, I would say without hesitation: "love's victory over death." I'd be obliged, though, to elaborate on that reflex explanation at some length. And at three levels!

On the surface level of narrative events and primary themes, in "love's victory over death," we see a story of political correctness: tolerance and diversity conquer racism and prejudice. The disenfranchised and marginal Mudbloods, half-breeds, and peripheral magical creatures join together to win a great victory over Voldemort, his neo-Nazi Death Eaters, and the evil Ministry.

In the underlying religious symbolism layer, Harry is a Christian everyman who, because of the Scar Horcrux Voldemort-nature within him, must die to himself and the world to save his friends. Because of the "bond of blood" he has with a savior who died for him (Lily), Harry's loving willingness to sacrifice himself saves his life. This resurrection and victory over the Voldemort-within secures his victory over the very real external Voldemort, whose power has been broken by Harry's sacrifice. "Love's victory" at this level is very much a pointer to the Christian hope of victory over death via participation in the sacrificial death and resurrection of Jesus of Nazareth, *Christus Victor.*

And on the anagogical or metaphysical level? "Love's victory over death" is about illumination and apotheosis. "Death" here is the false life of ego, power, and individual advantage. Here, "death" is of the false life of ego, power, and individual advantage. Harry masters death in Dobby's grave by choosing to believe, and by renouncing the pursuit of power (the Hallows) in obedience to his mentor's direction, and against his private opinions. "Love" is the resolution of contraries which Harry accomplishes in faithfully completing the hero's journey and his alchemical transformation from spiritual lead to gold. Returning to the creative center by closing the circle, Harry completely transcends his narrow view, having learned the broader Snape and Dumbledore perspectives. With this relative omniscience that equates to omnipotence in a world created by vision and knowledge, he easily dispatches the fragmented and unknowing Dark Lord.

The book's title points us to this last level of meaning. "Hallows" refers to the only use of that word in common English, the Lord's Prayer, in which Christ teaches his disciples to pray to "our Father" in heaven, "hallowed be thy name" (Matthew 6:9). The "name" of the Father, the Absolute and First Person of the Trinity, is both His authority ("stop in the name of the law!") and that by which he is known. God, being simultaneously transcendent and immanent in His Creation, is known by the polarity of everything within the world (Romans 1:20), and most especially, in the resolution of these contraries in life, love and peace. "Hallowing" his name means, then, to revere God's authority and to make "hal" or "whole," to see and to become a conscious vehicle of His life, love, and peace in the world.

This "hallowing," though, requires a death to self and ego. "Deathly Hallows," taken together, is a restatement of the alchemists' favorite gospel passage, John 12:24: "Verily, verily, I say unto you, Except a corn of wheat fall into the ground and die, it abideth alone: but if it die, it bringeth forth much fruit."

This esoteric understanding of the finale's title and "love's victory over death"—the meaning common to all three layers of interpretation— is the same as the tri-part explanation of the Hallows' "triangular eye." In seeing things as God—the "All-Knowing Eye"—sees, knows, and creates all things, we transcend the personal "I" or ego and share in His life. We are able, as well, to see the resolution of the Mirrored Image that

Deathly Hallows symbol

is His Creation in the Tree of Life/World Axis, and to know the peace there "that passeth all understanding" (Philippians 4:7). It is a symbol of illumination and theosis in communion with God's creative principle. The symbol *from* the book, that is a mystery to solve *within* the book, is a symbol *of* the book's story events and meaning.

Or is that too neat? Could I be wrong? Could this esoteric breakdown and exegesis of the Hallows symbol be just what I want to see in it?

Sure it could. I'd be crazier than I want to think I am to believe that the conjunction of this interpretation—with both Harry's burying Moody's eye and the alchemical level of understanding of what the series is about—amounted to a proof or demonstration of this view. I don't need to have Moody's magical eye to know I don't have the "All Seeing Eye," and that I don't know what these stories mean at every level.

Even if Ms. Rowling were to break with her historical pattern tomorrow, though, and hold a press conference to say the "triangular eye" is just a triangle, circle, and line representing the Cloak, Stone, and Wand, I wouldn't be very embarrassed. First, with George MacDonald, I doubt any author knows the full meaning of their works; Ms. Rowling can speak with some authority about how she consciously understood the books, but she does not have any more authority than the serious reader in explaining their meaning *en toto*.[2]

Second, I don't think I'd blush reading Ms. Rowling's interpretation because, even if I am wrong, I have created a useful tool for 1) understanding the anagogical meaning of her books and 2) introducing interpretation of stories and symbols to people uncomfortable in an ontologically flat world. Helping readers to understand Harry Potter – and inviting them to read Shakespeare, Dickens, and Dante at depth – is a lot more important than hitting the interpretation equivalent of a "walk-off home-run."

Conclusion: So What?

Okay. Reading Harry Potter with a "triangular eye" ourselves – that is, looking for surface, moral, and metaphysical layers of meaning in the text – helps us *how*?

Seeing the books in these three dimensions throws light on what caused the magic controversy, explains global Potter-mania, and suggests why reading the best books is the short cut to a more human life.

The weirdness of the whole magic controversy to me – and I was neck deep in it for a few years – was that very intelligent and generous people who had read the books were able to argue, with a straight face and clear conscience, that they thought the books were dangerous. I'd explain the magic as incantational, I'd lay out the panoply of Christian symbolism, and walk them through an introduction and AP course in literary alchemy. And I would be dismissed.

I understood and even admired those who chose not to read the books (and to ask others not to) in obedience to their pastors or spiritual directors. That was a potentially edifying obedience. But those who read the books and called "black" "white;" those folks left me shaking my head.

Viktor Krum's response to the Hallows symbol and noting my own aversion to the swastika helped me understand the 'Magic' controversy. The Biblical literalists and culture warriors that found Harry a "menace" and "spiritually dangerous" – even a "gateway to the occult" – were responding to the story's magic the way Viktor does to the "triangular eye" and I do to the *hakenkreuz*. They associated it with what they understood as a "real world" threat to their children – Wiccans, witches, New Age spirituality, the occult – and, even though the magic of these stories has nothing to do with those threats, the surface association was the only "meaning" they could get their heads around.

As we saw with the swastika and the "Jesus fish," reading the story-symbol exclusively on the surface   level – therefore associating it with noted users, a la Krum – is the way to get the meaning wrong. Mechanical interpretation at surface level gets the meaning of the story-magic backward; while Ms. Rowling's stories use magic in counterpoint to postmodern materialism, atheism, and ugliness, her critics counted her with their enemies without attempting to see either the edifying worldview or anagogical reality represented in this magical fiction.

As one Orthodox Christian bishop (with degrees from Princeton and Berkeley in psychology and liturgics) observed, critics condemning Harry Potter seem to be unable to discern the "spiritual forest for the magical trees."[3] Being incapable of reading with either penetration or understanding (and being distracted by culture war triggers), Harry Haters, with few exceptions, miss the moral, religious, and anagogical meanings of the stories.

Understanding Potter-mania

I wrote in my first book, *The Hidden Key to Harry Potter*, about Ms. Rowling's novels, that the reason for Harry's popularity was the Christian content, training in stock responses, and the alchemical symbols and work in the stories. I leaned heavily on Mircea Eliade's thesis that entertainments, especially fiction, are a major focus of modern life because they serve a mythic or religious function in a secular culture. Those writers and filmmakers who stuff edifying and metaphysical material into their stories will be more successful than those who don't. *Harry Potter* has inspired global fascination, even mania, because to postmodern hearts, reading his story is like finding water in the desert.

My belief that Harry is best understood as operating on three levels simultaneously, hasn't changed my thinking at all about the cause of Potter-mania. Eliade's observation is still true, and the desire for edifying and esoteric experience remains the engine of Ms. Rowling's success. The 3-D theory does, however, explain why no copycat writers have cloned Ms. Rowling's formulaic success.

In a nut-shell, all three levels of meaning fire simultaneously within the story line and succeed independently. That's not easy to accomplish. It's so hard I have to wonder if Ms. Rowling can do it again. As you read in chapter three, *Deathly Hallows* combined Harry's postmodern "struggle to believe" with his alchemical transformation laid over the Christian calendar. His struggle for faith and his battle with the Death Eater Nazis are right on the surface. His journey from doubt to faith and something like apotheosis runs beneath the surface, but the edifying, religious elements in the story almost seamlessly mesh with the alchemical stages of the story.

If you can't see that the surface, exoteric, and esoteric meanings work together, reinforcing one another, remember Xenophilius Lovegood. He disdained the Hallows' surface meaning that Viktor shared with him and the "instructive story" in *Tales of Beedle the Bard*; he was therefore unable to appreciate the dangers of the Hallows. Even Dumbledore hadn't read the story of the Three Brothers as a young man and understood it as a tale of caution about those who try to cheat death through magical objects, be they Hallows or Horcruxes. Lovegood, a caricature of New Age goofiness, wants esoteric knowledge and spiritual accomplishment, without exoteric grounding in edifying understanding and moral practice.

Without the three levels working together, a person won't experience the story as body, mind and spirit, and will not experience the transforming, edifying power of story, consciously or unconsciously.

Ms. Rowling's stories, though, have the three levels of meaning working so closely together that those who only understand consciously the surface meaning get the profound extras as a bonus. The "good guy-Rainbow Coalition" versus "bad-guy-Pureblood-Nazi-Death Eaters" drama of postmodern political correctness carries other meanings with its obvious "love over death" message. On board are the "love over death" meaning of the second and third layers, the edifying education and experience of exoteric Christian imagery and themes, and the way-under-the-radar esoteric alchemical initiation that transforms Harry and his readers.

"Is Ms. Rowling aware that she's doing this?" I think this is people's nice way of telling me I'm full of it. Suggesting she has pulled off this kind of three dimensional artistry *by accident,* or that it's unlikely she's as smart as all that, is to insist on flattening the levels of meaning into just the storyline events. If you recognize and understand the five keys, though, and how each key works, this skepticism is not an intellectually honest position.

Ms. Rowling tells her stories in the tradition of the best English writers, from Shakespeare to Lewis, in writing three levels of story meaning in one – the surface or topical, the edifying and moral, and the alchemic or metaphysical. I'll close by explaining one possible meaning of *The Tales of Beedle the Bard* title that I promised pages ago. I think it confirms the second and third levels of meaning she gives us in *Deathly Hallows* and all the books.

We know from Dumbledore's testimony that the power of "children's stories" is "a power beyond the reach of any magic." The only book of children's stories we come accross in *Harry* Potter, a book we have to read as closely as we can for the key to defeat Voldemort, is titled *Tales of Beedle the Bard*. A "Beedle" is a Dickensian-era word for a Church Warden. "Bard" in England can be used for any accomplished storyteller, poet, singer, or songwriter, but, if used by itself or prefixed by "the," it is another name for Shakespeare. You'd expect the tales of a Church Warden to be edifying morality tales, with encouraging examples for good behavior and faith. I'd expect tales from a Bard like Shakespeare to be alchemical dramas that assume like Dante that I am "saved," and which work on the much more difficult work, namely, my sanctification.

Even though I haven't yet read *The Tales of Beedle the Bard*, I think it's probable Ms. Rowling's fairy tales, like her novels, have a second and third layer – a moral and metaphysical meaning – in addition to the surface fun of the stories themselves. Ms. Rowling tips her hat to those meanings in the *Beedle the Bard* title.

Although *Beedle* is the only children's book we meet in the series, each time we pick up a *Harry Potter* novel, we have a children's book in our hands. Certainly it has been our individual and collective experience that there is a magic here greater than any used by witches and wizards in the stories. Along with Ms. Granger and the book he left her, Albus Dumbledore, in his conversation with Harry at King's Cross, invites us to find the key to defeat our Voldemorts – through close study and appreciation of the deeper messages and meanings in our favorite kids' books. Ms. Rowling, in the many eyes used in *Deathly Hallows* – Dumbledore's eye in the mirror shard, Tom Riddle's eyes in the Locket Horcrux, the green eyes of Snape's Beatrice, Moody's Mad-Eye, and the

Hallows symbol's triangular eye – asks us to think about how we see, and gives us examples of corrected, transforming vision that enables us to transcend a surface view for triangular and symbolic understanding.

I hope this discussion of the books' "seeing eye/sacred I" artistry and three layers of meaning will help serious readers to appreciate consciously what they have already experienced and enjoyed, to some degree, without "seeing" or knowing it. Ms. Rowling, writing in the tradition of symbolist poets, dramatists, and novelists from Shakespeare and Coleridge to MacDonald and the Inklings, asks her readers to "suspend empirical disbelief," and experience people and reality, as well as books, poems, and plays, with triangular, even Trinitarian vision. By taking that trip with Harry to King's Cross – the intersection of worlds and point of creation – we can be transformed in the *Logos*/Christ visible everywhere.

Endnotes

1   See *The Secret of Shakespeare*, Martin Lings, Inner Traditions (1984), page 14

2   *The Form of the Transformed Vision,* James Cutsinger, Mercer University Press, pages 79-80:

> Thus, symbols serve true unity because they reveal an open existence in which the being of all is made possible by the fluidity and transparency of each. Symbolization is akin to "Gravitation, all in all/nothing in any one part, as fluid, either, or such like"; like gravity, and like the soul, which is also "all in every part," and to which it is analogous, a symbol is "that nothing-something, something-nothing." It is with this in mind that Coleridge offered his most commonly quoted definition: "A Symbol . . . is characterized by a translucence of the Special in the Individual or of the General in the Especial or of the Universal in the General. Above all by the translucence of the Eternal through and in the Temporal." In each case, a thing becomes a symbol by allowing the precedence of something more, something higher and other, to shine through it.

3   *Symbolism of the Cross*, Rene Guenon, Luzac (1975), page xiii

> The cross is a symbol which in its various forms is met with almost everywhere, and from the most remote times; it is therefore far from belonging peculiarly and exclusively to the Christian tradition as some might be tempted to believe. It must even be stated that Christianity, at any rate in its outward and generally known aspect, seems to have somewhat lost sight of the symbolic character of the cross and come to regard it as no longer anything but the sign of a historical event. Actually, these two viewpoints are in no wise mutually exclusive; indeed the second is in a sense a consequence of the first; but this way of looking at things is so strange to the great majority of people today that it deserves dwelling on for a moment in order to avoid possible misunderstandings.

> The fact is that people too often tend to think that if a symbolical meaning is admitted, the literal or historical sense must be rejected; such a view can only result from unawareness of the law of correspondence which is the very foundation of all symbolism. By virtue of this law, each thing, proceeding as it does from a metaphysical principle from which it derives all its reality, translates or expresses that principle in its own fashion and in accordance with its own order of existence, so that from one

order to another all things are linked together and correspond in such a way as to contribute to the universal and total harmony, which, in the multiplicity of manifestation, can be likened to a reflection of the principial unity itself.

For this reason the laws of a lower domain can always be taken to symbolize realities of a higher order, wherein resides their own profoundest cause, which is at once their principle and their end; we would recall in this connection the error of the modern "naturalistic" interpretations of ancient traditional doctrines, interpretations which purely and simply reverse the hierarchy of relationships between the different orders of reality. Thus, the purpose of symbols and myths has never been - as often wrongly alleged - to represent the movement of the heavenly bodies, the truth being that they often do contain figures inspired by that movement and intended to express, analogically, something very different, because the laws of that movement are a physical translation of the metaphysical principles on which they depend. What is true of astronomical phenomena can equally and for the same reason be applied to all other kinds of natural phenomena; these phenomena, by the very fact that they are derived from higher and transcendent principles, truly serve to symbolize those principles. Obviously, this in no way affects the reality possessed by the phenomena as such in the order of existence they belong to; on the contrary, it is the very basis of that reality, for apart from their dependence on their principles, all things would be mere non-entity.

This holds good for historical facts no less than for anything else; they likewise conform to the law of correspondence just mentioned, and thereby, in their own mode, translate higher realities, of which they are, so to speak, a human expression. We would add that from our point of view (which obviously is quite different from that of the profane historians), it is this that gives to these facts the greater part of their significance. This symbolical character, while common to all historical events, is bound to be particularly clear-cut in the case of events connected with what may be called "sacred history"; thus it is recognizable in a most striking way, in all the circumstances of the life of Christ. If the foregoing has been properly grasped, it will at once be apparent not only that there is no reason for denying the reality of these events and treating them as mere myths, but on the contrary that these events had to be such as they were, and could not have been otherwise; it is clearly impossible to attribute a sacred character to something devoid of all transcendent significance.

In particular, if Christ died on the cross, it can be said that this was by reason of the symbolic value which the cross possesses in itself and which has always been recognized by all traditions; thus, without diminishing in any way its historical significance, the latter may be regarded as directly derived from the symbolical significance that goes with it.

4   God as "Seer," sees Himself as well as the world, including the minutest contingency – an "ant in the desert," to quote an expression of the Prophet. This, by the way, excludes all pantheism as well as all deism. (*The Eye of the Heart*, Schuon, World Wisdom, 1997; page 5)

FAQ – Frequently Asked Questions

31 Questions About the Artistry and Meaning of Deathly Hallows

The day *Deathly Hallows* was published I started posting topics for discussion at my weblog, HogwartsProfessor.com ('HogPro'). Within days, I had thirty different threads rolling and conversation was as good as it gets online. The regulars at the site, the HogPro All-Pros, are from all over the world and represent a real diversity of backgrounds. All are serious readers, some have advanced degrees, I'd guess the majority are Christians, and everyone of them enjoys discussing books they love with like-minded friends. Much of the book you have read, I'd say the better parts, began and was much improved in HogPro discussion rooms.

I took a greatest hits collection from those *Deathly Hallows* threads, added questions I have heard at conferences, universities, and churches where I have spoken, and then wrote answers reflecting I hope what I've already written and the important things I couldn't fit anywhere else. Please join the conversation at HogwartsProfessor and email me if you have other questions I should answer in the second edition.

Thank you for buying and reading this book, and, in advance, for writing me to share what you think, your comments and corrections. Your letter is the best part of writing this book, if my past experience holds true, and I promise a response to whatever you write.

Gratefully,

John

john@HogwartsProfessor.com

1. C'mon! It's a kid's book! Get a life. Aren't you embarrassed to be taking *Harry Potter* so seriously?

I'm thinking that more people want to ask me this question than do. One person who did ask was Stephen McGinty, a reporter for *The Scotsman* newspaper.[1] He was writing an article about the Prophecy 2007 Harry Potter conference in Toronto. His question was: *How would you respond to outsiders that you are taking "children's books" too seriously?* I responded:

> First I'd say that since Prisoner of Azkaban was published more adults have been reading these books than children or adults reading to children. The themes, symbols, and compost of great literature (Ms. Rowling's description of her inspiration) evident in these books make them substantive reading.
>
> Second, and more important, the Harry Potter books are a cultural phenomenon of the first order. No book not inspired by God or penned by Chairman Mao has ever achieved the global popularity and holding power that Ms. Rowling's novels have. Anyone not interested in exploring why these books are as popular as they are, frankly, is not a thinking person. My approach has been to "take Harry seriously" as literature rather than as a cultural artifact; my answer to the question of "whence Potter-mania?" is (a) the artistry of her work, (b) the postmodern themes themes that resonate with the beliefs and concerns of our age, and (c) the transcendent meaning she reaches at and hit in her use of traditional symbols and story points.

Mr. McGinty, who hasn't written some of the best articles on the Potter-beat, wrote a mocking piece about the convention with the headline: 'Harry Potter and the Weird Academic Theories.'

This same question was asked at a luncheon I moderated at Prophecy 2007. Prof. Philip Nel of Kansas State University, a leading figure in the study of children's literature, made the best response, I think, because it rings of common sense. No written work is as influential on the formation and orientation of the human person than books written for children; what is read in the nursery is reflected in the soul. If *any* books, then, are worthy of study, it is books that children are reading or learning about. I would only add to that paraphrase of Dr. Nel's remarks that children's literature read by adults is similarly more powerful and potentially transformative than adult and more realistic fiction because of its archetypal content, simplicity, and how much more vulnerable we make ourselves to its message. Not taking Harry Potter seriously or just as an entertainment, our defenses go down -- and our receptivity to its message rises respectively.

2. Just what is going on with the cover of the Scholastic Deathly Hallows?

It is a depiction of the final battle in the Great Hall of Hogwarts Castle between Harry and Lord Voldemort.

> The bang was like a cannon blast, and the golden flames that erupted between them, at the dead center of the circle they had been trading, marked the point where the spells collided. Harry saw Voldemort's green jet meet his own spell, saw the Elder Wand fly high, dark against the sunrise, spinning acorss the enchanted ceiling like the head of nagini, spinning through the air toward the master it would not kill, who had come to take full possession of it at last. And Harry, with the the unerring skill of the Seeker, caught the wand in his free hand as Voldemort fell backward, arms splayed, the slip of pupils of the scarlet eyes rolling upward. (Chapter 36, page 743-44).

There is, of course, quite a bit of artistic license involved. The curtains and Harry's posture are echoes of the cover of the first Scholastic book cover and this opening and closing of the drama with curtains is a nice touch. The wreckage at their feet that looks like splintered timbers as artful representation of chaos and ruin, the coliseum backdrop to suggest gladiatorial combat, the hooded figures seeming to sit in judgment, and the brilliance of the dawn breaking across the magical ceiling are flourishes and largely atextual. The wands are left out out lest too much were revealed. It's not a snapshot, consequently, but it is haunting and a pointer to the climactic confrontation towards which the seven books point.

3. Why is the dedication of *Deathly Hallows* in the shape of a serpent?

Serpent? I guess if this is taken as a Rorschach ink-blot test that is as good an answer as any. I think two other ideas are a little better.

First, the last words of the Epilogue are "All was well." This may be an echo of the last words in Henry Scott Holland's poem, 'Death is Nothing At All,' the last words of which are are often given as "All is well" (Holland was Canon of St. Paul's Cathedral and the poem is excerpted from a longer piece). That poem is sometimes printed with every line centered on the page[2] rather than left-justified which gives it a shape not unlike if not exactly like the *Deathly Hallows* dedication and Aeschylus quotation. This would be appropriate hat-tipping both because the beginning and end would be meeting, something of a Rowling signature, and because the poem and book are about understanding death. The dedication concludes, too, with "until the very end" which is a pointer to death and the last words of the book.

Second, and more obviously, the layout is in the shape of Harry's lightning bolt scar. Ms. Rowling had said for years that the last word of the last book was going to be "scar." She changed her mind. Lest we forget the scar Harry lost momentarily in his trip to King's Cross, however, she gives us its shape right up front.

4. Who are Aeschylus and William Penn – and why do their quotations open Deathly Hallows?

Ms. Rowling said in Los Angeles on her 'Open Book Tour' that:[3]

> "I really enjoyed choosing those two quotations because one is pagan, of course, and one is from a Christian tradition," Rowling said of their inclusion. "I'd known it was going to be those two passages since 'Chamber' was published. I always knew [that] if I could use them at the beginning of book seven then I'd cued up the ending perfectly. If they were relevant, then I went where I needed to go.
>
> "They just say it all to me, they really do," she added.

This, sadly, doesn't tell us much we couldn't have guessed. Clearly she thought they were meaningful and "cued up" the last story; but how? Here are some thoughts to cue your thinking about this.

Ms. Rowling opened *Deathly Hallows* with quotations from Aeschylus' *Libation Bearers* and William Penn's *More Fruits of Solitude*. Penn (1644-1718) was a notable Quaker and non-conformist; Aeschylus (524-486 BC) was a notable Athenian soldier and playwright. The play from which the Aeschylus quotation is from, the *Libation Bearers*, is the story of Orestes, a young man with a scar on his forehead, and his taking revenge on the muderers of his father, Agamemnon. Both quotations are about life after death and both the reality and accessibility of those who are dead that we have loved.

The Aeschylus quotation, on first reflection, is there for two reasons: (1) Ms. Rowling is a classicist and probably disturbed that more people don't make the Orestes/Harry connection, especially in light of the Prophecy (and was there another way to invite her uninitiated serious readers to the *Oresteia*?) and (2) there is a theme throughout the books of the survival of the dead in the living who loved them. This quotation is an invocation of the beloved dead for their help in overcoming a wrong — and we see Harry do much the same thing "In The Forest" on his way to his sacrificial death (and victory over death).

William Penn's quotation is on the same theme (without the agony or bloodlust of Orestes!) and makes a secondary point. Penn, as Quaker and non-conformist, is one of Ms. Rowling's historical models for the "underground" resisting the Ministry; though the Nazi parallels are many and obvious, the tradition of resistance to tyranny in England is much more about government regulations concerning worship and the State Church (Catholic and Anglican!). Ms. Rowling may be "instructing while delighting" a la Spencer in urging her readers to dare to be non-conformists in a morally courageous way after the fashion of Penn and the Society of Friends (a very different brand of non-conformity than is the rule of individualism in the West today).

Two more off-the-cuff reflections about these opening quotations:

(1) Ms. Rowling opens the story with quotations from authors that are almost certainly all but unknown by the great majority of her readers — citations she has not felt necessary to make in any other book and authors she has never mentioned in interviews. The simple uniqueness of her doing this to open her finale screams, "look very closely!"

(2) Aeschylus was a warrior and veteran/hero of the Battle of Marathon whose epitaph says nothing about his writing plays. Penn is a Quaker and pacifist who is remembered not for his writings as much as "Penn's Woods," the state where I live, which was founded as a place for the more difficult Christian sects to be transported to live as "non-conformists."

Aeschylus fought the good fight in arms to keep the Persians from extinguishing the free polis of Athens and all of Greece. Penn went to jail rather than cut his beliefs about man and God to the prescribed fashion of his government and the State Church.

Both quotations are about the life of the dead in the hearts of those who loved them and each is from the polar opposite of the heroic Western tradition (warrior/pacifist). Potter, of course, embodies both ideals in the Battle of Hogwarts, offering himself as non-resisting sacrifice and defeating Voldemort in combat.

No one speaks for Aeschylus but the Quakers can speak for Penn. Here is what Christopher Densmore, Curator of the Friends Historical Library of Swarthmore College, wrote about the William Penn-Harry Potter conjunction:

> When I opened the new and final volume of the J.K. Rowling's saga, HarryPotter and the Deathly Hallows, I found the narrative preceded by two quotations, one from Aeschylus and the other from that arch-Quaker, William Penn (1644-1718). Being director of a Quaker library, the idea that even a little bit of William Penn was now being disseminated with the twelve million or so copies of the latest Harry Potter book is gratifying.
>
> The quotation, "Death is but crossing the world, as friends do the seas." is from Penn's More Fruits of Solitude (1702), a book of aphorisms that was a sequel to his earlier Fruits of Solitude (1693). The two works have been reprinted many times in the past three centuries. They were even included in the first volume of the Harvard Classics along with the journals of Benjamin Franklin and (Quaker) John Woolman.
>
> While Harry Potter literally (if one can use that term for a fictional character) takes up the sword, where the Quaker William Penn (figuratively) put down the sword, there does seem to be much in the ethical position of Potter and Penn that would seem to be sympathy. "A good end cannot sanctify evil means; nor must we ever do evil, that good may come of it." (Fruits, 537) "Force may subdue, but love gains." (Fruits, 546).[4]

5. What is the golden potion that Severus Snape gives to Dumbledore to keep him alive?

Kathy Leisner of The Leaky Cauldron speculated at what was then Barnes and Noble University just after *Half-Blood Prince* was published (2005) that Severus "stoppered" Albus Dumbledore's death when he tried to destroy the Ring Horcrux and that he was a dead man walking in the sixth book. Her reasoning was essentially that there were several references in *Prince* to the first Potions Class Harry had with Severus Snape was back in *Philosopher's Stone*. In that class, the Potions Master tells the first year students he can "brew fame, bottle glory, and stopper death."

Ms. Leisner's theory became known as "Stoppered Death" in Harry Potter fandom and was explored at length in *Who Killed Albus Dumbledore?* and *Unlocking Harry Potter: Five Keys for the Serious Reader* prior to *Deathly Hallows'* publication. It wasn't much of a surprise, consequently, when this was revealed in 'A Prince's Tale,' if learning it was golden was interesting!

6. Is *Deathly Hallows* a Christian allegory or generic Monomyth with Dying/Rising God?

It isn't either one.

You will find Christians who assert that Harry's death and resurrection in *Deathly Hallows* is allegorical, that is, a point-for-point retelling of Christ's Passion and Resurrection after three days. There are strong parallels and the symbolism is both meaningful and edifying (see chapters 2, 3, and 6) but Harry is not a Christ stick-figure or stand-in. If anything, he is a Christian Everyman and spiritual seeker whose life comes to resemble or echo Christ's because of the hard choices he makes about what to believe and with respect to death. This resemblance -- in his response to temptation, his acceptance of his destiny as sacrifice, his victory over death -- is not negligible, certainly, but, as Harry is purified by his death, what we could call "redeemed," makes him more an Everyman Christian allegorical figure than a Jesus of Nazareth stand-in.

You'll also find Christian critics who dismiss *any* Christian meaning in the series finale and who argue with a straight face that the resurrection theme in Harry Potter is just another secular use of the "*dying-rising, savior-deliverer myth motif.*"

The maven at the Behold A Phoenix web site responded to this assertion:[5]

> The concept of dying and rising gods in antiquity was popularized a century ago by Sir James Frazer in The Golden Bough. Scholars in the fields of anthropology and comparative religion have mostly rejected this concept, citing that Frazer over interpreted the evidence in his conclusions. Glenn Miller of Christian Thinktank (a great website on Christian Apologetics) quotes from Jonathan Z. Smith, who contributed the entry "Dying and Rising Gods" for *The Encyclopedia of Religion* (Edited by Mircea Eliade; Macmillian: 1987:)

The category of dying and rising gods, once a major topic of scholarly investigation, must now be understood to have been largely a misnomer based on imaginative reconstructions and exceedingly late or highly ambiguous texts.

Smith examined the cases of ancient deities such as Adonis, Baal/Hadad/Adad, Attis, Marduk, Osirus, and Tammuz/Dumuzi and came to the following conclusion:

As the above examples make plain, the category of dying and rising deities is exceedingly dubious. It has been based largely on Christian interest and tenuous evidence. As such, the category is of more interest to the history of scholarship than to the history of religions.

Deathly Hallows is not a Christian allegory, per se, but what Christian content it has and traditional symbolism it employs (and if you've read this far in the book, I'm hoping you understand how much there is) preclude the bizarre 'Dying and Rising God' thesis.

7. Did Rowling win the 'Biggest Twist' prize she said she was hoping to get?

Ms. Rowling is a big Austen fan, which is the genesis of this "Big Twist" question. As she has said:

"My favorite writer is Jane Austen and I've read all her books so many times I've lost count."[6]

I re-read Austen's novels in rotation - I've just started Mansfield Park again. I could have chosen any number of passages from each of her novels, but I finally settled on Emma, which is the most skilfully managed mystery I've ever read and has the merit of having a heroine who annoys me because she is in some ways so like me. I must have read it at least 20 times, always wondering how I could have missed the glaringly obvious fact that Frank Churchill and Jane Fairfax were engaged all along. But I did miss it, and I've yet to meet a person who didn't, and I have never set up a surprise ending in a Harry Potter book without knowing I can never, and will never, do it anywhere near as well as Austen did in Emma. [7]

"The best twist ever in literature is in Jane Austen's <u>Emma</u>. To me she is the target of perfection at which we shoot in vain."[8]

Many of Ms. Rowling's readers, having read the first six books many times and mapped out possibilities, predicted much of the twist in *Deathly Hallows*. 'Stoppered Death' theory, the idea of a Severus-Lily relationship being important, and the possibility that Harry was a Horcrux were all common-places among serious readers in 2005, if none of them was universally accepted. These were important plot points but not the heart of Ms. Rowling's surprise or "twist" reserved for *Deathly Hallows*. That was the combination of Albus Dumbledore's history, his Machiavellian planning of Harry's strategic demise, and Snape's sympathetic backstory. I'm sure someone out there saw that one coming but I didn't see it or read about it until I read *Deathly Hallows*. I don't know if this qualifies as surpassing Miss Austen, but it surprised me a lot more than the ending of *Emma*!

8. How different was this story from all the other Rocky-wins-against-all-odds stories?

I think I see what you mean. *Harry Potter* has quite a lot of the lovable underdog conquering against all odds story-staple to it and just about every movie and best-selling book of our time has these elements in it, too. It would be weird if Ms. Rowling's books were as popular as they are and were *completely* different or sui generis when compared to other stories we like. She is, after all, a writer of our times writing for an audience of postmoderns, all of whom like the underdog motif a lot.

Please read my *Unlocking Harry Potter: Five Keys for the Serious Reader* for an in-depth discussion of Ms. Rowling as a postmodern writer. I explain at length there that one of the reasons for why these books are so popular is that "we buy and read them because we like them." That's not as vapid and circular as you might think because "why we like them" is that "the books resonate with the concerns and our beliefs of this historical age." I explain in the fifth key of *Unlocking* that there are ten qualities of Postmodern Story-Telling, and, as you'd expect, Ms. Rowling hits a perfect 10 in Harry Potter.

Deathly Hallows is no exception; it is a great finish to her several postmodern themes, most notably, that government, media, and schools are the agencies of the Grand Myth that makes us as prejudiced as we are, that these cultural prejudices make us effectively blind to the way things really are, and that only the excluded or "other" ("freaks!") have something like a true view of things. The Orwellian Ministry of Magic in *Deathly Hallows* proclaiming that Magic is Might is taken over by the Dark Lord so easily because it is already evil at the core. Harry's odyssey or "life on the run," too, only seems to solidify his place in people's heart as the hoped for Deliverer of the Oppressed. Harry's victory is in large part due to his respecting all magical creatures and Hogwarts houses; he is a "Postmodern hero" in leading the magical "rainbow coalition" against the Nazi Slytherins.

Travis Prinzi understands more about postmodernism than I even care to know. He wrote:[9]

> It's postmodern because, not only did Harry see through the exceedingly obvious Nazi-like prejudices, but he even saw through the prejudices of the "Good Guys," the oppressive stories that even the best members of the Order still live by. As Griphook said, Harry is an "odd wizard." Calling Harry an "odd wizard" is the best way to get at his postmodern character - he sees, because he learned from Dumbledore, that even the "good guys" take part in the oppression of house-elves and goblins. Even Sirius treated a house-elf so badly that it resulted in his own death.
>
> So, yeah, it's postmodern, not because of the opposition to the the overtly Nazi-like ideology (after all, even most rationalistic modernists could see the obvious injustice there), but because he saw the oppression that even the story's best moral characters overlooked (and in so doing, perpetuated).
>
> That said, he didn't fully accomplish a postmodern turnaround of all oppression, and I'm glad for the sake of the story's credibility that he didn't. Rowling knows that evil and prejudice are far too complex to be solved in one year by one person. It would be an utter insult to the complexity of the problems of racism, prejudice, and slavery to have wrapped up that whole storyline by the end of Book 7. Harry represents a shift in the right direction in the Wizarding World. There's still a long battle to be fought to overcome oppression.

So it's not just another *Rocky*, even if its resonance with the way we see things *is* at the heart of Harry's popularity.

9. Are you disappointed that Harry wasn't beheaded?

Just a little! It seemed that this demise was Harry's likely end, a la Sydney Carton in Dickens' *Tale of Two Cities*.

We had something of a smoking gun about Ms. Rowling and *The Tale of Two Cities* in a story from her year in Paris studying French.

> Lecturers remember Rowling as nervous and insecure, but a fellow student, Yvette Cowles, told Sean Smith, her biographer, that she

was popular and striking. "She wore long skirts and used to have this blue denim jacket she liked to wear. Jo was very shapely and she had this big hair, kind of back -combed and lacquered, and lots of heavy eyeliner. I think she was quite popular with the guys." In her first year she signed up for French and Classics but an attitude to academia best described as minimum work, maximum fun led to her abandoning Classics after she failed to register properly for an exam. Her third year was spent teaching in a school in Paris and sharing a flat with an Italian, a Russian and a Spaniard. She found the Italian disagreeable and would avoid him by spending whole days in her room reading. During this time she read Charles Dickens' A Tale of Two Cities, a literary discovery that may have influenced her alleged intention to kill off Harry Potter at the end of book seven. The death of Charles Darnay, sacrificing his life for a friend, and his moving last words had a major impact on Rowling: "It is a far, far better thing that I do than I have ever done; it is a far, far better rest that I go to than I have ever known."

{Hat Tip and many thanks once again to Lisa Bunker for hunting down this 2003 *Scotsman* article[10] about Ms. Rowling that my search engines couldn't locate.}

Supposedly, the full story has Ms. Rowling weeping in a cafe after finishing the book and saying that Carton's line (not Darnay! ouch) was the single greatest line in English, period. True or not, *Tale of Two Cities*, its resurrection motif, and its cathartic ending deserves a closer look by Potter-philes. Not only do the *Harry Potter* novels share an alchemical structure with *Tale of Two Cities*, Harry dies a figurative death every year on his Hero's Journey and rises from the dead in the presence of a symbol of Christ. The resurrection theme — love's victory over death — is evident in both and presented in a similar black-white-red sequence.

And the killer connection? (Forgive me that, please.)

Ms. Rowling has laced every one of her *Potter* books with references, characters, and plot events involving or pointing to a beheading of some kind. When I read the books this past year with my Valley Forge Military Academy fourth classmen (ninth graders), by the time we reached *Goblet* the cadets were groaning at each new reference to someone having their head cut-off. [Grateful Bow and a Hat Tip to Linda McCabe for bringing this grisly motif to my attention in 2003.]

Struggling to think of any?

- How about Nearly Headless Nick and the gang of the beheaded on the Headless Hunt?
- Buckbeak's near-miss decapitation?
- Ron's Severing Charm on his Dress Robes?
- The fake-wand battle in which the parrot eats the head off Harry's fish?
- Harry's prediction of his own death by decapitation in a homework assignment for Professor Trelawney?
- The Weasley twins' Headless Hats?

There are a daunting number of beheadings and decapitation in the first six books.

Ever hear of "Chekhov's Gun"? Anton Chekhov apparently felt strongly about what Janet Batchler calls "set-ups" and "pay-offs." As he wrote to several friends and demonstrated in his own plays, Chekhov thought that a dramatist shouldn't show a loaded gun on stage in the first act if it wasn't going to be fired before the final curtain. Given the number of times Ms. Rowling has shown us the axe or the shadow of an axe falling in her first six books, this rule from the stage might be re-christened "Rowling's Razor." I thought someone, probably Harry, was almost definitely going to take it in the neck in *Deathly Hallows*.

And it didn't happen.

There is plenty of neck action in *Deathly Hallows*, most of it murderous, but Harry and friends escape it. As "Kathy" scored it at HogPro:[11]

As far as other beheadings or "taking it in the neck (or head)," here is my count:

- *George Weasley (loses an ear)*
- *Mad-Eye Moody (not sure exact manner of death, but his magical eye was removed from his head and placed in Umbridge's office door)*
- *Bathilda Bagshot (Nagini comes out of her neck)*
- *Harry, Ron and Hermione (all physically injured to some degree by wearing the locket horcrux around their necks)*
- *Hermione (throat almost slit while in captivity at Mafoy Manor, blood is drawn)*

- *Wormtail (strangles himself after Harry reminds him of his life debt)*
- *Snape (bitten by Nagini in the neck)*
- *Neville Longbottom (Sorting Hat bursts into flame while on his head)*
- *Nagini (Neville beheads snake with Sword of Gryffindor...)*

So Snape, Wormtail, and Nagini are the characters Ms. Rowling was pointing to in her death-by-strangulation, decapitation, or neck injury and the good guys should have been wearing helmets and neck braces, too.

10. Is Severus Snape's love for Lily and life of unrequited love a Wuthering Heights echo?

Yes and no.

Severus Snape's allegiance and motivations had become the central question surrounding the series; we learn in The Prince's Tale, Severus' memories given by him at his death, that his service to Dumbledore and Harry is all a consequence of his unrequited love for Harry's mother, Lily, Severus' childhood friend. Severus vows to Dumbledore that he will do anything for him if the Headmaster will save Lily from Voldemort; at Lily's death, Severus is convinced that his continuing love for her means he must stay on at Hogwarts to protect her son. Are Severus' thoughts about Harry an echo of Heathcliff in Wuthering Heights and his bizarre relationship with Catherine Earnshaw (or another tip of the hat to Sydney Carton love for Lucie in *Tale of Two Cities*)?

Certainly Severus' life after Lily Evans Potter's death is shaped absolutely by his love for her and his remorse for his part in her death. He is something of a Heathcliff echo and the caricature of a Gothic anti-hero in this respect but he's too positive a character in the end, despite his sadism as a teacher, to be squeezed into a Heathcliff mold. I think Carton and Dante are more important (see chapter 4).

11. Why does Rowling mix in the Hallows temptation with Harry's Horcrux hunt?

The books are largely about the corruptive influence and temptations of power on the hero's journey to "corrected vision" and theosis (see chapters 5-7). For Harry to complete the journey he began in *Philosopher's*

Stone, in which ending he was able to get the Stone because he didn't want to use it, he would have to become Master of Death by overcoming the temptation of immortality available to him in possessing all three Hallows. Dumbledore wasn't equal to this temptation as a younger man or even in old age.

12. Is *Deathly Hallows* really just Prof. MacGonagall's final exam in Transfigurations?

Could be!

If you make a list of the people who become different and better people through their actions and decisions and through the events of *Deathly Hallows,* you come up with these transfigurations, not to count what happens to Harry, Ron, and Hermione: Dudley Dursley,Remus Lupin, Grawp, Kreacher, Aberforth Dumbledore, Prof. Trelawney, Percy Weasley, Neville Longbottom, Draco Malfoy and his parents, and the Centaurs.These are much different folks at the end of *Deathly Hallows* than they were at the beginning or when we left them in *Prince*.

The changes range from the almost instantaneous and very surprising changes of heart (Kreacher, Aberforth, the Centaurs) to the more developed and longer-in-coming (Neville, Remus, Draco). Each Harry Potter novel has been about choices and change, especially Harry's transformation over the book's adventures, but *Deathly Hallows* takes the cake for numbers and depth of changes.

13. *Deathly Hallows* seems more about Ron's transformation than Harry's. Wassup with that?

I'm not sure I'd go so far as saying the finale is more about Ron than Harry, but I see your point.

If the terrible trio, Ron, Hermione, and Harry, are a body - mind - spirit triptych a la *The Brothers Karamazov* and more recent depictions in Star Trek and Star Wars, Ron represents the "body" or "passions" soul faculty. They decide to wear the Locket Horcrux (shades of Frodo!), and Ron is, naturally, the most affected by its evil heart. Nonetheless, his departure for the better part of four chapters is easily the *nigredo* and nadir of *Deathly Hallows* and his transformation and return one of the more inspiring and exciting moments of the book (the series?).

The apotheosis of the change in Ron, gaged by Hermione's reaction, is his concern about the house-elves in The Battle of Hogwarts. I'm not sure Ron "gets" house-elves even then (his suggestion is patronizing and borderline racist rather than recognizing the power of these creatures) but, if it is a given that their species-being seems to be about service or slavery, then he has come to accept responsibility without feeling disdain.

The final union of Hermione (Ms. Hermes or Alchemical Mercury) and Ronald (middle name 'Bilius' meaning Joe Choleric or Sulfur) is the Alchemical Wedding we've been waiting on for the Great Work's "quarreling couple." Their two children even have alchemical names: 'Rose' is a synonym for the Philosopher's Stone, believe it or not, in alchemical texts and 'Hugo's name has two consonants, that like his mother's initials, are the chemical sign for mercury.

14. Am I crazy or was *Deathly Hallows* a WWII allegory? How many Nazi echoes are there?

You're not crazy for noting all the WWII points of correspondence. There are a bunch.

Beside the Orwellian *1984* hat-tips in the "Magic is Might" statue and policies of the Voldemort directed Ministry of Magic, I was struck by three different *Deathly Hallows* plot points right off that seemed conscious signs connecting the Dark Lord and the German National Socialists of the '30's and '40's. The first was the symbol that Xenophilius Lovegood wears to the wedding which so offends Viktor Krum (as discussed in chapter 7). The swastika similarly is an ancient spiritual symbol that cannot be shown anywhere without drama (it is illegal in Germany, for instance) because of its use by the Nazis. Voldemort's desire to find the Elder Wand or "Wand of Destiny," too, points to Hitler's desire to find and use the so-called "Spear of Destiny" in building the Third Reich. Ms. Rowling even has Dumbledore as a young man fall to this temptation of overlooking individual rights and freedom "for the greater good," a signature quality of totalitarian regimes.

The Weasley/Delacour wedding, too, is an echo of the Anglo/Gallic alliance against Hitler, which brings us to the Voldemort and Death Eaters in control of the Ministry parallels with the Third Reich:

- The Mudblood/PureBlood distinction screams Aryan racist nonsense about the Master Race.

- The persecution of Muggle-Born wizards and crimes against Muggles results from this madness.

- Voldemort kills teachers who resist by speaking out.

- The Ministry makes school attendance mandatory to insure control of young hearts and minds.

- They create a culture of fear with legal taboos that restrict free speech.

- The rounding up of dissidents by "Snatchers" is reminiscent of the vigilantes who gathered Jews and "undesirables" during the Nazi Final Solution.

- Grindelwald being defeated in 1945, the end of WWII, and being placed in a prison that sounds very much like "Nuremburg," the city in which Nazi war criminals were tried.

- "For the Greater Good" reminded me that fascism is a disease of the political left (Nazi is an abbreviated way of saying "National Socialist").

- The Potter underground radio broadcast and the peripatetic existence of Harry, Ron, and Hermione calls up images of the French Resistance to the occupying Nazis (Ms. Rowling no doubt grew up hearing these stories and then read about them in her French studies).

- Harry's being sorted as "Undesirable Number One" is another pointer to the "other" created by the metanarrative of National Socialism and all millenialist totalitarian regimes.

- *The rising up of the house-elves, Centaurs, and the students of Hogwarts in the final battle had an echo of the Warsaw ghetto uprising or Treblinka more than the great battles at the end of the Hobbit, LOTR, and Narnia's finish.

- Anybody think the Voldemort-Hitler equation is silly? Ms. Rowling grew up in a country scarred by war with the German fascists, a country that believed that Hitler had Jewish ancestry and still persecuted Jews.

And there are the smaller touches like the Nazi salute the Death Eaters exchange before entering Malfoy Manor and Rowling's depiction of Scimgeour as Churchill following Chamberlain/Fudge.

But, having said all that, I am NOT saying that Harry Potter is a WWII allegory. There are a bunch of parallels that are used to advance Ms. Rowling's anti-authoritarian message. Ms. Rowling's postmodern beliefs about the world and the constitutive "other" are tempered by her modern beliefs shaped by the Rowling parents who were born during or just after the Blitz. There is evil in the world and individuals need to sacrifice themselves to combat it. I think we've established a background of "resistance to totalitarianism" in *Deathly Hallows*; we don't have to stretch for allegorical one-for-one correspondence.

15. What are we supposed to make of the Name Taboo?

The Name Taboo in *Deathly Hallows* referred to here is a law making it a criminal offense to say the name of Voldemort. This Ministry-enforced Taboo immediately brings bounty hunters ("Snatchers") and breaks protective spells to the place where anyone has said the name. It is supposedly to catch Death Eaters but, of course, is used to round up Resistance fighters who are not afraid to say the name.

Ms. Rowling here is playing with a few ideas here, I think. The Name Taboo is certainly a "Pay Off" for the "Set Ups" in all the other books about the wizard convention of not using Lord Voldemort's name -- even when everyone believed he was dead! This is a combination of noting how evil is often a mockery of the good and Ms. Rowling's thoughts about restrictions of free speech in the name of "the Greater Good."

God Himself in the Hebrew Scriptures forbids using "His Name in vain." This is not necessarily a prohibition against ever invoking the Deity; the three Abrahamic religions each have spiritual paths based on attentive saying of the Name of God to invoke His presence in the heart. It is to clarify how powerful and potentially dangerous this is, however, if done impiously or casually. Voldemort, who is pursuing a personal immortality and quasi-divine power status by murder, violence, and fear, apes the true God's power by making his assumed name a legal taboo. Harry and Dumbledore's refusal to conform to convention by not saying Voldemort's name is Ms. Rowling's pointed message that we are obliged to resist those who would make themselves our Lords.

I suspect, too, based on Ms. Rowling's comments in the media as well as her depiction of the Ministry under Pius Thicknese that she is no admirer of governments, especially those who justify power-grabs from the people in the name of protecting the people. Could the Name Taboo be a pointer to the irony of the Patriot Act? Americans, according to critics of the Bush administration, have lost their civil liberties or allowed them to be rolled back, by government officials saying these rights if unchecked leave the nation vulnerable to terrorist attack. The loss of prized liberties, however, is not tallied as a terrorist victory.

I do not share and I do not disagree with Ms. Rowling's expressed desire for a Democrat in the White House rather than a Republican. The Name Taboo, though, in *Deathly Hallows* may be a reflection of her political views.

16. There seem to be quite a few wand-as-male-sexual-organ jokes in Deathly Hallows – or am I a pervert for seeing this?

If you're a pervert, then you're in good company. Ms. Rowling doesn't duck making wand-as-peter jokes for those willing "to go there," and it's not just bathroom or bedroom humor.

I had a pointed, if private, exchange in 2003 with a film critic, who wrote me to say that he thought my ideas about the battle in *Chamber of Secrets* were risible; that story, he said, could as easily be understood as a Freudian adventure in phallic and yonic imagery (giant serpents, swords and broken wands, chutes and floods in the girls bathroom, etc) than as the traditional Morality Play that I described. He saw these two interpretations as exclusive rather than complementary so neither being true was possible, both being true was impossible, and the Freudian interpretation was as likely as an edifying, spiritual one.

We return to the meaning of swords, wands, wand cores, and wand mastery in *Deathly Hallows* with a vengeance, and, necessarily, to how Ms. Rowling is using these phallic images. Men and women pursue more powerful wands, have their wands broken or taken, replaced or not, discuss "wand performance," and the decisive battle turns on who is the Master of the Elder Wand. Harry ends the drama by a semi-miraculous "healing" of his broken holly and phoenix feather original. Ms. Rowling uses wands as tokens of power, identity, ego, *and* sexuality here. "Wands are only as powerful as the wizards who use them. Some wizards just like to boast that theirs are bigger and better than other people's" (*Hallows*, Chapter 21, p. 415).

I disagree strongly with readers who think that books are just projection-platforms for beliefs that people bring with them. There is a better and a worse reading of text; relativism is not a guide for thoughtful interpretation. I resist as adamantly, though, exclusivists who insist that a Christian and Freudian reading cannot be *simultaneously* valid (in a fantasy coming-of-age novel, no less). Novels can have sexual and religious undertones; the question is predominance and priority which is a matter of interpreting the author's intentions.

I think the sexual elements of the Harry Potter books are lightly shaded relative to the religious elements, especially in the final novel. The jokes about the trolls comparing the sizes of their clubs and Ron's "it's not all wand-work" line on Harry's birthday are funny throw-aways. That Voldemort has his big snake "soul member" decapitated publicly, though, by a young man who finally is using his own sword rather than his father's wand is a psycho-sexual symbol of no little power. That it is also a shade of the last being first and David versus Goliath and of the victory of Christ over the serpent in the Garden is also undeniable. If simultaneous symbolism, which representation is predominant? The whole last chapter turns on the last battle of wand-powers and virtue with very heavy *Christus Victor* symbolism after King's Cross. The sexual shading highlights and buttresses the religious under-tow and tones.

It is masterful artistry — and the relativists and exclusivists both miss it. You're no pervert for noting this symbolism; please don't restrict its meaning to physical body parts.

17. What are we to make of the White Lady's fairy tale just before the Battle of Hogwarts?

That was a weird break in the action, wasn't it? The whole wizarding world is breaking into camps for Ms. Rowling's version of the Last Battle and Calvary when Harry tracks down the Gray Lady and hears the 'Tale of the Ravenclaw Tiara,' or, alternately, 'Ballad of the Bloody Baron.' He does get the information he needs – there is a tiara, Voldemort learned about its Albanian location – but the story-hour moment as the world around him unravels is very curious.

I think it's about Severus Snape and the power of fairy tales.

We learn from the haughty Lady that the Bloody Baron had loved her but she had not loved him. When he was unable to convince her to return to see her dying mother, the Slytherin House Baron in a rage murdered the woman he loved in anger and frustration. His life-as-a-ghost ever since has been spent in remorse and chain-bound penitence for his mistake.

Sound familiar? Slytherin House master responsible for the death of the object of his unrequited love? Spending his days in painful remorse and regret? That's right, the story of the ghosts is echoed in the life of Severus Snape.

So what?

Ms. Rowling spends a significant part of *Deathly Hallows* demonstrating in her narrative that we are obliged to take stories seriously, especially fairy tales. Dumbledore leaves Hermione the original (if glossed by symbols) runic version of *The Tales of Beedle the Bard*, in which Grimm Brothers-like collection we find 'The Tale of the Three Brothers.' This story turns out to be a cipher of sorts for the "real-world" Peverell Brothers, of whom Harry is a descendant, and which story drives much of the three Deathly Hallows action of the book.

Ms. Rowling seems to be suggesting that literature, even kids' fairy tales, need to be taken very seriously, even as "real-world" events. Hermione and Ron think this is so much rot; these stories are for instruction about good manners and hygiene, not history or even psychology. Harry, however, understands intuitively and almost immediately that the fairy tale has a core in fact that changes everything about his situation, namely, that the three Hallows exist -- and Voldemort is in pursuit of the Deathstick or Elder Wand. (See Chapter 7.)

I'm not suggesting that Ms. Rowling wants us to read fairy tales as factual events ("find the Gingerbread House with a large oven for bread and with a cage in the yard large enough for a good-sized boy"). It is important to note, though, that Harry succeeds in his mission *only* because he takes fairy tales very *seriously* and acts on what he learns from them. I put it to you as a possibility that the author's purpose in this is to urge via Harry's example her readers to read Harry very seriously and to learn from his example and his adventures. If we don't value what Harry shows us, namely, those greater realities we experience in our heads, as Dumbledore mentions to Harry at King's Cross, we are destined to Tom Riddle, Jr.'s fate. As Dumbledore explained:

> That which Voldemort does not value, he takes no trouble to comprehend. Of house-elves and children's tales, of love, loyalty, and innocence, Voldemort knows and understands nothing. Nothing. That they all have a power beyond his own, a power beyond the reach of any magic, is a truth he has never grasped. (Chapter 36, pages 709-10; emphasis in original)

Did Snape know the story of the Bloody Baron? I doubt it. Would he have learned enough from it to have avoided his fate, a fate much like the Baron's? I'm inclined to think that's unlikely, too. Ms. Rowling, in her urging us to value children's tales, however, and to recognize in them an other-worldly power and truth, believes if we will read and reflect that our lives won't have to be Grimm tales or shades of the agonies experienced by Severus Snape and Tom Riddle, Jr.

18. Is Dumbledore a good guy or a bad guy?

He is a deeply flawed hero.

Much of the action of *Deathly Hallows* is the peeling of the onion to get to the truth about Albus Dumbledore and his relationship with Harry. We learn with Harry (and everyone else) a lot of information about the late headmaster, much of it gossip, most of it true, from Rita Skeeter in *The Daily Prophet* and in her book, *The Life and Lies of Albus Dumbledore*. These facts even when shorn of the Skeeter/Ministry spin are still very disturbing. What we learn on the trio's travels, from Aberforth, and from the Pensieve and Severus' memory don't do much to reassure us about Dumby's personal history, his intentions, *and* his methods. "Secrets and lies" are his natural currency, it seems; using people his forte. Santa Claus has turned out to be a secret admirer, even a disciple of Nicolo Machiavelli.

And yet Harry willingly sacrifices himself in 'The Forest Again' on the Headmaster's orders and is even happy to see and speak with the man in King's Cross. Harry pays the price all along and in the end for Dumbledore's secrecy and duplicity but definitely believes the leader of the Order is a good guy. Harry names his second son 'Albus' in case you had any doubts.

The surprise-inside the beloved Headmaster, the Michael Gambon-nasty we never would have guessed was hiding within all-father Richard Harris, was Ms. Rowling's big finale twist. Harry's success in defeating Dumbledore, oddly, though, isn't in understanding Dumby for who he is but choosing to believe in his plan, the ultimate goodness of his intention, and in the man himself. As I explained in chapter one and three, this struggle to believe, I should say 'the critical necessity of choosing to believe,' is Ms. Rowling's most important spiritual message for her skeptical postmodern readers. Even if it is only in the power and truth of fairy tales, we need to believe in something good, true, and beautiful outside of ourselves if we are to conquer our internal and external Voldemorts.

I don't know if Dumbledore can be called a 'good guy' or 'bad guy' without qualification or stuttering. I'm sure if Harry hadn't believed in him that Voldemort would have carried the day within Harry and in the world at large.

19. What about Dumbledore being gay? What are we supposed to do with that?

Not much.

Ms. Rowling revealed on her Open Book Tour that she "always thought of Dumbledore as gay." I think three things can be safely asserted about that announcement.

First, it was something done very much in the heat of a poignant exchange with a fan. Dr. Amy Sturgis described the Carnegie Hall public conversation and specific question that brought Ms. Rowling to share this thought about the Headmaster's sexual orientation. The author was sufficiently moved that she said as preface to her remark that she felt the woman deserved an "honest answer" to her question, i.e., that she was going to depart from script. [Read Dr. Sturgis' account of that evening at her web log: http://eldritchhobbit.livejournal.com/175955.html]

Second, Dumbledore's sexuality isn't important beyond the least significant of character shadings. We know this for certain because it is nowhere mentioned in the 4100 pages of the novels. We do not need author confirmation of this but we have it. Ms. Rowling said in her Adeel Amini interview:

> From one controversy to the next, it seemed inevitable that the topic of Dumbledore's sexuality would crop up. How did Rowling deal with the fallout? "It was funny, mostly!" she exclaims. "I had always seen Dumbledore as gay, but in a sense that's not a big deal. *The book wasn't about Dumbledore being gay.* It was just that from the outset obviously I knew that he had this big, hidden secret and that he flirted with the idea of exactly what Voldemort goes on to do, *he flirted with the idea of racial domination*, that he was going to subjugate Muggles. So *that was Dumbledore's big secret.*
>
> "So why did he flirt with that?" she asks. "He's an innately good man, what would make him do that? I didn't even think it through that way, it just seemed to come to me, I thought, 'I know why he did it. He fell in love.' And whether they physically consummated this infatuation or not is not the issue. The issue is love. *It's not about sex.* So that's what I knew about Dumbledore. And it's relevant only in so much as he fell in love and was made an utter

fool of by love. He lost his moral compass completely when he fell in love and I think subsequently became very mistrusting of his own judgement (sic) in those matters so *became quite asexual. He led a celibate and a bookish life."* ...

She continues: "He's a very old single man. You have to ask: why is it so interesting? People have to examine their own attitudes. It's a shade in a character. Is it the most important thing about him? No. It's Dumbledore, for God's sake. *There are 20 things that are relevant to the story before his sexuality."* Bottom line, then: he isn't a gay character; he's a character that just happens to be gay. Rowling concurs wholeheartedly. (emphasis added) http://www.adeelamini.com/JKR/ESTE012C_adeelaminicom_JKR.pdf

The important revelation about Dumbledore, the big twist of the final chapter and the whole series, is that the Headmaster had feet of clay, was borderline Machiavellian, and, if he probably didn't have a Grindelwald action figure hidden in a desk drawer, he did have some embarrassing skeletons in the closet. These revelations set the stage for Harry's "struggle to believe" and his eventually "corrected vision" and apotheosis. The "gay Dumbledore" issue only distracts from these essential points. [See John Mark Reynold's essay on 'Taking Stories More Seriously than the Author:' http://www.scriptoriumdaily.com/2007/10/23/dumbledore-is-not-gay-taking-stories-more-seriously-than-the-author/]

Which brings me to my third and last thought on this subject here: I can think of two very good reasons to think of Dumbledore as a gay man, albeit a celibate bookish one. He is an alchemist *and* the hero of a postmodern novel. All the other good guys in the Potter saga are somehow "other;" they're poor, they're orphans, they're Muggle born, they're half-breeds, they have a "little furry problem" or have escaped from Azkaban. Dumbledore was the exception to this rule. His adolescent same sex attraction experience, however, at least to many American readers, resolves that exception. Would that his short-lived desire to rule the world was considered as much the mark against that him that Dumbledore grieved about as this "secret love."

We know, too, that an Alchemist, at least an accomplished one, is a qualitative androgyne or *rebis*. This kind of hermaphroditism, a resolution of contraries, is usually represented sexually as a man-woman. If I had to represent this kind of figure in story form, I confess that I would probably have chosen a celibate man with a history of same sex attraction.

This is an important question only because so many people ask about it. To serious readers, though, of the books, it is little more than another interesting detail among thousands of such details that do not enter into any of the layered meanings of the books. Folks that get worked up about it, "for" or "against," need to reflect on the value of reading the series in light of a throw-away comment at a public reading that is atextual. I don't think there's much there to get excited about myself.

20. Am I the only fan who was really disappointed with *Deathly Hallows*?

Oh, no. Lots of folks were (and are) disappointed with the last book. I edited a collection of essays about *Half-Blood Prince* called *Who Killed Albus Dumbledore?* (Zossima Press, 2007). Of the five very serious Potter-mavens other than myself who contributed chapters to this delightful book, full to the brim with speculation about how *Deathly Hallows* would turn out, more than half have written me to say that Ms. Rowling blew it. I don't think this is a reaction peculiar to Potter experts who went out on a limb with their guesses. It seems, based on informal questions I ask at the talks I give in churches, book stores, and universities, that *most* fans didn't like the Epilogue.

This is a function of unreasonable expectations and elements of surprise.

I predicted before *Deathly Hallows* was published that there were only three 'sure things' about this book's publication: Bloomsbury/ Scholastic were going to sell a lot of books, the book would be leaked before it officially went on sale, and millions of people were going to be disappointed. I knew the last was a sure thing only because it was *impossible* for any book to have equaled the level of expectations. Each book would have had to have come with a check equal or greater than the 2008 economic spending check from the IRS for this not to be true.

And *Deathly Hallows* is different. Harry spends relatively little time at school, where all the other adventures have been centered. There's no Quidditch, little Snape, and a bunch of unanswered questions and unresolved story-lines. Worse, Ms. Rowling introduces details in the last book that are necessary for the ending, little things like Snitches having flesh-memory, how Horcruxes can be destroyed, expansive wand-lore, and the existence of the three Deathly Hallows. For folks who lived and breathed these books for more than a few years and had created on-line identities around characters and plot-points, this was all a bit jarring.

And disappointing.

I hoped, even expected the book would be a 'big twist' and an alchemical carnival with no little transcendent meaning. I was and am delighted with Ms. Rowling's book, which I think is clearly her best work. I respect those who had different expectations for and experiences reading *Deathly Hallows*.

21. How does *Deathly Hallows* fit in with or complete the seven book series?

As I wrote in chapter one's discussion of the Hero's Journey, *Deathly Hallows* seems to complete the circle started in *Philosopher's Stone*. There are multiple references back to every book, certainly, but the biggest overlap seems to be between first and last. Here is a chart in no particular order of the echoes that suggest Ms. Rowling wrote *Deathly Hallows* as an end.

Deathly Hallows	Philosopher's Stone
Hagrid with Harry on Sirius' Bike	Hagrid with Harry on Sirius' Bike
Hagrid carries Voldemort-attacked Harry (17)	Hagrid carries Voldemort attacked Harry (1)
Harry, Ron, and Hermione rescue dragon	Harry and Hermione rescue Norbert(a)
Harry's resurrection after King's Cross	Harry's resurrection after three days
Neville out of nowhere is Gryffindor Champion	Neville surprise points cause Gryffindor victory
Dumbledore's Deluminator key to Ron's return	Dumbledore's Deluminator up front
Stoppered Death potion revealed	Snape mentions ability to "stopper death"
Harry rides the rails at Gringotts with Griphook	Harry rides the rails at Gringotts with Griphook

Hermione to Ron at Whomping Willow: "*Are you a wizard, or what*!?"	Ron to Hermione at Devil's Snare: "ARE YOU A WITCH OR NOT!?"
Driving Mystery: The Deathly Hallows and, specifically, the Resurrection Stone	Driving Mystery: Finding the Philosopher's Stone and keeping it from Snape
Harry found worthy of Hallows and Mastery of Death because he doesn't want to use them	Harry able to "find" Stone and take it from Mirror because he doesn't want to use it
Harry abandons magical objects giving him faux immortality with Dumby's approval	Dumbledore explains why he and Flamel agreed to destroy the Philosopher's Stone
Ron uses "Wingardium Leviosa" on a stick	Ron uses "Wingardium Leviosa" on a club
Harry learns origin of Invisibility Cloak and receives Resurrection Stone from Dumby	Harry receives Invisibility Cloak as gift from Dumbledore at Christmas and receives Philosopher's Stone from mirror
Harry learns his family story at Christmas in Godric's Hollow	Harry sees his family for the first time in the Mirror of Erised on Christmas Day
Harry hates Severus but learns in the end that Snape was Dumbledore's closest ally	Harry hates Severus but learns in the end that Snape protected him from Qirrelldemort
The Centaurs break their rule of non-involvement to fight Lord Voldemort	The Centaur Firenze breaks Centaur custom by rescuing Harry from Quirrelldemort

Harry in obedience goes into Forbidden Forest to confront Lord Voldemort	Harry serves a detention in Forbidden Forest and has near death experience with Voldy
Harry goes underground seven times in trials and opens Snitch and uses Resurrection Stone.	Harry overcomes seven obstacels underground to reach Philosopher's Stone.
Harry decides he must seek Horcruxes and tries to convince R&H to stay behind	Harry decides he must protect the Stone and tries to convince R&H to stay behind
Harry, Ron, and Hermione have adventure and leave Neville at Hogwarts	Harry, Ron, and Hermoione have adventure and leave Neville in Gryffindor Common Room
Order of Phoenix parents die in battle leaving orphan boy named "Gift from God" (Theodore)	Order of Phoenix parents die in battle leaving orphan boy named "Heir of Father" (Pater)
Voldemort kills Hogwarts Professors Burbage and Snape	Voldemort kills Hogwarts Professor Quirrell
Harry's Victory is won and celebrated in Hogwart's Great Hall	Harry's Victory is revealed and celebrated in Hogwart's Great Hall

22. The battle scenes in *Deathly Hallows* were straight out of Lewis and Tolkien, no?

I'd say "no," at least not "straight out of."

The battle scenes in *Deathly Hallows*, specifically, the Battle of Hogwarts and the Last Battle consequent to Harry's death that ends in the wizard duels in the Great Hall, like everything else in the series, comes from the compost heap of all the all the things Ms. Rowling has read (or so she tells us). Her battle scenes seem a remarkable mix of Biblical, historical, and Inkling literature, which seems to support her point. Without neglecting the artistry with which she put together these stories, I thought I saw glimpses or reflections of the battles in *The Lion, the Witch, and the Wardrobe*, *The Lord of the Rings*, *The Hobbit*, and *That Hideous Strength*, among others.

Many readers have noted the hat-tip to Tolkien's Frodo struggling to wear the ring even as a necklace in the trio's trouble wearing the Locket-Horcux. There was another Tolkien echo, the Mouth of Sauron with Frodo's mithril coat at Mordor's gate, when Voldemort showed Harry's body to his friends. When Voldemort attacked Harry's body after Narcissa said he was dead, were you thinking of Hektor's body being dragged around Priam's towers? When Buckbeak soared into the final fray did you look up to the sky and say, "The Eagles!"? Me, too.

One of my favorite Potter commentators, Reyhan Yazar, has noted that the last three Potter books read more like screen-plays than the first four. He suggests this was inevitable because of Ms. Rowling's involvement with film production while she was writing those novels. The *Lord of the Rings* movies and the first *Narnia* film, too, were big events during these years as well. It is only speculation, of course, but it would be unusual if there weren't some kind of bleed between these cinematic events -- all of which feature dramatic, large scale battles at the finish -- and Ms. Rowling's mental picture and exposition of Harry's last stand against the Death Eaters and Voldemort.

23. Have any notable Harry Haters come to embrace him post-*Deathly Hallows*?

No.

24. Why does Molly Weasley call Bellatrix LeStrange a "bitch" in their fight to the death?

Because she's a choleric, Gaelic, angry woman, whose son has just died in battle, whose two brothers were killed by Death Eaters, and because Bellatrix is threatening to kill her only daughter, Ginevra. I think that combination of love, grief, mama bear adrenaline, and memory of sorrows when mixed with fear and menopausal angst is combustible. The word and explosion certainly seems in character -- and, given the paucity of cursing in the books, certainly cranks up the intensity of the moment.

Why, though, aren't there any objections to Harry's use of the word "Bastard" in the Ravenclaw Common Room?

25. Harry and friends use Unforgiveable Curses in the Battle of Hogwarts. Is that legal?

I think so.

Look at the context. Amycus Carrow has just physically threatened and spat in the face of Professor McGonagall, Harry's Head of House as a Gryffindor. Carrow and McGonagall had been arguing about what they would tell the Dark Lord when he arrived because they didn't have Harry Potter as Alecto Carrow thought. Amycus' plan was to blame the students and let Voldemort torture them. McGonagall told him that wasn't going to happen and gave him the short course on right-and-wrong. She gets spit in the face and a threat for her trouble.

And Harry blasts Amycus with an Unforgiveable Curse.

Note two things about this: McGonagall's response in the Ravenclaw Common Room and Harry's behavior later.

McGonagall reprimands Harry, not for using the Cruciatus Curse successfully (which requires real hatred; she commends him for being "gallant" in this regard), but for being "foolish" in revealing himself (Chapter 30, page 594). *She* then uses an Unforgiveable Curse, Imperio, on Amycus to disarm him and position him next to his sister for binding with ropes. Voldemort's imminent arrival at the castle, the context of both Harry's and McGonagall's use of the Unforgiveable Curses, means the Battle of Hogwarts has begun. Their use of the strongest possible magical spells on the enemy is no more surprising or a moral failure than Molly Weasley's using a killing curse on Bellatrix at the Battle's climax.

Incredibly, though, Harry does not use any Unforgiveable Curses in the Great Hall after his execution in the Forest and return to life and action after a trip to the limbo King's Cross. He uses "jinxes and curses" against the Death Eaters while under his Invisibility Cloak (Chapter 36, page 734) and a host of shielding charms to protect his friends. He doesn't run wild with the Unforgiveable Curses, however; he even uses a disarming spell on Voldemort rather than the killing curse, Avada Kedavra!

Why not? Because his sacrificial death and resurrection have changed him. I don't think he's equal to the hatred necessary to use those spells, He even seems to be loving to Voldemort in advising him to try and feel some remorse. Harry's and Prof. MacGonagall's use of

Unforgivable Curses in the Ravenclaw Common Room signals that the war has begun and the rules of engagement have changed. Harry's use of protection and disarming spells up to and in his battle with the Dark Lord mark the profundity of the victory he won in the Forbidden Forest over his inner-Voldemort.

26. What is the difference between Dumbledore's death and euthanasia?

Not much. And a whole lot.

One of Ms. Rowling's signature techniques is something called "narrative misdirection." In brief, she fools us in every book by restricting the point of view from which the story is told to "just above Harry's head." We think we know what's going on, but we never know what Dumbledore, Snape, Voldemort, or even Ludo Bagman are up to. At the end of the story, consequently, when we find out something has been going on outside of Harry's line of sight, we're blown away by what we missed (see chapter 1's first key for why Ms. Rowling does this).

What's the big surprise of *Deathly Hallows*? That Albus Dumbledore, greatest wizard of the age and Harry's *de facto* parent and mentor through most of the series, was all too human – and, to risk stretching a point, not always on target ethically. When Harry finds out from the likes of Rita Skeeter and Ron's batty aunt some of the things the Headmaster never told him about Dumbledore's life, Harry realizes Dumbledore has told him almost nothing and begins the struggle to believe that largely defines the book.

The two most disturbing things we learn about the Headmaster both involve Severus Snape. The most dramatic thing is that Harry has been kept alive, not out of any grand love for Harry or the memory of his mother, but so he might die at the right time, in Severus' words, like a "pig to slaughter." As Ms. Rowling has said, Dumbledore has a strong "Machiavellian" streak, a side of planning and secretiveness that his brother Aberforth despised, and quite rightly.

The second thing we learn is that Dumbledore's death on the Tower was planned. There are apologists for this plan with interesting arguments:

- Dumbledore was already dead so this was not murder or assisted suicide;

- By dying on the Tower as he does, Dumbledore saves Draco

from having to commit the murder, Severus from failing to keep the Unbreakable Vow, and Snape's status inside Lord Voldemort's camp (i.e., it is a heroic and noble sacrifice);

• Snape has to kill Dumbledore in order to gain control of the Elder Wand and be safe from the Dark Lord's attack (this explains Dumbledore's plan and intention but Draco's disarming Dumbledore ruins the plan, albeit providentially); and

• As Dumbledore says to Snape, his being killed by his friend prevents the potentially horrible death he might otherwise suffer at the hands of the Death Eaters (he mentions the blood thirsty Fenrir Greyback in particular.

All of these defenses are decent arguments, but they fail ultimately on ethical grounds. Dumbledore is still alive on the Tower and, however justified, heroic, even Christ-like the Headmaster's sacrifice is there, it still requires Severus Snape to kill an innocent, living man. As Mark Shea wrote at *First Things* magazine (*Harry Potter and the Christian Critics,*[12] Thursday, September 13, 2007):

> But the fact remains that "You shall not do evil that good may come of it." It is evil to kill an innocent man, as Snape himself points out. Mercy killing isn't just wrong for Muggles. And "I was just following orders" was shown to have limited traction in 1946.

The point of *Deathly Hallows* is in large part coming to terms with the fact that the beloved Headmaster and the greatest wizard of his age was not the man we thought he was and perhaps not even a very good man. Dumbledore apologizes to Harry with tears in King's Cross for just the failings we have mentioned and confesses that he has known for some time that Harry was "the better man."

How is Harry a "better man"? Look at his battle with Voldemort for some clues. That was no agape fest they were having in the Great Hall in the darkness before the dawn, but Harry is transparent in telling Voldemort what he knows and urging him to take the only path that had any hope of saving his atrophied, fragmented soul a life of eternal torment, i.e., feeling remorse. Voldemort is incapable of this but Harry is obliged to call him to repentance because of the stakes involved and his obligation, for lack of a better phrase, to love his enemy. Voldemort kills himself, figuratively and literally, because Harry's disarming spell will only kill Voldemort if he is right about being the master of the Elder Wand and Voldemort disregards Harry's advice and tries to kill him.

Ms. Rowling offers Harry's love for an enemy and transparent service to the truth as the way to fight internal demons and external evils. Dumbledore's Hemlock Society Machiavellianism is what we must come to terms with to understand the Headmaster; we are not meant, however, to embrace or defend the command decision that ordered another man to commit murder. As Dumbledore said at King's Cross to Harry, "Poor Severus."

On the other hand, we are reminded at Dobby's funeral on Easter, when Harry thinks of Dumbledore and his death again and again, that the Headmaster's sacrifice on the Tower was all he felt he could for his friends, even if it involved Severus in euthanasia. However sad this choice is, it is hard to miss. There is also a strong story parallel between the death of the true King of Gondor in the *Silmarillion*. As a friend wrote me:

> The kings of Númenor (extended to their descendant Aragorn) were given the gift of abnormally long lives and the privilege of simply willing their own deaths at a time of their own choosing. If they clung to life at the end, they would completely drop into full senility. Aragorn, who is King of Arnor and Gondor, does this when he's over 200 years old against the pleas of his wife Arwen.... Check out the story in Appendix A-I in LOTR.

Arwen doesn't kill Aragorn but we have a "willing death" in the face of senility. The folks who jump all over the supposed euthanasia rarely refer to this parallel in the works of the hallowed J. R. R. Tolkien. That's too bad. This is a fascinating plot point for discussion because it makes "Dumbledore-as-Christ" more than a little ambivalent, especially when his *realpolitik* thinking is revealed in 'The Prince's Tale.' I'd be suspicious of anyone who makes this death a black-and-white issue, whichever answer they feel is correct.

27. Is *Deathly Hallows* an exception to the rule that the end chapters reflects the beginning chapters?

I don't think so, at least, not if you are willing to see something turning into its opposite as a reflection in addition to a parallel.

The first chapter, a meeting of Death Eaters with the Dark Lord at Malfoy Manor, ends with the murder of Prof. Charity Burbage by

Lord Voldemort and her being fed to Nagini. Yecch. 'Charity' is another word for 'love' and the ending chapters, in which Harry dies for the love of his friends and is saved again by the sacrificial love of his mother, are essentially love's victory over death in general and Lord Thingy specifically. In between, we see the world turned upside-down by Harry's choice to believe and consequent transformation.

In Harry's first appearance in the book, he stumbles over tea that Dudley had left outside his bedroom door as something of a peace gesture or sign of affection. Harry cuts himself on the broken china and wonders if it it hadn't been left there as a booby-trap or dirty trick. He learns as the Dursleys depart that Dudley doesn't think he's "a waste of space" and that Harry misunderstood the tea-trap.

It isn't an especially affectionate farewell, but, as Harry says, this is as close as a Dursley has ever come to saying "I love you."

In Harry's appearance in the book's Epilogue, unlike all the previous closing chapters at King's Cross Station, the Dursleys aren't there to pick Harry up for summer vacation on Privet Drive. Harry and Ginny are bringing their children to the Hogwarts Express for Albus Severus Potter's first trip. We're not going to see if Harry and Dudley are good friends as a bookend to the story's ending.

Harry and company, though, do notice the man that Harry, beginning in *Philosopher's Stone* and through the remaining books, felt was the only person he could hate more than Dudley: Draco Malfoy.

> *Draco caught sight of Harry, Ron, Hermione, and Ginny staring at him, nodded curtly, and turned away again.* (Epilogue, page 736)

So what? As with Dudley, not an especially affectionate or heart-wrenching exchange but the relationships have changed. Harry no longer hates Slytherin. He explains to his 11 year old son, named for a Slytherin House master, that, if he is sorted into Slytherin, that is okay. For the man who grew up with two hatreds, the Dursleys and all Slytherins but especially Dudley and Draco, the beginning and end of the books are supposed to represent a closed loop.

28. Will we ever see another series as good as this one?

I think we're obliged to understand the tsunami of Potter-mania and Ms. Rowling's seventeen year effort to plan and write these books as a once in a lifetime event. If she writes another series as good as this one, I will be delighted (and very surprised). God allowing, her success has inspired other brilliant story tellers with both a remarkable understanding and "compost pile" of reading to draw from to take up a pen and begin their *magnum opus*.

29. What would you ask Ms. Rowling if you were able to interview her?

If I were invited to enter the Presence and ask Ms. Rowling a few questions (or just allowed to fly a paper airplane over her gate), I hope very much I could resist asking her questions about plot points or for interpretations of her work (see Chapter 7, note v).

I think, though, I would ask her a question about the alchemy books she said in a 1998 interview she had read before writing the first book, which reading helped her establish the "magical parameters" of the series. I'm interested in learning if those books were primarily historical, traditional, literary psychological, "spiritual" (the faux alchemy of New Age writers), or a combination of the lot. I'd love to know which books on this subject were especially helpful to her, if any.

I'd probably also ask her, too, what French books and plays are favorites of hers or which she spent the most time studying while at Exeter and in Paris. In my survey of her more than ten years of interviews, I don't remember anyone asking her what she thinks of Hugo, Dumas, Sartre, or Guenon. I think this would be helpful in understanding the Gallic edge of her mental compost heap.

And, if this were an interview in her home, I'd ask to stand in front of her book shelves with her and to be allowed to ask her about the books there. I'd be especially interested in seeing if titles like Swift's *Battle of the Books*, Dante's *Comedia* (with Dorothy Sayers' notes), Coleridge's *Aids to Reflection*, Spencer's *Faerie Queen*, or Agatha Christie's mysteries are there and asking her thoughts on them and other 'Greats.' As a daddy, I'd be curious to hear, too, if her children enjoy *Hank the Cowdog* and Brian Jacques' *Redwall* series (mine do).

If the guards hadn't thrown me out or cut me up and fed me to the pet Greyhound by then, I'd ask to play a game of Minesweeper with her on the computer. She is supposed to be very good at it and I'd like to confirm that and leave on an upbeat note. I stink at Minesweeper and so, even if she is only average, she is sure to win easily.

30. What do you think of Ms. Rowling's decision to sue the publishers of the *Harry Potter Lexicon*?

I understand that it is none of my business and only feel sympathy for everyone involved. The New York judge opined that the case was "lawyer-driven" and asked the parties to settle. I hope he is wrong -- and, if he is right, that the parties have settled their disagreement amicably by the time this book has been published. In a world possessed by the spirit of celebrity, every controversy and media event of this kind, however well-intentioned everyone may be, obscures the brilliance of Ms. Rowling's achievement, and, if she is to be believed, distracts her from her writing.

31. Why would Ron and Hermione name their son 'Hugo'?

The common sense answer – and I wasn't the first to see this – is that Hermione Granger Weasley, whose first name means 'feminine mercury' and whose maiden name initials are 'Hg,' the Periodic Table abbreviation for 'mercury,' was having a little fun. The consonants in Hugo's name are 'Hg.' Element chipped off the old block.

My thought when reading in the Epilogue that Ron and Hermione had named their son Hugo was not alchemical. It struck me that a French major like Ms. Rowling would have to sneak a reference to Victor Hugo into this epic before the finish.

Here are three reasons for thinking Ms. Rowling wants her readers to have the great French poet, essayist, artist, and novelist in mind as they finish her 4100 page serialized novel:[13]

(1) Hugo's novels are also very long, engaging, and "character driven;"

(2) Hugo was "spiritual but not religious," in fact, something of an anti-clerical bore, but his books challenge serious readers to reflect on their prejudices, their willingness to confront injustice, and on their capacity to love sacrificially; and

(3) Hugo was no friend of the political or media establishment. He spent the last years of his life in forced and then voluntary exile from France because of his disdain for the government of his native country.

Sound familiar? Ms. Rowling may not be in exile but she has told her fans not to trust the government or the press to tell them the truth. Ms. Rowling has not waved any anti-church banners to date, it is true, but I suspect "Pius Thicknesse" as the agent of Lord Voldemort in the Ministry of Magic, Confundus Charmed or not, was a reflection of her thoughts about the "religious right." And *Les Miserables*, when it was first published, came out in much anticipated volumes, two and the finale, over a period of time.

Is it any accident that *Les Miserables*, the most famous of Hugo's novels, is a huge hit on Broadway and film? I know it was the first really long book I had to read in high school (Mrs. Smith's 9th grade honors English class, Mtn Lakes High School, 1975...) and, as much as my classmates and I were prepared to despise the unabridged Hapgood monster-sized translation, we loved Jean Valjean and hated Javert despite ourselves. It is the stuff of Generation X, post-Watergate, post-Vietnam head space: "the government is your enemy; only the sacrificial choices of ostracized individuals will change the world."

The link of Hugo to Harry Potter, I guess, is a natural one, especially given Ms. Rowling's French studies background and the popularity of the musical version of *Les Miserables*. When I was picked up at the Bob Hope airport for Sonorus 2007, the three people in the car sang along *in magno voce* with the CD of a Broadway version on the long drive to the high desert, talked about other productions, how the musical was staged, and what the story meant to them. I didn't know anything about "Les Mis" the musical (still don't, really) but I was impressed by the similarity of these Potter-philes' feelings for Hugo's epic and their embrace of Ms. Rowling's novels. That this show has been in continuous production in Paris, the West End, and Broadway since 1985 I guess means Zossima Press should publish a book[14] about why people are so crazy about this play.... "Whence *Les Mis* Mania?"

Anyway, my thought on Ron and Hermione choosing the name "Hugo" for their son, a name revealed only in the last pages of the books, was that Ms. Rowling was suggesting the next book her readers should pick up "if they like Harry Potter" is something long by Victor-Marie Hugo, fire-brand Romantic artist and citizen.

Endnotes

1   http://news.scotsman.com/topics.cfm?tid=3&id=1201052007

2   http://www.wowzone.com/death.htm

3   http://www.mtv.com/news/articles/1572107/20071017/index.jhtml

4   http://hogwartsprofessor.com/?p=135#comment-11850

5   http://beholdaphoenix.blogspot.com/2007/08/comment-on-richard-abanes.html

6   http://www.quick-quote-quill.org/articles/1999/0099-amazon-staff.htm

7   http://www.accio-quote.org/articles/2000/0500-heraldsun-rowling.html

8   http://www.quick-quote-quill.org/articles/2000/1200-readersdigest-boquet.htm

9   http://hogwartsprofessor.com/?p=129#comment-11591

10   http://www.accio-quote.org/articles/2003/0616-scotsman-mcginty.html

11   http://hogwartsprofessor.com/?p=127#comment-11324

12   http://www.firstthings.com/onthesquare/?p=844

13   http://en.wikipedia.org/wiki/Victor_Hugo

14   *To Love Another Person,* Zossima Press, 2008

Bibliography

Abraham, Lyndy. *A Dictionary of Alchemical Imagery.* Cambridge, UK: Cambridge University Press, 1998.

Aeschylus. The Oresteian Trilogy. Translated by Philip Vellacott. Baltimore: Penguin, 1974.

Ariosto, Ludovico. Orlando Furioso. Translated by Guido Waldman. New York: Oxford University Press, 1991.

Austen, Jane. Emma. Vol. IV: The Oxford Illustrated Jane Austen. New York: Oxford University Press, 1988.

Baird Hardy, Elizabeth. *Milton, Spenser, and The Chronicles of Narnia: Literary Sources for the C. S. Lewis Novels.* Jefferson, North Carolina: McFarland, 2007.

Barfield, Owen. What Coleridge Thought. Middletown, Connecticut: Wesleyan University Press, 1971.

Battistini, Matilde. *Astrology, Magic, and Alchemy in Art.* Translated by Rosanna M. Giammanco Frongia. Los Angeles: J. Paul Getty MuseumPublications, 2007.

Bloom, Harold. *The Western Canon: The Books and School of the Ages* . New York: Harcourt Brace, 1994.

Booth, Wayne c. *The Rhetoric of Fiction (Second Edition).* Chicago: University of Chicago Press, 1983.

Borella, Jean. *The Secret of the Christian Way: A Contemplative Ascent Through the Writings of Jean Borella.* SUNY series in Western esoteric traditions. Translated and edited by G. John Champoux. Albany: State University of New York Press, 2001.

Bunyan, John. The Pilgrim's Progress. Chicago: Donohue, Henneberry, 1907.

Burckhardt, Jacob. The Civilization of the Renaissance in Italy. Translated by S. G. C. Middlemore. New York: Harper Torchbook, 1958.

Burckhardt, Titus. *Alchemy: Science of the Cosmos, Science of the Soul.* Translated by William Stoddart. Baltimore: Penguin, 1972.

_____. *Mirror of the Intellect: Essays on Traditional Science and Sacred Art.* Translated and edited by William Stoddart. Cambridge: Quinta Essentia, 1982.

Cahoone, Lawrence (ed.). *From Modernism to Postmodernism: An Anthology.* Malden, Massachusetts: Blackwell, 2001.

Carroll, Lewis. *Alice's Adventures In Wonderland* and *Through the Looking-Glass.* New York, Barnes & Noble, 2004.

Cirlot, J. E. *A Dictionary of Symbols (Second Edition).* Translated by Jack Sage. New York: Dorset, 1971.

Coleridge, Samuel Taylor. *Aids to Reflection.* New York: Chelsea House, 1983.

_____. *Biographia Literaria.* Vol. III: *The Complete Works of Samuel Taylor Coleridge.* New York: Harper & Brothers, 1868.

Cutsinger, James. *Advice to the Serious Seeker: Meditations on the Teaching of Frithjof Schuon.* Albany: State University of New York Press, 1997.

_____. *The Form of the Transformed Vision: Coleridge and the Knowledge of God.* Macon, Georgia: Mercer:, 1987.

_____. *That Man Might Become God: Lectures on Christian Theology.* Unpublished: available at www.cutsinger.net.

Dickens, Charles. *A Tale of Two Cities.* London: The Folio Society, 1985.

Dostoevsky, Fyodor. *The Brothers Karamazov.* Translated by Constance Garnett. New York: Barnes & Noble, 2004.

Duriez, Colin. *Field Guide to Harry Potter.* Downers Grove, Illinois: IVP Books, 2007.

Dante, Alighieri. *The Divine Comedy.* Translated by Henry Cary and edited by Ralph Pite. Rutland, Vermont: Everyman, 1994.

_____. *The Divine Comedy 1: Hell.* Translated by Dorothy Sayers. Baltimore: Penguin, 1975.

_____. *The Divine Comedy 2: Purgatory.* Translated by Dorothy Sayers. Baltimore: Penguin, 1975.

_____. *The Divine Comedy 3: Paradise.* Translated by Dorothy Sayers. Baltimore: Penguin, 1975.

_____. *The Divine Comedy 2: Purgatorio.* Translated with commentary by John D. Sinclair. New York: Oxford University Press, 1967.

Eliade. Mircea. *The Forge and the Crucible: The Origins and Structures of Alchemy (Second Edition).* Translated by Stephen Corrin. Chicago, University of Chicago Press, 1978.

_____. *Images and Symbols: Studies in Religious Symbolism.* Translated by Philip Mairet. New York: Sheed and Ward, 1969.

_____. *The Myth of the Eternal Return: Cosmos and History.* Translated by Willard Trask. Princeton: Princeton University Press, 1971.

_____. *The Sacred and the Profane: The Nature of Religion*. Translated by Willard Trask. New York: Harvest Books, 1968.

_____. *The Two and the One*. Translated by J. M. Cohen. New York: Harper, 1965.

Evola, Julius. *The Hermetic Tradition: Symbols and Teachings of the Royal Art*. Translated by E. E. Rehmus. Rochester, Vermont: Inner Traditions, 1995.

Ford, Paul. *Companion to Narnia: A Complete Guide to the Enchanting World of C. S. Lewis's The Chronicles of Narnia (Fourth Edition)*. San Francisco: Harper, 1994.

Frye, Northrop. *Anatomy of Criticism: Four Essays*. Princeton: Princeton University Press, 1957.

_____. *The Double Vision: Language and Meaning in Religion*. Toronto: University of Toronto Press, 1991.

Granger, John. *How Harry Cast His Spell: The Meaning Behind the Mania (Third Edition)*. Carol Stream, Illinois: Tyndale, 2008.

_____. *Unlocking Harry Potter: Five Keys for the Serious Reader*. Wayne, Pennsylvania: Zossima Press, 2007

Guenon, Rene. *The Esoterism of Dante*. Translated by C. D. Bethell. Ghent, New York: Sophia Perennis, 1996.

_____. *Fundamental Symbols: The Universal Language of Sacred Science*. Compiled and edited by Michel Valsan, translated by Alvin Moore, Jr., revised and edited by Martin Lings. Cambridge: Quinta Essentia, 1995.

_____. *The Lord of the World*. Translated by Carolyn Schaffer, et alii. Oxford: Coombe Springs Press, 1983.

_____. *Symbolism of the Cross*. Translated by Angus McNab. London: Luzac, 1975.

Haeffner, Mark. *Dictionary of Alchemy: From Maria Prophetissa to Isaac Newton*. San Francisco: Aquarian Harper, 1991.

Hamilton, Edith and Huntington Cairns (eds.). The Collected Dialogues of Plato. Princeton: Princeton University Press, 1978.

Hooper, Walter. *C. S. Lewis: A Companion and Guide*. San Francisco: HarperSanFrancisco, 1996.

Jacobs, Alan. *The Narnian: The Life and Imagination of C. S. Lewis*. New York: Harper, 2005.

Key, William Bryan. Subliminal Seduction. New York: Signet, 1974.

Klossoswki de Rola, Stanislas. *The Golden Game: Alchemical Engravings of the Seventeenth Century.* New York: Thames & Hudson, 1997.

Lewis, C. S. *The Voyage of the Dawn Treader: Book 3 in the Chronicles of Narnia.* New York: Collier Books, 1970.

_____. *The Magician's Nephew: Book 6 in the Chronicles of Narnia.* New York: Collier Books, 1970.

_____. *The Last Battle: Book 7 of the Chronicles of Narnia.* New York: Collier Books, 1970.

_____. *The Discarded Image: An Introduction to Medieval and Renaissance Literature.* Cambridge: Canto, 1994.

_____. *English Literature in the Sixteenth Century excluding Drama.* New York: Oxford University Press, 1954.

_____. *Essay Collection.* [Toronto:] Harper Collins (Canada), 2003.

_____. *An Experiment in Criticism.* Cambridge: Cambridge University Press, 1961.

_____. *Literary Impact of the Authorized Version.* London: The Athlone Press, 1950.

Linden, Stanton. *Darke Hieroglyphicks: Alchemy in English Literature from Chaucer to the Restoration.* Lexington, Kentucky: University of Kentucky Press, 1996.

Lings, Martin. *Ancient Beliefs and Modern Superstitions.* Cambridge: Quinta Essentia, 1991.

_____. *The Eleventh Hour: The Spiritual Crisis of the Modern World in the Light of Tradition and Prophecy,* Cambridge: Quinta Essentia, 1987.

_____. *The Secret of Shakespeare.* New York: Inner Traditions, 1984.

_____. *Symbol & Archetype: A Study of the Meaning of Existence.* Cambridge: Quinta Essentia, 1991.

Marinelli, Peter V. *Ariosto & Boiardo: The Origins of Orlando Furioso.* Columbia, Missouri: University of Missouri Press, 1987.

McGillis, Roderick (ed.). *George MacDonald: Literary Heritage and Heirs.* Wayne, Pennsylvania: Zossima Press, 2008.

Machiavelli, Nicolo. *The Prince.* Translated by Liugi Ricci, revised by E. R. P. Vincent. New York: New American Library, 1980.

Morrison, John. To Love Another Person: A Spiritual Journey Through Les Miserables. Allentown, Pennsylvania: Zossima Press, 2008.

Mulvey-Roberts, Marie (ed.). *The Handbook of Gothic Literature.* Washington Square, New York: New York University Press, 1998.

Paris, Jean. *Shakespeare*. New York: Grove Press, 1960.

Pearl, Matthew. The Dante Club. New York: Random House, 2004.

Penn, William. Some Fruits of Solitude/More Fruits of Solitude. Rockville, Maryland: Wildside Press, 2007.

Perry, Whitall. *The Widening Breach: Evolutionism in the Mirror of Cosmology*. Cambridge: Quinta Essentia, 1995.

Prinzi, Travis. *Harry Potter and the Imagination: The Way Between Two Worlds*. Allentown, Pennsylvania: Zossima Press, 2008.

Roberts, Alexander and James Donaldson (eds.). Fathers of the Second Century: Clement of Alexandria (Entire). Vol. II: The Ante-Nicene Fathers. Peabody, Massachusetts: Hendrickson, 1994.

Robertson, D. W. Jr. A Preface to Chaucer: Studies in Medieval Perspectives. Princeton: Princeton University Press, 1962.

Ruskin, John. The Queen of the Air. New York: John Wiley and Sons, 1873.

Sayers, Dorothy. *Introductory Papers on Dante*. Vol. I: *The Poet Alive in His Writings*. Eugene, Oregon: Wipf & Stock, 2006.

Schuon, Frithjof. The Eye of the Heart: Metaphysics, Cosmology, Spiritual Life. Bloomington, Indiana: World Wisdom Books, 1997.

Shakespeare, William. *Romeo and Juliet: The Pelican Shakespeare*. Edited by John Hankins. New York: Penguin, 1985.

Tillyard, E. M. W. *The Elizabethan World Picture: A Study of the Idea of Order in the Age of Shakespeare, Donne, and Milton*. New York: Vintage, 1959.

Virgil. Aeneid. Translated by Robert Fitzgerald. New York: Random House, 1983.

Ward, Michael. *Planet Narnia: The Seven Heavens in the Imagination of C. S. Lewis*. Oxford: Oxford University Press, 2007.

Williams, A. N. *The Divine Sense: The Intellect in Patristic Theology*. Cambridge: Cambridge University Press, 2007.

Williams, Charles. The Figure of Beatrice: A Study in Dante. Berkeley, California: Apocryphile Press, 2005.

Yates, Frances A. Giordano Bruno and the Hermetic Tradition. Chicago: University of Chicago Press, 1979.

Yates, Frances A. The Art of Memory. Chicago: University of Chicago Press, 1974.

Index

Note: With few exceptions, book titles are listed under the author's name.

Zossima Press Titles for November 2008

"What we achieve inwardly will change outer reality." Those words, written by Plutarch and quoted by J.K. Rowling her 2008 Harvard commencement speech, sum up both the importance of the *Harry Potter* series and the argument of Travis Prinzi's analysis of the best-selling books in *Harry Potter & Imagination: The Way Between Two Worlds*. Imaginative literature places a reader between two worlds: the magical world on the page and the world of daily life, and challenges this reader to imagine and to act for a better world. Starting with discussion of *Harry Potter*'s more important themes, *Harry Potter & The Imagination* takes readers on a journey through the transformative power of those themes for both the individual and for culture by placing Rowling's series in its literary, historical, and cultural contexts. Prinzi explores how the world of fairy stories in general, and *Harry Potter* in particular, are not merely tales that are read to "escape from the real world," but stories with the power to transform readers and the world.

Hog's Head Conversations: *Brilliant Essays on Harry Potter*
Zossima Press Collection, Vol. 1 2008 – Travis Prinzi, editor

---

A professor of literature for over thirty years, Dr. James W. Thomas (Pepperdine University) takes us on a tour back through the Potter books in order to enjoy them in different ways upon subsequent readings. Re-readers will be pleasantly surprised at what they may have missed in the books and at what secrets Rowling has encoded for us to decode as we revisit these rich texts. The professor's informal and often lighthearted discussions focus on puns, humor, foreshadowing, literary allusions, narrative techniques, and various other aspects of the *Potter* books hard-to-see on the hurried first or fifth reading. Throughout, Dr. Thomas also draws parallels between passages in Harry's story and various literary classics. *Repotting Harry Potter* is not concerned with spoilers. After all, it's for re-readers; and, as the professor points out, for the serious student of serious literature there are no spoilers, and nothing can really be spoiled. Dr. Thomas shows us too that a "serious" reading of literature can be as much fun as it is edifying and rewarding.

REPOTTING
HARRY POTTER

A Professor's Book-by-Book
Guide for the
Serious Re-Reader

by JAMES THOMAS

NOVEMBER 2008

Daily reflections by two poets from different times and places, but with a common love.

Betty Aberlin's close readings of George MacDonald's verses and her thoughtful responses to them speak clearly of her poetic gifts and spiritual intelligence.

Luci Shaw, poet

A Book of Strife in the form of

The Diary of an Old Soul

George MacDonald

Let your white page in ground, my print be seed. Growing to golden ears, that faith and hope shall feed.

The White Page Poems

Betty K. Aberlin

To Love Another Person:
A Spiritual Journey Through Les Miserables
by John Morrison (November 2008)

"I've just put down your manuscript. I had not got far into it before I knew that I was sitting at the feet of an excellent teacher, theologian, and literary and drama critic. Quite seriously – I feel that I have no possible comment on your work except, "Publish it! Whenever you can!""

Thomas Howard, author

Fourteen essays that truely place MacDonald in context. Important, challenging, and exciting.

This comprehensive collection represents the best of contemporary scholarship on George MacDonald.

Rolland Hein, author

GEORGE MACDONALD
LITERARY HERITAGE AND HEIRS

14 essays on the background
and legacy of his writing
Roderick McGillis
editor

Sixteen of the best presentations from the international C. S. Lewis convention in Wake Forest, NC. Walter Hooper shares his important essay "Editing C. S. Lewis," a chronicle of publishing decisions after Lewis' death in 1963.

"A magisterial work, chock full of fresh historical tidbits and penetrating analysis."

David Baggett
editor of *C.S. Lewis as Philosopher*

"Indespensible"
James Como

Why I Believe in Narnia:
*33 Essays and Reviews
on the Life and Work of C.S. Lewis*
by James Como

"A valuable, wide-ranging collection of essays by one of the best informed and most astute commentators on Lewis' work and ideas."

Peter Schakel, author
Imagination & the Arts in C.S. Lewis